D1602770

Competition, Monopoly, and Differential Profit Rates

Competition, Monopoly, and Differential Profit Rates

On the Relevance of the Classical
and Marxian Theories of Production Prices
for Modern Industrial and Corporate Pricing

Willi Semmler

Columbia University Press
New York . . . 1984

Library of Congress Cataloging in Publication Data

Semmler, Willi.
  Competition, monopoly, and differential profit rates.

  Bibliography: p.
  Includes index.
  1. Industrial concentration. 2. Competition.
3. Monopolies. 4. Price policy. 5. Profit. 6. Class-
ical school of economics. 7. Marxian economics.
I. Title.
HB238.S45 1984   338.5′2   83-23168
ISBN 0-231-05616-8
ISBN 0-231-05617-6 (pbk.)

Columbia University Press
New York   Guildford, Survey

Clothbound editions of Columbia University Press books are Smyth-
sewn and printed on permanent and durable acid-free paper.

Contents

Contents

Preface and Acknowledgments

The original incentives to work on these ideas of competition and monopoly within the context of the Classical and Marxian economic theory go back to the time when I taught at the Free University of Berlin and enjoyed very lively discussions with my colleagues and the students about this topic. A grant from the American Council of Learned Societies for the year 1978–1979 and my affiliation with the economic departments of Columbia University and the New School for Social Research made it possible to undertake extensive theoretical and empirical studies on this subject without teaching obligations. During the preparation of this work I enjoyed the extremely helpful discussions and comments by Anwar Shaikh and Ulrich Krause from the time of the original conception and by Duncan Foley at a later stage. I am also very grateful for discussions and comments on earlier drafts of the manuscript or particular chapters, especially for those by Ghislain Deleplace on section 2.3, as well as to James Clifton, Peter Flaschel, Alfred Eichner, and David Kotz. All of them have helped me with a detailed critique and valuable suggestions concerning the theories and the material treated in this book. Several colleagues and friends with whom I have shared discussions of ideas have provided useful comments on parts of the manuscript or on earlier papers that were integrated into the final version of this book. Among them are Robert Heilbroner, David Schwartzman, Edward Nell, Paul Sweezy, Harry Magdoff, Pierangelo Garegnani, Elmar Altvater, Juergen Hoffmann, Bertram Schefold, Neri Salvadori, Howard

Wachtel, Ian Steedman, and John Weeks. Many other friends, colleagues, and students forced me to clarify ideas and to present the empirical material more clearly when I was teaching at the Free University of Berlin, American University (Washington, D.C.), and the New School for Social Research (New York). I also want to acknowledge the useful discussions and the help of many students at the New School, especially for assisting me in the extensive empirical research and for editing several versions of the manuscript. Among them, those whom I want to thank most are Hassan Farrah, Carl Ward, Barry Robertson, and Mark Glick. Last but not least, I want to acknowledge the stimulating discussions with Alain Lipietz, Gérard Duménil, and Dominique Levy, which I had while I was visiting scholar at the LEPREMAP in Paris in the fall of 1983.

New School for Social Research
New York
January 1984

Symbols

$\mathbf{A}$	input matrix (intermediate inputs)
$\overline{\mathbf{A}} = \mathbf{A} + \mathrm{d}\mathbf{l}$	sociotechnological matrix (input matrix and matrix of consumption goods for labor power)
$\tilde{\mathbf{A}} = \mathbf{A} + \mathbf{B}'$	input matrix and depreciation matrix for fixed capital
$\mathbf{A}^+ = \overline{\mathbf{A}} + \mathbf{B}'$	sociotechnological matrix and depreciation matrix for fixed capital
$\mathbf{B}'$	depreciation matrix for fixed capital
$\tilde{\mathbf{B}}$	fixed capital stock matrix (fixed capital only)
$b'_{ij} = \tilde{b}_{ij}/t_{ij}$	depreciation coefficients derived from the matrix of fixed capital stock and turnover time
$\mathbf{B}^+$	matrix of total capital advanced
$b^+_{ij} = a^+_{ij} \cdot t_{ij}$	coefficients of the matrix of total capital advanced, derived from the sociotechnological matrix, depreciation matrix, and turnover time
$\mathbf{B}$	output matrix
$\mathbf{B}^* = (\mathbf{I} - \mathbf{A})$	identity matrix minus input matrix
$\mathbf{C} = (\mathbf{B} - \mathbf{A})$	net product matrix
$\langle \mathbf{C} \rangle$	diagonal matrix of cost per unit output
$\mathbf{d}$	real wage vector per unit labor
$\mathbf{l}$	vector of direct labor coefficients
$\mathbf{p}$	price vector

$\mathbf{Q'} = (\mathbf{I} - \mathbf{A})^{-1}$	Leontief-inverse including only the input matrix
$\mathbf{Q} = (\mathbf{I} - \tilde{\mathbf{A}})^{-1}$	Leontief-inverse including the input matrix and the depreciation matrix
$\mathbf{S}$	surplus product matrix
$\mathbf{r}$	uniform profit rate
$\langle \bar{\mathbf{r}} \rangle$	diagonal matrix of profit rate differentials r_i
t_{ij}	turnover time
$\mathbf{x}$	gross output vector
$\mathbf{y}$	net output vector
$\langle \alpha \rangle$	diagonal matrix of reduction coefficients α_i
μ	markup
$\langle \mu \rangle$	diagonal matrix of markups μ_i
$\langle \delta \rangle = [\mathbf{I} + \langle \mu \rangle]$	diagonal matrix of $1 + \mu_i$
π	profit rate in empirical price equations
Λ	vector of direct and indirect labor requirements
λ	eigenvalue
$\langle \Pi \rangle$	diagonal matrix of gross profit per unit output
$\| \; \|$	Euclidean vector norm

Competition, Monopoly, and Differential Profit Rates

Part 1. On Theories of Competition and Their Empirical Predictions

After locating the approach pursued here in the history of economic thought, I will present the notion of competition in three different theoretical frameworks: the neoclassical theory, the classical/Marxian theory, and the post-Marxian/post-Keynesian theory. These theories of competition are reviewed in order to clarify their empirical predictions for pricing and profit rate differentials.

1. INTRODUCTION AND OVERVIEW

Industrial concentration and the rise of large corporations since the end of the nineteenth century have been a challenge to liberal as well as Marxist economic analysis. In both streams of thought, the idea was developed that the economies of advanced capitalist countries have moved away from a perfectly working competitive economy toward one with imperfections. In the liberal tradition, a differentiated theory of imperfect competition has been elaborated since the turn of the century to provide a framework for the analysis of modern market structures. In the Marxist tradition since Hilferding (1968) and later in post-Keynesian theory, the ideas of the classics and of Marx on competition and the working of the market system have been replaced by a theory of monopoly capital, finance capital, and corporate economy. Accordingly, it has been stated that due to industrial concentration, vertical integration, diversification, and oligopolistic coordination in the markets, large firms possess discretionary market power. Thus, discretionary price-setting power, markup pricing, and target rate of return pricing were considered new forms of pricing and profit determination by large firms in modern economies. Prices have seemingly become an arbitrary phenomenon, or as Paul Sweezy (1968:271) puts it, "No reasonable general laws of monopoly prices have been discovered, because none exist." Moreover, a persistence of differential profit rates between monopolized and nonmonopolized industries and between large and small firms were expected, giving rise also to an increasing instability of advanced capitalist market systems.

The classical and Marxian concepts of competition, price, and profit have been thought to be obsolete and were no longer utilized as a framework for explaining modern industrial and corporate pricing and profit determination. Although post-Marxian economists (such as Rudolf Hilferding, Maurice Dobb, Paul Baran, Paul Sweezy, Oscar Lange, Michael Kalecki, and Joseph Steindl) have analyzed structural and institutional changes in capitalist development since the end of the nineteenth century in great depth, still, doubts have been raised as to whether the classical and Marxian concepts of competition, production price, and profit determination were sufficient to serve as a guideline for analyzing modern market structures and their impact on pricing and profits. Indeed, in unorthodox economics the idea persisted that the classical and Marxian theories of value are a good and transparent approximation for prices and profits even for modern industrial production. Classical political economy distinguished between scarce and reproducible commodities. The theory of value was developed especially for reproducible commodities. Smith's theory of natural prices, the Ricardian critique of the Smithian measure of value (the labor-commanded concept), the Ricardian labor-embodied theory of value, the search for an absolute measure of value, and the Marxian concept of value and its transformation into prices of production were still considered a sufficient basis on which to build a theory of price and profits for modern industrial production. Especially in the Marxist discussion on the problem of the transformation of values into prices, starting with Marx's own contribution and further developed by Bortkiewicz, Dmitriev, Winternitz, Seton, Brody, Morishima, Okishio, and recently Shaikh, the idea remained that the classical and Marxian theories of value and prices of production are still a useful first approximation for the analysis of modern industrial price and profit determination.

The rediscovery of the classical and Marxian theories of price—Smith's natural price, Ricardo's theory of embodied labor, and Marx's theory of value and prices of production—as relevant theories of modern industrial prices and profits was recently initiated again by Sraffa's interpretation of Ricardo and by Sraffa's book *Production of Commodities by Means of Commodities* (1960). Numerous books and articles were published in order to show the relevance of Ricardo's theory of value and price for modern economies; they have also provided a starting point for a critique of neoclassical economics. The best-known books that have attempted to show the relevance of this theoretical heritage for modern economies include Pasinetti, *Lectures on the Theory of Production* (1977); Roncaglia, *Sraffa and the Theory of Price* (1978); Steedman, *Marx after Sraffa* (1977); and Garegnani, *Marx e gli economisti classici* (1981). On the other hand, there have also been many fruitful Marxist attempts to apply the theory of value and prices of production to industrial prices and profits. The most advanced book recently published in this field is Brody's book *Proportions, Prices and Planning* (1970), which may perhaps be considered a basic work in the Marxist discussion of prices and profits of reproducible commodities. Other important works in this field are Abraham-Frois and Berrebi, *Théorie de la valeur, des prix et de l'accumulation* (1976), Fujimori, *Modern Analysis of Value Theory* (1981), and a paper by Shaikh, "A Transformation from Marx to Sraffa" (1982).

The common ground for both classical and Marxian views is the assumption that the conditions of the markets are dominated by the conditions of production and reproduction of a commodity. The fundamental assumption is that there are *centers of gravity* for prices and profits, given by the long-run *conditions of social reproduction*, which regulate market phenomena. Thus, two laws for pricing and profits are discussed: one determines the long-run prices and profits, the other the deviations from it—the market phenomena (see Deleplace 1981). Although the question of what determines the long-run prices and profits themselves is given different answers by writers in the classical and Marxian traditions, they all share the view that the conditions of *production and reproduction* are more important than market structure and demand. These concepts are obviously very much alive both in the neo-Ricardian and in the modern Marxist discussion of prices and profits. Modern writers have utilized linear economic models to a greater extent in order to describe these characteristics of the classical and Marxian theories. In doing so, authors have assumed that the centers of gravity for prices and profits are the solutions of linear economic systems, which in turn seem to assume some kind of "perfectly competitive economy." Yet the basic question that has been raised here is whether the classical theory of natural price (Smith), the labor theory of value (Ricardo, Marx) and the theory of prices of production (Marx) can be represented on the basis of a theory of perfect competition and its stability assumptions.

It is well recognized that the central problem in defining the long-run prices and profits and their relation to the market price and market profit rate, in the classical and Marxian sense, is that of how to define the classical and Marxian *theories of competition*. If it is true that the classics and Marx maintain specific theories of competition that are different from the neoclassical theory of perfect/imperfect competition, as well as from the post-Marxian and post-Keynesian theories, then the next question is, Are there differences between the classical and the Marxian theories (see Cartelier 1979; Benetti 1981; Deleplace 1974, 1981; Schefold 1981; Levine 1981; Nikaido 1983; Flaschel and Semmler 1984)?

It is well known that the theory of competition was worked out most comprehensively in Marx. By reinterpreting both the classical and the Marxian theories in the first part of the book, and their concepts of long-run prices and profits, I hope to present a useful framework, one that makes possible the interpretation of the empirical phenomena of modern industrial and corporate pricing and profits, which the post-Marxian and post-Keynesian theories have been so concerned with.

Given these considerations, the following issues will be addressed in this book. In part 1, I will discuss three kinds of theories of competition and work out their essential characteristics and differences with regard to their empirical predictions on prices and profit rate differentials. The first theories to be discussed are the classical and Marxian theories of competition and the notion that natural prices (Smith), labor values (Ricardo, Marx), and prices of production (Marx) serve as centers of gravity for market prices. Second, I will compare those theories with the neoclassical notion of perfect/imperfect competition, where variations in demand and the number of firms are the main determinants of industrial prices. Third, I will discuss the notion of competition found in the post-Marxian and post-Keynesian theories of oligopoly or monopoly pricing. In this context, the interpretation of the classical and

Marxian notions of competition is given some emphasis, since both theories are very often misinterpreted by modern writers. In part 2 of the book (chs. 3 and 4), a survey of empirical studies on competition, pricing, and profit rate differentials will be provided. Empirical evidence for the above-mentioned three kinds of theories of competition will also be discussed. The empirical studies are examined in order to find out whether or not they support one of the following three views:

> Market prices are determined by the competitive mechanism and by supply and demand; prices converge toward equilibrium prices, and differentials of profit rates are eliminated in the course of time. Here, variations in demand and industrial concentration are considered to be the main determinants of prices and price changes (neoclassical theory).
>
> Market prices are determined by monopoly or oligopoly power and markup or target rate of return pricing, thereby allowing systematic differentials of profit rates in the long run (post-Keynesian and post-Marxian views of monopoly).
>
> Market prices are regulated by production prices, which serve as their centers of gravity, and long-run prices change when the center of gravity changes; differentials of profit rates are due not to market power but to other causes (classical and Marxian views).

After theories of competition and empirical evidence on industrial and corporate pricing and differential profit rates have been presented, it will be necessary to come back to the question of how the modern empirical findings can be reconciled with the classical and Marxian theories of competition, production prices, and average profit rates. This will be the main topic of part 3. In section 5.1, an evaluation of the empirical findings on prices and profits will be given in light of the classical and Marxian theories of competition and production prices. In section 5.2, an extended concept of production prices is discussed that allows for deviations of market prices from production prices and for deviations of market profit rates from the average profit rate. In section 5.3, the question of whether modern industrial and corporate pricing based on markup or target rate of return pricing is consistent with the classical and Marxian theories of competition and the production price concept will be discussed. Whereas in chapter 5 single-product industries are assumed in my discussion of industrial pricing, in chapter 6 I discuss the problem of joint production, corporate pricing, and their relation to the classical and Marxian concepts of production prices. As mentioned before, since the 1920s, the pricing policy of multiplant and multiproduct corporations has become a theoretical problem as a result of industrial concentration and the rise of large corporations. By going back to the concepts, discussed in the 1920s, on which modern industrial and corporate pricing were based originally, I will provide a new interpretation of so-called oligopolistic price-setting behavior. I will show that modern industrial and corporate pricing do not necessarily contradict, but can be made consistent with, the classical and Marxian theories of price and profit determination. In working out these new results, we have to differentiate in a fundamental manner between market or *monopoly power*, as defined in relation to *market structure* (concentration, entry barriers, collusion), and *corporate power*, as power not so much over markets as over production processes and production relations. This is also the topic of the last chapter of this book, where I give a short summary of the findings and discuss the difference in the concepts of market power on the one hand and corporate power on the other.

2. ON THEORIES OF COMPETITION

$\mathbf{R}$ecent discussion has raised doubts not only about the correctness of the notion of competition in the post-Marxian theory of monopoly (see Clifton 1977; Weeks 1981; Shaikh 1978, 1980) but also about the concept of competition and equilibrium in modern Marxist literature, which uses the framework of *linear production models*. Here we assume the existence not of "monopoly prices" and differentials of profit rates but of a kind of "perfectly competitive economy" with uniform profit rates and prices of production as equilibrium prices. In order to interpret the Marxian theory of exploitation, reproduction, and accumulation, and to discuss the so-called transformation problem, it seemed to be sufficient to consider an equilibrium situation where market prices are prices of production and where the profit rate is uniform (see Brody 1970; Morishima 1973). Some attempts have been made to discuss the relation of market prices to prices of production due to disequilibrium situations (see Koshimura 1975) and the relation of so-called monopoly prices to prices of production due to monopoly power in the market (see Okishio 1956; Koshimura 1975, 1977; Teplitz 1977); but the classical and Marxian notions of competition have not been discussed until recently (see Nikaido 1983).

The reorientation to the classical and Marxian theories of production prices was particularly influenced by Sraffa's book *Production of Commodities by Means of Commodities* (1960). However, in the work of some important followers of Sraffa, assumptions pertaining to perfect competition were also made in presenting a theory of production prices (see Steedman 1979a). The concept of production prices was not related to the concept of competition, the market process, and market prices in the classic theory (see Roncaglia 1978:16). The classical theory of competition and the relation of actual prices to production prices and of actual profit rates (market profit rates) to a "normal profit rate" did not become a theoretical issue until the whole discussion turned into a critique of neoclassical general equilibrium theory. Since then it has been realized that the concept of prices in classical political economy was different from the neoclassical concept of competitive prices (see Roncaglia 1978). It was recognized that classical political economy had a developed concept not of equilibrium prices but, as mentioned above, of a "center of gravity." Natural prices or prices of production are not equilibrium prices but centers of gravity around which actual prices or market prices fluctuate. Thus, the classical concept of competition was discussed again in a new light (see Eatwell 1981; Garegnani 1976). But in comparing the fundamental assumptions of the classical and neoclassical theories of prices, many writers thought that there was no difference between the classical and the Marxian theories of production prices, market prices, and competition. The different conceptual frameworks underlying the classical and the Marxian theories of competition were also mostly overlooked. In section 2.1 I want to give a short introduction to theories of competition in order to clarify the particular frameworks to which different notions of competition and prices belong. Moreover, since empirical literature also refers to different concepts of competition, it is necessary to discuss these different concepts before we can give a survey of the main empirical findings on industrial and corporate pricing and profit rate differentials.

2.1. On Neoclassical Theory: Competition and Convergence Toward Equilibrium

The classical theory of competition has been interpreted not only by writers who base their position on Sraffa's book (1960) but also by neoclassical economists (see Stigler 1957; Arrow and Hahn 1971: 2). In fact the classical theory, especially the theory of Adam

Smith, has been considered the foundation of the neoclassical general competetive analysis. According to Arrow and Hahn (1971: 2), Smith was the "creator of the general equilibrium theory."

There are, of course, some elements in classical theory, particularly in Smith's *Wealth of Nations*, that could be interpreted from the neoclassical point of view (see Smith 1976, ch. 7). Competition in Smith's sense meant "free competition": everyone should be able to act according to one's own interests. There should be as few barriers as possible to economic activities. Given these preconditions, economic resources would be allocated efficiently and the society as a whole would be enabled to realize a welfare maximum. The market is the place where individuals and their interests are coordinated and disturbances are eliminated. The fundamental mechanism which would produce these results is the supply and demand mechanism. Moreover, the market mechanism is considered to operate in a political milieu of perfect liberty. To a great extent this is the neoclassical interpretation of Smith's theory of "free competition," and in that respect Smith was seen as the most important forerunner for the neoclassical theory of competition (see Stigler 1957; Arrow and Hahn 1971). The neoclassical theory formulated several conditions for a "perfectly competitive economy," for which a welfare maximum would be realized. These conditions, generally regarded as the necessary and sufficient conditions for a perfectly competitive economy, are as follows (see Arrow and Hahn 1971, chs. 1–3):

> The participants in the economic activities (the producers and consumers) show a maximizing behavior: the producers, transforming inputs into outputs, maximize profits under production constraints, and the consumers maximize their utilities under income constraints. The decisions of the agents in the markets are independent of each other. There are no coalitions or collusions and no external effects of production or consumption decisions.
>
> A large number of buyers and sellers is assumed so that no firms or consumers have a significant influence on the quantity sold or bought in the market. All firms produce under constant or decreasing returns to scale. The production possibility set of producers is convex, as is the set of preferences for consumers. For firms as well as for consumers, both of which are price takers, prices are given by the aggre-

gate demand and supply on each market through a tatonnement process.

Resources are perfectly mobile between the production possibilities, so that differential profit rates can be eliminated. The perfect mobility of resources between production possibilities thus assumes free entry and free exit of firms to and from industries, which also presupposes nonindivisibility of the resources.

Producers and consumers have complete information about the production and consumption possibilities.

Given the initial endowment of resources and the structure of the preferences of consumers according to the general equilibrium theory, these conditions will guarantee properties of a perfectly competitive economy as follows (see appendix 5): They will provide the market system with an *equilibrium price vector*. The equilibrium price vector does not necessarily have to be unique. However, it allows for a consistent exchange of commodities between the market agents. Thus, it will allow the economic agents to make decisions that are mutually compatible. This competitive equilibrium is considered to be a *Pareto optimal* one, i.e., an equilibrium that provides a perfect allocation of resources such that the firms have maximized profits and consumers maximized utilities (see Arrow and Hahn 1971, ch. 5). Moreover, according to the neoclassical theory of a perfectly competitive economy there is also—as usually assumed—*high stability* of the decentralized market system. For the most part, it is assumed that the equilibrium is stable with regard to small changes in prices (local stability) or with regard to large changes in prices (global stability). The latter holds only if the equilibrium is unique. The fundamental law that brings about these results is the law of *supply and demand* (Arrow and Hahn 1971: 265), according to which supply and demand are continuously dependent on actual prices (market prices) and market prices respond to supply and demand. The law states that variations in market prices are due to variations in *excess demand*. Excess demand is considered a continuous function of actual prices. Only at equilibrium prices is excess demand zero. Thus, in neoclassical economics the *variation in demand* is the most important determinant of actual prices (I will discuss this point further in ch. 3).

These characteristics of the standard neoclassical view of competition, which are used as a framework for interpreting the classical theory of competition, require some preliminary qualifications.

First of all, in this theory of competition the intensity of competition in the markets among producers, for example, is measured by the quantity of firms in the industries. It is assumed that the more firms in the industries, the closer to optimal the market results will be. Second, the assumption that prices and quantities converge toward an equilibrium—driven by competitive forces— is very strong. According to this theory, a disequilibrium between supply and demand will be eliminated by price and quantity reactions, and exogenous distortions of the market mechanism will disappear in the course of time. A change in the technique used by firms and a change in the structure of demand will, through a smooth adjustment process, lead to a new competitive equilibrium. An equilibrium will not be brought about by severe disruptions but is a result of a continuous and smooth process of convergence, during which disequilibria will be eliminated. Third, it is characteristic of this theory that uncertainty, risk, and expectation are excluded (in more advanced versions it is assumed that they can be modeled by mathematical expectation).[1] Fourth, since in neoclassical theory individual buyers or sellers do not have an influence on prices, the neoclassical theory needs the fiction of an auctioneer, i.e., an agent who is external to the participants in the market and is neither a buyer nor a seller.

Once these idealized market conditions are accepted as prerequisites for perfect competition and optimal performance of firms, deviations from these conditions can be considered to lead to "imperfect," "restricted," or "monopolistic" competition that does not result in a welfare maximum. According to this theory, deviations from these idealized conditions are caused by industrial concentration, which allows a greater share of the market for leading firms; coalitions, agreements, and collusion among participants in the market (cooperative behavior); and limited mobility of resources among the different industries (market entry and exit barriers). All three factors allow leading firms to have an influence on prices and quantities (by withholding production and raising prices). Thus, once the theory of perfect competition is accepted, the notion of monopoly or oligopoly power is determined in advance by the assumptions of the theory. Deviations of actual prices from "competitive prices" and the existence of differentials of profit rates seem to be explainable on this basis.[2] Whether this theoretical approach is powerful enough to explain the empirical phenomena or not is a question to be discussed later.

On the other hand, the question remains whether or not this standard neoclassical theory has interpreted correctly the classical theory of competition. Don't we have to discuss the classical theory of competition within another framework?

2.2. On the Classical Theory: Center of Gravity and Fluctuation of Market Prices

As mentioned above, classical, and especially Marxian, political economy has developed a notion of competition and long-run position of the economy that is quite different from the neoclassical theory of perfect competition. As many writers have recently pointed out, the main features of classical political economy are its concept of *reproduction and economic surplus, center of gravity* concept of price, and particular notion of *equilibrium* (see Pasinetti 1977; Garegnani 1976, 1981; Roncaglia 1978; Eatwell 1981; Benetti 1981; Deleplace 1981; Walsh and Gram 1980). These three features are essentially related to the concept of competition in classical political economy. In the following section, I mainly want to deal with Smith and Ricardo.[3] Since Marx's dynamic theory of competition requires a special treatment, we will refer only occasionally to Marx here.

2.2.1. REPRODUCTION AND SURPLUS PRODUCT

Pre-Smithian economic theory had already developed a notion of economic surplus (see Walsh and Gram 1980, chs. 1 and 2); however, it became clearer in Smith and Ricardo, and especially in Marx. Using modern input-output techniques, we can define what was meant by the notion of reproduction and physical surplus. As Garegnani (1981) has shown, the classics started with a given physical system and a given structure of production. In order to keep the model simple, I abstract from stocks, which will be introduced later, and exemplify the ideas of the classics by using only a flow matrix, a circulating capital model in Marxian terms. Classical political economy assumed that once the technical conditions of production, represented by a productive flow matrix **A**, the real wage vector **d**, and the vector of direct labor requirements **l**, are given, the economic system generates a surplus product that can be appropriated by the owners of capital. Since in the classics, workers' consumption is regarded as a necessary part of the social reproduction, the surplus can be defined as follows:[4]

gross product − (replacement of means of production + necessary consumption) = surplus product

Using matrix notation, there is a surplus product if

$$\mathbf{x} - (\mathbf{A} + \mathbf{dl})\mathbf{x} > 0,$$

where **x** is the gross output vector. The difference represents the surplus product. In this context, profit can be considered as the dual of the surplus product. If the same equation is written $\mathbf{p} - \mathbf{p}(\mathbf{A} + \mathbf{dl}) > 0$, with **p** the price vector, the difference represents the profit per unit output.

As Walsh and Gram (1980:56) have pointed out, Smith already considered the profit to be the dual of the surplus product. According to Smith, in a freely operating market with no restrictions on the mobility of capital and no "artificial" or "natural" monopolies or state interventions, the private owners of the surplus would "allocate the surplus available as capital stock so as to put in motion the greatest quantity of productive labor" (Walsh and Gram 1980: 63). Thus, in Smith, free competition for private capital would guarantee an allocation of the surplus such that the maximum accumulation of capital is generated. Commodities are assumed to be freely reproducible in the relevant model. The cost of the reproducible commodities, according to the classical political economists, are determined by the cost of their reproduction. Thus, the normal price should cover, as Smith saw it, the normal wage, the normal rent, and the normal profit. As mentioned by Walsh and Gram, Smith, although he did not speak of an equilibrium profit rate, assumed the profit to be extracted as a normal or usual one, in proportion to the amount of stock invested: The profits of the stock "are regulated altogether by the values of the stock employed and are greater or smaller in proportion of the extent of this stock" (Smith 1976:66). At the same time, Smith is already very clear about the existence of differential profit rates due to risks, different accidents, temporary monopolies, and relation of supply and demand (ch. 9). However, in his theory of a production price or normal price, he maintains that the normal price, which he calls the *natural price*, is composed of the normal wage, normal rent, and normal profit. The natural price is considered a center of gravity around which the market price fluctuates.[5]

2.2.2. CENTER OF GRAVITY

As Benetti (1981) and Deleplace (1981) have shown, in Smith and Ricardo, but also in Marx, there are two laws determining prices. One law determines the center of gravity for prices; the other regulates the fluctuations of the actual price, or market price. As Smith put it, "The natural price itself varies with the natural rate of each of its component parts, of wages, profit, and rent; and in every society this rate varies according to their circumstances, according to their riches or poverty, their advancing, stationary or declining conditions" (Smith 1976:80).

Market prices are determined by a different law, by supply and demand, expectation, risk, and different accidents creating shortages or gluts. Because of these influences, the market prices fluctuate around the centers of gravity. Smith (1976, ch. 7) also discusses the influence of temporary monopolies on market prices. The *natural prices* for the commodities and the natural or normal factor rewards, in the sense of Smith, are independent from short-run demand and supply. It is assumed that an equalization of rates of return on factors of production takes place, enforced by the tendency of the factors to move from areas of low to high rate of return. With input-output techniques, the meaning of Smith's concept of natural prices regulating market prices can be demonstrated by referring only to a circulating capital model (a capital stock matrix will be introduced later).

If we assume normal profits and normal or natural wage rates, and neglect rent, then according to Pasinetti (1973), we may write the natural prices—the centers of gravity in Smith's concept—as vertically integrated wages and profits:

$$p = w\mathbf{l} + \mathbf{pA} + r\mathbf{pA} \tag{2.1}$$

$$\mathbf{p(I - A)} = w\mathbf{l} + r\mathbf{pA}$$

$$\mathbf{p} = w\mathbf{lQ'} + r\mathbf{pAQ'}, \tag{2.1a}$$

where $\mathbf{Q'} = (\mathbf{I - A})^{-1}$ is the Leontief inverse, which multiplied by $w\mathbf{l}$, gives us the vertically integrated wages and multiplied by $r\mathbf{pA}$, gives us the vertically integrated profits. $\mathbf{I}$ is the identity matrix, $\mathbf{A}$ is the flow matrix (stocks are not included in this case), $\mathbf{p}$ the price vector, r the uniform profit rate, w the uniform wage rate, and $\mathbf{l}$ the vector of direct labor requirements per unit of output. Thus, we can write the price for a commodity (see Shaikh 1976):

$$p_i = w'_i + \Pi'_i,$$

where w'_i and Π'_i are the vertically integrated wages and profits. Thus, relative prices can be expressed as follows:

$$\frac{p_i}{p_j} = \frac{w'_i + \Pi'_i}{w'_j + \Pi'_j} . \tag{2.1b}$$

Even if there is a circularity in Smith's argument, which has been the main criticism of the adding-up theory of Smith, we can clearly see his argument that the center of gravity of prices, the natural prices, are determined independently of supply and demand and the forces that regulate the fluctuations of the market prices. The normal wage and profit rates, together with the structure of production, assigning weights for the integrated wages and profits, will determine the long-run prices. Therefore, these centers of gravity are also called production prices or reproduction prices (see Brody 1970; Levine 1980).

As can also be seen from this formulation of the center of gravity, changes in the regulating price are determined by the changes in the structure of production $(\mathbf{l}, \mathbf{Q'})$ and changes in the normal wage w and normal profit rate r. However, it has to be mentioned here that Smith, as well as Ricardo and Marx, does not assume that in any *actual* state of the economy the profit rate will necessarily be uniform for all sectors. There will be differential profit rates because

The establishment of any new manufacture or any new branch of commerce, or of any new practise in agriculture, is always a speculation from which the projector promises himself extraordinary profits. These profits sometimes are very great and sometimes, more frequently, perhaps, they are quite otherwise; but in general, they bear no regular proportion to those of other trades in the neighbourhood. If the project succeeds, they are commonly at first very high. When the trade or practise becomes thoroughly established, and well known, the competition reduces them to the level of other trades. (Smith 1976:131)

As we will see later, this potential for differential profit rates, as well as the fact that profit is calculated on the stock of capital, will have an influence on the formulation of the production price. In Ricardo and in Marx, the *direct* and *indirect labor requirements* were considered approximate centers of gravity of market prices. As has been shown in the literature (see Pasinetti 1977; Schefold 1976), the direct and indirect labor requirements Λ are exactly the regulating prices if the profit rate r is zero or if the proportion of capital to labor is the same in all production processes.

In the first case, if $r = 0$ the price equation (2.1) will be reduced to

$$\mathbf{p} = w\mathbf{l}(\mathbf{I} - \mathbf{A})^{-1},$$

and setting $w = 1$ we get $\mathbf{p} = \Lambda$, with

$$\Lambda = \mathbf{l}(\mathbf{I} - \mathbf{A})^{-1}. \tag{2.2}$$

Relative prices are equal to relative values. Thus, if λ_i/λ_j is the ratio of direct to indirect labor requirements, we can write $p_i/p_j = \lambda_i/\lambda_j$, and the change in relative prices is equal to the change in relative values. The vector $\mathbf{l}$ or the input-output matrix $\mathbf{A}$ can change. An exact estimate of the change in values due to a change in the direct labor requirements or the matrix $\mathbf{A}$ is developed in appendix 1.

For the second case, the price equation can be written as

$$\mathbf{p} = w\mathbf{l}[\mathbf{I} - (1 + r)\mathbf{A}]^{-1}. \tag{2.3}$$

Here too, as can be shown, we get[6]

$$p_i/p_j = \lambda_i/\lambda_j.$$

Estimations of the change of relative values can be developed in the same way as for equation (2.2). In all other cases, when the capital/labor ratio is different for all industries *and* the profit rate $r > 0$, relative prices will be a function of the wage rate w or the rate of profit r, provided that the structure of production is given and does not change. Thus, relative prices will be

$$\frac{p_i}{p_j} = \frac{\{w\mathbf{1}\, [\mathbf{I} - (1 + r)\mathbf{A}]^{-1}\}_i}{\{w\mathbf{1}\, [\mathbf{I} - (1 + r)\mathbf{A}]^{-1}\}_j} \, . \tag{2.3a}$$

If we set $w = 1$, all prices for a given structure of production will be a function of the rate of profit r.[7] Also, in this case, the estimate in appendix 1 can be used to predict the possible price changes due to a change in the rate of profit for given types of matrices $\mathbf{A}$. Ricardo and also Marx maintained that the direct and indirect labor requirements are still a good first approximation for the centers of gravity of prices. Marx, for example, speaks of a *regulation* of relative prices by relative values (Marx 1967b:177). These statements by Ricardo and Marx can be illustrated as follows (see Shaikh 1976). Rewriting the price equation for relative prices (2.1b), we get

$$\frac{p_i}{p_j} = \frac{w\lambda_i + \Pi'_i}{w\lambda_j + \Pi'_j} \, . \tag{2.3b}$$

Since λ_i, λ_j represent the direct and indirect labor requirements, assuming a uniform wage rate w, which cancels out, we get for relative prices

$$\frac{p_i}{p_j} = \frac{\lambda_i(1 + \Pi'_i/w'_i)}{\lambda_j(1 + \Pi'_j/w'_j)} \, . \tag{2.3c}$$

As demonstrated by equation (2.3c), relative prices are determined by the relative direct and indirect labor requirements and the vertically integrated ratio of profits and wages. Ricardo and Marx maintained that the most important variable for long-run relative prices and price change would be the first term, the direct and indirect labor requirements, which reflect the structure of production. The second term was thought to be a disturbance term (Shaikh 1976, 1982), which was regarded as very stable in the course of time.[8]

However, in spite of the differences in the concepts of the center of gravity in Smith, Ricardo, and Marx—which will be discussed more extensively in section 2.3—all three shared the view that the centers of gravity have the characteristics of production prices. The level of output or the variation in demand does not play a role in the determination of the regulating price. Ricardo (1951:384), for example, explicitly states, "If the demand for hats should double, the price would immediately rise, but that rise would only be temporary, unless the cost of production of hats or their natural price were raised." In chapter 4, Ricardo develops further the idea that the natural price is independent of the level of output or demand. He shows how a sudden demand change, for example, makes the market price increase and an inflow of capital ensues, which increases production and brings down the market price to the natural price. On the other side, of course, Ricardo—and later Marx— knew that the change in effectual demand can lead to a change in the "facility" or "difficulty" of production and therefore also to a change in the natural price. This problem was worked out further in Ricardo's theory of rent and in Marx was also applied to industrial production (see also appendix 3.2). However, this problem is mainly worked out in their theories of accumulation and technical progress (see sec. 2.3.3).

2.2.3. LONG-RUN POSITION AND DEVIATIONS

As discussed, the classics (Smith, Ricardo) and Marx distinguished between the laws that determine the centers of gravity (natural price in Smith, direct and indirect labor requirements and price of production in Ricardo and Marx) and the laws that determine the fluctuation of the market price, the actual price. The centers of gravity reflect the long-run position of the economy (see Garegnani (1976, 1978, 1981); however, the long-run position cannot be called a competitive equilibrium in the sense of the general equilibrium theory. The centers of gravity around which the actual prices fluctuate are not necessarily equilibrium prices. The assumption of the competitive equilibrium theory, that prices react according to the excess demand or supply and converge toward equilibrium, need not be made. Marx, for example, maintains that demand and supply can be equated only "when the whole is viewed over a certain period, but only as an average of past movements" (Marx 1967b:190). The regulating price itself is a result of long-run effects of "natural forces" in Smith and the "forces of production" in Marx (see Deleplace 1981) and the average or normal rewards for capital and labor used up in production. Actual prices are equal to natural prices, labor values, or prices of production only by mere accident. Moreover, in Smith, Ricardo,[9] and Marx—as will be shown later—profit rates of industries and firms are never equal to the social average. Competition produces a deviation from the center of gravity and the normal profit rate as well as a tendency toward them.

As has been shown, in the long run, the centers of gravity are changing. Competition of capital, capital accumulation, and technical progress produce a change in the natural prices or in the direct and indirect labor requirements (see also sec. 2.3.3). The direct and indirect labor requirements are changing when the productivity of labor increases or decreases. The development of labor productivity and the direct and indirect labor requirements are considered in the classics—at least in Ricardo and Marx—to be a first approximation of the determinants of the development of the long-run price. Moreover, as shown above, the level of output and the variation in demand do not play as important a role in the classics and Marx as they play in modern competitive equilibrium theory (see appendix 3.2). Demand and supply, like other forces (random events, speculation and uncertainty, restricted mobility of money capital, or temporary monopolies) cause *deviations* from the center of gravity, but they do not determine the center itself (see Ricardo 1951, ch. 4). Thus—as will be discussed in chapters 3 and 6—the classical theories of competition and long-run price show a certain similarity to the modern markup theory for oligopolistic pricing, where again variations in demand do not play an important role for the long-run prices.

2.3. On the Marxian Theory: Competition and Disequilibrium

Even though the three essentials of the classical theory of competition have already been found in the pre-Smithian, Smithian, and Ricardian economic theories, the concept of competition was worked out most comprehensively by Marx (see Kuruma 1973). In

Marx we can see a more elaborated concept of competition than we can find in Smith and Ricardo.[10] We can also see essential differences between the classical (Smith, Ricardo) and the Marxian concepts of competition.[11] First, in Marx, competition is a derivative concept; it is not considered a self-contained starting point for his economic theory. The starting point of Marxian economic theory is the production of surplus value and the self-expansion of capital. Second, more so in Marx than in the classical theories, competition is not only an equilibrating force but also a force that produces disequilibria, distortions, and misallocation due to the rivalry of capitals. Thus, the centers of gravity for prices or profits cannot be considered optimal or equilibrium prices or profit rates as with the neoclassical works. The center of gravity concept in Marx is clearly elaborated more than it is in the classics. This is especially true for the treatment of the relation of market forces to long-run prices. Third, Marx elaborates the causes of the long-run changes of the centers of gravity either through direct and indirect labor requirements or through prices of production. (This point is worked out more in Marx than in Smith and Ricardo.) Fourth, since the center of gravity concept is not an equilibrium concept, fluctuations of market prices around prices of production and of industry or firm profit rates around the average profit rate are considered to be the normal state of an economy.

2.3.1. SURPLUS PRODUCTION, SELF-EXPANSION OF CAPITAL, AND COMPETITION

According to Marx, the laws immanent in capitalist production, like the production of surplus value and the self-expansion of capital, "manifest themselves in the movement of individual masses of capital, where they assert themselves as coercive laws of competition, and are brought home to the mind and consciousness of the individual capitalist as the directing motives of his operations. But this much is clear, a scientific analysis of competition is not possible, before we have a conception of the inner nature of capital, just as the apparent motions of the heavenly bodies are not intelligible to any but him, who is acquainted with their real motions, motions which are not directly perceptible by the senses" (1967a:316). Like classical theory, Marx's theory deals with the laws of economic reproduction and the production of surplus in capitalist societies. The starting point of his economic analysis is the production of surplus and the self-expansion of capital. Competition is the result of the self-expansion of the different units of capital. Thus, Marx does not have a "quantity theory of competition" (the fewer suppliers, the less the intensity of competition, the worse the market results). According to Marx, competition is not eliminated if the number of competing capitals decreases. Competition is a lasting struggle which is connected with the downfall of old capitals and thus with the centralization and concentration processes, but simultaneously with the creation of new capitals and of new disequilibria. Marx speaks of the "battle of competition." Competition does not apply only to the sphere of exchange. In Marx's theory, competition affects the production, realization, distribution, and accumulation of the economic surplus. The striving of individual capitals for surplus profit causes increases in productivity and decreases in costs of production (see Marx 1967a, ch. 12; Shaikh 1980; Semmler 1984b).[12] For individual capitals the competitive fight also involves the use value of the goods, the changes in quality of the products which influence the *realization* of the commodity value and thus the market shares of the individual capitals. Moreover, competition includes the fight over *distribution* of the surplus value among the different lines of business and forces capital to *accumulate* and to expand. In the production, realization, distribution, and accumulation of surplus value through the competition of capitals, Marx distinguishes between two essential aspects: competition of capitals within one industry, which produces a uniform market price for a given use value and defines the market value as the regulating center of gravity; and the competition of capitals between industries through the inflow and outflow of capital, which brings about a tendency toward an equalization of profit rates in the different spheres of production. Referring to this concept of competition—competition as a result of the production of surplus and self-expansion of capital, which is not equivalent to a free mobility of capital between industries—makes it possible to analyze the behavior of modern corporations, not in terms of theories of imperfect competition and monopolistic behavior, but in terms of a theory of competition (see chs. 6 and 7).

2.3.2. MARKET VALUES AND PRICES OF PRODUCTION
AS CENTERS OF GRAVITY

Like the framers of the classical theory of competition, Marx seems to have a concept of two laws for prices and profits (see Deleplace 1981). Since in Marx competition is not only an equilibrating force but also a force that creates disequilibria and distortion, the concept of long-run prices and profits cannot be viewed as an equilibrium concept as formulated in the neoclassic theory. I want to summarize the Marxian concept of long-run prices by raising the following questions: What determines long-run prices and what is their relation to market prices? To what extent do market forces influence long-run prices? and, What is the difference between the Marxian concept of center of gravity and the equilibrium concept of price?

I will begin with the discussion of market values as centers of gravity and the relationship of the latter to the market prices.[13] Like Smith and Ricardo, Marx considers the market value to be independent of the level of production or demand. As Marx put it, "There is no necessary connection between the quantitative volume of the commodities in the market and the market value" (1967b: 186). Marx assumes that for a *given* state of the society and for a *given* "labor productivity, the production of a certain quantity of articles in any particular sphere of production requires a definite quantity of social labor" (p. 187). The *change* of the relative market values—and later the prices of production (sec. 2.3.3)—are determined by laws that are different from those of supply and demand, which regulate the *fluctuations* of the market prices.

For a given state of the society, the demand is considered to be given. It is "effectual demand" in the sense of Smith, predetermined by the income distribution and the "social needs." Thus, demand is oriented not toward actual prices but toward market values (in the theory of Smith, toward natural prices). Therefore, the commodity should "satisfy social needs" and the "quantity of labor contained in the commodity should represent socially necessary labor" (p. 182).

On the production side, Marx assumes the coexistence of different techniques producing the same commodity, not a unique technique. The market value is understood as a weighted average of the individual values of the commodity.[14] There are producers with most efficient, average, and least efficient techniques. However, as long as we do not know the output mix of the different types of producers producing one type of commodity, which is supposed to match the "social needs," we do not know the direct and indirect labor requirements and thus the market value. (see ch. 6.2.1) Marx assumes that the output mix of the different types of production activities is *given* for a "mass of commodities available in the market" (p. 182). Different combinations are possible, leading to different determinations of the market value of commodity. (However, as Marx demonstrates, the ratio of supply and demand and the change of the market price can shift the weights to the least or most efficient producers and to a new regulating market value, as explained below; see Marx 1967b:184).

If the supply or the "mass of commodities available in the market"[15] falls short of the quantity demanded, demand is oriented toward the market value,[16] or the commodity producers withhold output (p. 185), the market price will rise and the profit rate increase. Differential profitability leads to capital mobility, and an increase in supply would make the market price fall toward the market value, or even below it (the market value may also increase because of an increase in the weight of the least efficient producers).[17] The reverse will be true if the quantity supplied is greater than the quantity demanded. The market price will drop, the relative profitability will lead to an outflow of capital, and the market price may increase, even above the market value. Thus, we can find two sets of determinants, one for the market value, the other for the market price.

The market value is regulated by the given conditions of social reproduction, i.e., the "social demand" and the weights of the different techniques within an industry. The market price is regulated by the conditions of market interactions: shortages and gluts, speculation (p. 185), the degree of competition on each side of the market (p. 193), and the degree of capital mobility. This second set of forces makes the market prices fluctuate around the market values as their regulating centers. Marx has these two sets of forces in mind when he says that supply and demand cause the fluctuations of market prices around the market values but do not determine the market values themselves. "If commodities are sold at their market values, supply and demand coincides. . . . If supply and demand balance one another, they cease to explain anything, do not affect market values, and leave us so much more in the dark about the reasons why the market value is expressed in just this sum of money and no other. It is evident that the real inner laws of capitalist production cannot be explained by the interaction of supply and demand. . . ." (p. 189), but, we can conclude, have to be explained by different laws, i.e., the laws that determine the market values (or, as shown later, the prices of production).

The *long-run changes* of market prices and the changes in supply and demand are *regulated* movements, which follow the changes in the market values, the socially necessary cost of production and reproduction of the commodities. "Should the market value change, this would also entail a change in the conditions under which the total mass of commodities could be sold. . . . Should the market value rise, this would entail a drop in the social demand, and a smaller mass of commodities would be absorbed. Hence, if supply and demand regulate the market price, or rather the deviations of market price from market value, then in turn, the market value regulates the ratio of supply to demand, or the centre round which fluctuations of supply and demand cause market price to oscillate" (p. 181). The determinants for the long-run changes in the centers of gravity will be elaborated more in section 2.3.3.

Although Marx analyzed other forces determining the centers of gravity than Smith and Ricardo did, the concept of centers of gravity as the regulating centers for market phenomena seems to be similar in Smith, Ricardo, and Marx. However, Marx makes explicit some possible interrelations between the laws that determine the market value of the commodities and the laws that determine the fluctuations around them. The market forces (supply and demand) not only entail changes in the market price but also can influence which technique in the industries is dominant for the determination of the market value. For example, if demand is "weaker than supply, the favourably situated part [the most efficient technique], whatever its size, makes room for itself forcibly by paring its price down to its individual value. The market value cannot ever coincide with this individual value of the commodities produced under the most favorable conditions, except when supply far exceeds demand" (p. 184). If demand rises, "in some lines of production it may also bring about a rise in the market value itself for a shorter or longer period, with a portion of the desired products to be produced under worse conditions during this period" (p. 191). Thus, Marx assumes that the long-run changes in "social" (or "effectual") demand may influence which combination of techniques become the dominant ones for the determination of the market values.[18]

Contrary to market values, market prices are constantly subject to the constellation of supply and demand, speculation, restrictions on the mobility of capital, etc., which forces market prices to fluctuate around the centers of gravity (market values). In the long run, the regulating exchange values of the commodities —and therefore also the average market price—are determined by long-run changes in the technical and social conditions of the reproduction of the commodities and by the change of the weights of the different techniques in industries. This determination holds also when centers of gravity are no longer regulated solely by the direct and indirect labor requirements, as in the situation discussed here, but are regulated, as in fully developed capitalist production, by the cost of production, plus the average rate of profit on capital advanced. Here the regulating price, in its simple form, is

$$p = c + rK/x, \tag{2.4}$$

where r is the average rate of profit, K/x the capital advanced per unit of output, and c the cost of production per unit of output. However, r is derived from the structure of production and the cost of reproduction of labor power (see sec. 2.3.3). Here, then, the prices of production take the place of market values as the centers of gravity of market prices.[19] All of the other above conclusions remain in force, also for multiple techniques (Semmler 1984a).

The long-run determination of market prices by market values —which means, in capitalist commodity production, by prices of production $p = c + rK/x$—presupposes the competition of capital *between* industries. A short-term equilibrium of supply and demand, as well as a market price holding both in balance, is possible even without the existence of equal profit rates in all industries. Such an equilibrium, however, could not exist for a long period, because capitalist production implies the tendency toward the equalization of profit rates in all spheres of capital investment (see Levine 1980). In spite of a balance between supply and demand, the following capital movements ensue when unequal industry profit rates exist: From industries with lower profit rates capital flows out, whereby the capacity in these industries falls. This allows the profit rate in the areas in question to rise. On the other hand, additional capital flows into industries with an above-average profit rate, because it wants to participate in these high profit rate sectors. By increasing supply, it lowers the profit rate in these areas.[20] In any case, Marx assumes (1967b:195) that through these movements of capital between industries there arises a *tendency* toward the distribution of surplus value according to the capital advanced, i.e., a tendency toward the average profit rate and toward prices of production as more concrete regulating centers for market prices.

In Marx's concept of the adjustment process of market prices toward market values as their centers of gravity, it is clear that market prices *do not converge* toward the centers of gravity. Marx's center of gravity concept is quite different from the neoclassical one. In the Marxian concept, an equilibrium price never exists and supply is never brought into equilibrium with demand:

> Since, therefore, supply and demand never equal one another in any given case their differences follow one another in such a way—and the result of a deviation in one direction is that it calls forth a deviation in the opposite direction—that supply and demand are always equated when the whole is viewed over a certain period, but only as an average of past movements, and, only as the continuous movement of their contradiction. But this average is not merely of theoretical, but also of practical importance to capital, whose investment is calculated on the fluctuations and compensations of more or less fixed periods. (p. 190)

Since Marx's view is that competition keeps deviations from the centers of gravity within certain limits while it also creates new disequilibria and deviations, he assumes that market prices fluctuate around their centers of gravity and that profit rates fluctuate around the general rate of profit; they do not converge toward them.

2.3.3. CHANGES IN THE CENTERS OF GRAVITY

The next question is, What are the determinants of long-run change in the market values as centers of gravity for actual prices or in the prices of production as the more concrete form of the regulating price when commodities are the product of capital? As preliminarily pointed out in section 2.2.2, changes in the direct and indirect labor requirements are determined by changes in the structure of production, a conclusion which the classics and Marx derive from the theory of accumulation and technical change. Of course, as shown, Marx as well as Smith and Ricardo presupposed that there will be "social" (or "effectual") demand for the produced commodities. We cannot go here into an elaborate discussion on technical change in Marxian and classical economics (see Okishio 1961; Shaikh 1978, 1980; Roemer 1979; Schefold 1980a). On the basis of linear production models for values and for prices of production, I want to briefly work out the impact of technical change—or, in general, changes in the structure of production—on relative values and the impact of changes in the structure of production and in income distribution on relative production prices. The results are derived in appendixes 1 and 2. To work out this problem, we want to assume again that there is only one production process activated in each industry and thus that there is no coexistence of different techniques within an industry. The values derived from the structure of production are regarded as the market values, and the prices derived from the production price model are regarded as the prices of production.

The labor values for industries with single processes and single products were written as $\Lambda = l + \Lambda A$ or as $\Lambda = l(I - A)^{-1}$ We want to work out the *change of values*, referring only to single process and single product industries. Suppose now that there is technical change or, in general terms, change in the structure of production such that elements of one or several columns of the matrix A, representing the technical coefficients of production, change, or that one or some elements in the vector of direct labor requirements l alter. In Marx, the cause of technical change is the striving of capitals to produce a surplus profit. In this context, some authors (see Okishio 1961; Roemer 1979) have argued that we should allow only for a technical change that is cost minimizing— i.e., one that decreases the sum of inputs in a production process (summed up by the prevailing value or price vector). However, we also want to allow for a structural change that may lead to an increase in elements of columns of A or elements of l (see Marx 1977,

ch. 23). We want to allow, for example, for the possibility that more
raw material, means of production, or labor is used up in a production process than before.

By substituting for $\Lambda(I - A) = l$, the system of values, $\Lambda B^* = l$,
we can demonstrate in general the change of the value vector due
to a change in the elements in the vector l. We can write the effect of
change in the structure of production on the value vector as
follows:[21]

$$(\Lambda + \delta\Lambda)(B^* + \delta B^*) = l + \delta l, \qquad (2.5)$$

which can be written as

$$\tilde{\Lambda} = (l + \delta l)(B^* + \delta B^*)^{-1}, \qquad (2.5a)$$

where $\tilde{\Lambda}$ is the original value vector, B^* the matrix $I - A$, $\delta\tilde{\Lambda}$ the
change in the solution of the equation system, $\tilde{\Lambda}$ the new value
vector, δB^* the change in matrix B^*, and δl the change in vector l.
The sign for the altered matrix B^* and for l can be positive or negative. Thus, δ is the variation by which the coefficients can change.
The most sensitive part of the solution of $\tilde{\Lambda}$ is the change in the inverse $(B^* + \delta B^*)^{-1}$. (The inverse can even become singular if there
is a slight change in the elements of matrix A. In that case we will
have no solution.) From the formula above, we can derive the
change of the value vector:

$$\delta\Lambda = (\delta l - \Lambda\delta B^*)B^{*-1}(I + \delta B^* B^{*-1})^{-1}. \qquad (2.6)$$

A general method for the estimation of the change in the inverse, and
thus of the change in the vector value Λ, due to δB^* and δl, with
examples, is given in appendix 1. However, we need to make some
further remarks. By using linear production models for depicting
the Marxian theory of value, we might encounter some problems
with regard to the *economic adjustment process*, or the market
process, that leads to the new values as derived above as centers of
gravity for market prices (see Semmler 1984a). As shown in appendix 1, the new value vector $\tilde{\Lambda}$ may change quite strongly compared
with the old value vector Λ. The direction of the change seems to be
quite clear, but the *magnitude* of the change can become a problem.
The value vector may change in certain cases quite sensitively with
respect to small changes in the structure of production.[22] Consider-

ing the value vector as the market value—representing here only single process industries—we see that the centers of gravity, around which the market prices are supposed to fluctuate, can themselves change *strongly* in certain cases (worked out in appendix 1). Such cases, of course, would raise the problem of an economic adjustment process, i.e., the working out of the market process, which would allow the new market values to become the new centers of gravity for actual prices, the market prices. Such an adjustment process, however, may be hard to imagine, since not only does it presuppose a perfect mobility of capital and labor and very high flexibility of prices and quantities in industries, to allow the market process to establish the new centers of gravity; it also presupposes that during the adjustment process no new technical change is initiated by the prevailing market prices. We can conclude from this that long-run relative prices derived from linear production models, in certain cases, might not be very relevant as centers of gravity for market prices.[23] A similar problem can be analyzed when prices of production are derived from a linear model.

The analysis of the *change of prices of production* as more concrete centers of gravity for market prices in capitalist production is more complicated than that of values. Here we will assume that capital accumulation will lead to a change in the structure of production and income distribution. With reference only to a circulating capital model, the main determinants for production prices are the structure of production and cost of reproduction of labor power. (A more extended model is discussed in appendix 2 and sec. 3.1.3.) The system of prices of production is usually written in a linear production model, as follows:

$$p(A + dl) = \lambda p \qquad (2.7)$$

or with the substitution $(A + dl)' = \overline{A}'$

$$\overline{A}'p = \lambda p, \qquad (2.7a)$$

where λ is the maximum eigenvalue of the indecomposable matrix $\overline{A}'$ and p is the eigenvector associated with this maximum eigenvalue (see appendixes 2 and 3). We can now discuss three cases. A more detailed analysis is given in appendix 2.

1. If due to technical change elements a_{ij} in the matrix A alter

and the proportion of capital to labor changes, not only will the direct and indirect labor requirements change, but so will the profit rate and the prices of production. As is well known from Frobenius' theorem (see appendix 3), the profit rate is a continuous function of the elements of **A**. If the elements of **A** increase, the profit rate r decreases;[24] however, as shown in appendix 2, the direction and the magnitude of the change in relative prices of production cannot be so easily determined. What can be shown is that for certain technical conditions of production, i.e., for certain types of matrices, the relative prices can change quite sensitively in response to a small change in the elements of **A**.

2. Furthermore, we can see that the prices of production and the profit rate will alter when the real wage vector **d** changes. For example, if the real wage increases, the profit rate will decline, and the elements of the vector of prices of production will change too (see appendix 2).[25] But in this second case, the value vector remains the same, since neither **l** nor **A** is altered. We get disturbances only of prices of production (and of the profit rate). The values remain the same. This is a case to which Ricardo and Marx referred when they discussed the influence of wages on the values of commodities. They showed, contrary to Smith, that the values of the commodities are not influenced by a change in wages.

3. If the elements of **A**, which are used up as capital, and the direct labor requirements **l**—components of the matrix $(\mathbf{A} + \mathbf{dl})$ in equation (2.7)—alter, the values as well as the prices of production will change. The direction of the change in values is clear, while the magnitude remains a problem. But the direction and the magnitude of change in prices of production can become a problem under certain conditions (see appendix 2). For a change in the prices of production and the profit rate due to a change in the matrix **A** or in **dl**, we can develop a general estimate. Using an approach similar to that used for values, we can separate the disturbance effect on λ and **p** due to a disturbance in $\overline{\mathbf{A}}$, where $\overline{\mathbf{A}} = \mathbf{A} + \mathbf{dl}$, and write

$$(\overline{\mathbf{A}}' + \delta\overline{\mathbf{A}}') \, (\mathbf{p}^{(r)} + \delta\mathbf{p}^{(r)}) = (\lambda_r + \delta\lambda_r) \, (\mathbf{p}^{(r)} + \delta\mathbf{p}^{(r)}), \qquad (2.8)$$

where $\delta\overline{\mathbf{A}}'$ is the change in the matrix $\overline{\mathbf{A}}'$, $\mathbf{p}^{(r)}$ and $\delta\mathbf{p}^{(r)}$ the original eigenvector and the change in it, and λ_r and $\delta\lambda_r$ the original eigenvalue and the change in it. A general process for estimating these changes is developed in appendix 2.[26] Here again a warning is necessary. As mentioned, a similar sensitivity of the change in prices of production, as well as in the profit rate, to small changes in the structure of production or the cost of reproduction of labor power can be analyzed in production price systems, as it can be for the labor values (see appendix 2). This brings up again the problem of an economic adjustment process that could provide that the new production prices serve as centers of gravity for market prices. If linear production models for prices of production can reveal for certain matrices such properties of unstable solutions—as they did for certain value systems—and the economic adjustment processes do not exist, this would not allow the new production coefficients of the economy to determine the regulating production prices. Therefore, we can conclude again that in certain cases the equilibrium solution of the new production price system might not provide us with a very relevant determination of the long-run prices of production. Marx himself seemed to have the view that neither values nor the general profit rate nor prices of production as the long-run centers of gravity change significantly when there are short-run and small changes in the input-output relations of industries or in the allocation of capital among industries.

In regard to the general rate of profit as the major component of the prices of production, Marx explains this stability as follows:

> In view of the many different causes which make the rate of profit rise or fall one would think. . . . that the general rate of profit must change every day. But a trend in one sphere of production compensates for that in another, their effects cross and paralyze one another. . . . We shall later examine to which side these fluctuations ultimately gravitate. But they are slow. . . . Within each individual sphere of production, there take place changes, i.e., deviations from the general rate of profit, which counterbalance one another in a definite time, and thus have no influence upon the general rate of profit, and which on the other side do not react upon it, because they are balanced by other local fluctuations. Since the general rate of profit is not only determined by the average rate of profit in each sphere, but also by the distribution of total social capital among the different individual spheres, and since this distribution is continuously changing, it becomes another constant cause of change in the general rate of profit. But it is a cause of change which mostly para-

lyzes itself, owing to the uninterrupted and many sided nature of this movement (1967b:169).

Market values, prices of production, and the general profit rate are thought to be quite stable and not to change sensitively when the structure of production changes slightly. In Marx the production and circulation conditions are thought to reflect "regulating averages" (p. 860).[27] This would make them more stable, and they would not change drastically for a given period of time (chs. 9 and 10). (For industries, for example, it is also the existence of the firms and the coexistence of different techniques in industries which prevent the average production technique from being changed as easily).

Thus, summarizing the properties of the Marxian concept of long-run prices, we can say that short-run fluctuations in neither output and demand, nor relative input prices and production coefficients influence the regulating prices (see also Schefold 1981). Long-run changes in "social" (or "effectual") demand and output, accompanied by capital accumulation, affect the relative market values (or prices of production) by changing the direct and indirect labor requirements and/or by giving more weight to the least or most efficient producers in industries (see appendix 3.2).[28]

2.3.4. AVERAGE PROFIT RATE, DIFFERENTIAL PROFIT RATES, AND RENT

Up to this point, I have assumed that profit rates fluctuate around the average profit rate in the economy, and an average profit rate was regarded as part of the production price that allows the commodity to be produced and reproduced. In Marx, as well as in the classical theory, however, the effectiveness of the tendency toward an equalization of profit rates, and thus the fluctuation of industry profit rates around the general profit rate, as derived before, is based on the following conditions (see Marx 1967b:196):

The existence of "free" wage labor, i.e., the removal of barriers to the mobility of workers.

The removal of all artificial monopolies in production and trade, i.e., of all barriers which restrict the free inflow and outflow of capital.

The retreat of the state from production and circulation and the self-regulation of supply and demand on all markets by competition of the individual capitals.

Thus, free competition is based on mobility of capital, which permits the inflow and outflow of capital with as few restrictions as possible.[29] Compared with those commodities that are considered freely reproducible by the mobility of capital, Marx also speaks of another type of commodities that are unreproducible or reproducible only under restricted conditions. In areas where barriers to the mobility of capital exist, e.g., in the production of agricultural products, minerals, and raw materials, a rent can arise. Marx especially analyzed "artificial" or "natural" barriers to the mobility of capital in his theory of ground rent. Landowners can capture a rent because they have a monopoly in landed property. The access to land is limited, and if demand increases, agricultural products cannot be reproduced easily on an extended scale. The competition of capital for fields of production brings about a rent for landed property. As can be seen from the following quotation, landed property especially is considered in Marx an "artificial" or "natural" monopoly," which leads to restricted mobility of capital. Absolute rent arises "if equalisation of surplus-value into average profit meets with obstacles in the various spheres of production in the form of artificial or natural monopolies, and particularly monopoly in landed property, so that a monopoly price becomes possible" (Marx 1967b:861). On the other hand, "if the equalisation of the values of commodities into prices of production does not meet any obstacles, then the rent resolves itself into differential rent. . . ." (p. 860). As we can see from this quotation, the restricted mobility of capital in agricultural production—but also in the production of minerals and other raw materials—become a cause of the appropriation of surplus value in the form of a rent.[30]

As is well known, in Ricardo, scarcity and rent do not play a role in price determination. Since in Ricardo there is no rent on the marginal land and the regulating price is determined by the marginal producer, rent is not an element in price determination. Thus, even in the exceptional case, scarcity does not affect the relative prices. In Marx, since there is a rent even for the marginal producer, relative prices are affected by commodities with restricted reproducibility (like agricultural products and minerals).[31] However, the effect is limited and predictable.[32] Since I am concerned here not with the Marxian and Ricardian theories of rent but with competition and differential profit rates for industrial capital, I do not want to focus on these types of commodities.[33]

For commodities as products of industrial capital, Marx developed a very detailed analysis of the existence of differential profit rates, which is based on his dynamic theory of competition. In Marx, competition of capital does not bring about a smooth process of adjustment and convergence toward equilibrium prices and profits but rather is a force that leads to differentiation of production and market conditions, to disequilibria and deviations from the regulating price. Accordingly, we can analyze the existence of profitability differences of different industries, caused by deviations of market prices from production prices,[34] and interfirm profit rate differentials. The competition of firms within one industry brings about differentials of profit rates for firms. As discussed before, the technique of production is not the same for all firms within one industry. Firms with better techniques can capture surplus profits. Also, the size of the firms is not the same, and size advantages lead to cost differentials. Thus, differences of profit rates among firms of the same industry are quite normal, as they are between firms of different industries.

Whereas interfirm profitability differences always exist within an industry, due to the coexistence of different techniques, firm sizes, and other causes of cost differentials, without any tendency toward equalization of profit rates, the question arises of how long it will take for industry profit rates above or below the average to develop a "normal" rate of profit. The classical answer is that the time required to adjust supply to demand, market prices to prices of production, and profit rates to the social average depends on the concrete conditions of production and circulation of commodities; the time to build up new capacity in industries where the profit rate is above average, to withdraw money capital from fields of employment with low profit rates, to produce and to circulate commodities —that is, the turnover time of capital—is different in each industry. The amount of capital that is necessary to produce at the socially necessary cost of production also differs. These restrictions on the the mobility of capital could be overcome by the credit system and by borrowing and lending money capital, but these restrictions on the mobility of capital nevertheless exist and are different in each industry. No general theory about adjustment time to develop an average rate of profit is possible.[35]

In the classical and Marxian theories, these restrictions on the mobility of capital are seen as restrictions on the equalization of profit rates. Thus, the relation of supply and demand (and other causes that allow a deviation of the market prices from the production prices) can cause differential profits. For example, this is the case when new commodities are discovered and demand is still high, yet commodities cannot be or are not reproduced sufficiently fast to match demand. The market price will be above the normal or production price and the profit rate above the normal or average one. This had already been pointed out in Smith and Ricardo. In Marx, this is equivalent to the case in which the least efficient producer represents the dominant technique for the regulating price and other producers in that industry can enjoy profit rates above the norm. This will be the other way around for industries with declining demand. Moreover, Marx saw other possibilities of barriers to capital mobility. Barriers to the mobility of capital also exist, for example, for commodities that are regarded as reproducible. Commodities may be reproducible, but only under restricted conditions. This is the case when the access of capital to the conditions of production (like natural resources, special techniques, or other input factors) is limited and thus the entry of new money capital is restricted.[36] In this case, there will be constraints concerning the reproduction of commodities, the market price might be for a considerably long time higher than the production price, and interfirm as well as interindustry profitibility differences will appear, a point that is worked out well by Steindl (1952, ch. 2). On the other hand, however, there are also constraints on firms wishing to move out of industries where the profitability is declining. In certain industries, the transfer of capital faces considerable difficulties if large amounts of fixed capital are required which cannot be transferred easily when profit rates decline.[37] In those industries, the profit rate can stay below the average for a considerably long time.

Thus, the Marxian theory analyzes three causes of differentials of profit rates: deviation of supply and demand for a shorter or longer period due to shortages or gluts (and in Marx they will deviate because excess supply or demand will not approach zero in the course of time); restriction of the access of capital to conditions of production in certain production spheres and limitation of the entry of new money capital or the exit of old established capitals; productivity, cost, and size differences of firms in industries (surplus profits for more efficient and lower profits for less efficient firms, enforced by the deviation of the market price from the production price).[38]

We can see (especially in Marx 1967b, ch. 10) that Marx did not assume that profit rates will be equalized in all spheres of production in an actual economic system. The process of competition between capitals produces differentials of profit rates as well as an equalization tendency. As Marx (1967b:366) put it, "The general rate of profit is never anything more than a tendency, a movement to equalize specific rates of profits," and "The average rate of profit does not obtain as directly established fact, but rather is to be determined as an end result of the equalization of opposite fluctuations" (p. 368). To what extent the "fluctuations" of profit rates make it necessary to specify the concept of production price in the context of the Marxian theory will be discussed in section 5.2.

2.4. On Post-Marxian and Post-Keynesian Theories: The Rise of Oligopoly and Market Power

As mentioned above, the post-Marxian literature, since Hilferding and Lenin, has developed a theory of two stage of capitalist development: the stage of free competition and the stage of monopoly capitalism. In the literature since Hilferding and Lenin, three causes are posited as the main reasons for the genesis of monopoly capitalism and monopoly profits: concentration of production within industries, combined with centralization of existing capital across industries; increasing constraints on mobility of capital because of high proportions of fixed capital in certain industries; and collusive behavior of corporations and trusts within or across industries.

At the end of the nineteenth century, Engels (1978) was already describing the genesis of trusts and corporations in European countries. But Hilferding (1968) was the first European Marxist to analyze systematically the changing character of capitalism. In his book *Das Finanzkapital* Hilferding posited increasing concentration in production and circulation and the cooperation and collusion among capitals because of mergers, cartels, and trusts as the main causes of the develoment of monopoly capitalism. At the same time, he analyzed in detail the barriers to mobility of capital across industries. In his view, the increasing organic composition and the accumulation of fixed capital became the main barriers to capital mobility. As he saw it, competition was decreasing because competition among big capitals tended to be unstable and encouraged greater collusion and the formation of cartels. Competition among big capitals will not last long; it will end up in a general cartel. Production and distribution of income will be organized by the powerful, big cartel. But the cartelized industries are not the last stage of development; they will be overcome by a merger of bank capital and industrial capital with finance capital.

According to Hilferding's theory, the decreasing competition goes hand in hand with an increasing regulation of capitalism by cartels and the state. The instability of the capitalist economy is reduced. The laws of motion of capitalism are replaced by regulation. Power becomes the dominant force in the economy. Concentration, entry barriers, and collusion result in monopoly prices, monopoly profit, and the disruption of the tendency toward equality of profit rates. In competitive capitalism the existence of a uniform profit rate is assumed. The classical and Marxian theories of center of gravity, competition, and differentials of profit rates are no longer discussed. However, for Hilferding himself, who developed more a theory of "finance capital" and not of "monopoly capital," the centers of power are not the highly concentrated units of industrial capital, but the financial units. He did not assume that the highly concentrated industrial enterprises or even cartels can control their external environment, an assumption that was made in later theories on large corporations (see Hymer 1979). Hilferding still analyzed the possibility of a breakdown of oligopolistic collusions and cartels due to business cycles and crises. Moreover, his theory of decreasing immobility of industrial capital is very close to the Marxian theory of restricted mobility of industrial capital. However, more important than this similarity is the derivation of monopoly profit in Hilferding. Contrary to theorists in the later developments of the post-Marxian theory, where monopoly profit is related to the *behavior* of large corporations, Hilferding discusses very well the *economic* cause for monopoly profits. Hilferding regards monopoly profit basically as a rent for commodities with limited reproducibility (like agricultural products, minerals, and other raw materials). His category of cartel rent is derived from the excess profit in the production of primary products, where the collusion and cartelization of industries has its origin. The diversification and vertical integration of industrial firms are aimed at capturing a cartel rent by cartelization of the production and distribution of primary products, spreading from those areas to the industrial, trade, and banking sectors. The model for this analysis of monopoly can be found in the Marxian theory of *artificial* and *natural* monopoly, elaborated in his rent theory. Whereas Hilferding can indeed be called the most important forerunner of the post-Marxian theory of monopoly capital, his theory nevertheless differs in many respects from modern versions.

Lenin (1965), by referring to the empirical results of Hilferding, systematically analyzed the replacement of free competition by monopolistic competition. The concentration in production, cartels, trusts, and collusions in the market; the amalgamation of bank capital with industrial capital; and the amalgamation of the monopolies with the state were considered the main reasons for the increase of monopoly power. On the other hand, Lenin considered the capitalist mode of production to mean self-expansion and accumulation of capital. He assumed that competition is not abolished by concentration and collusion but renewed on a higher level (see also Weeks 1981). Thus, Lenin speaks not only of increasing monopolies but also of monopolistic competition and rivalry. Moreover, according to Lenin's theory, the concentration and oligopolization of industries imply not the increasing stability but the increasing instability of capitalism. Lenin regarded oligopolization, as well as increasing competition and rivalry in the production, circulation, and banking sectors, as a necessary tendency in capitalist development.

For Bukharin (1973), another famous post-Marxian writer of the twenties, competition and rivalry existed only among capitals of different nations, i.e., among the capitals on the world market. He extended Lenin's theory but at the same time limited it to national capitals on the world market.

In a very important article, Varga (1969) summarized the post-Marxian discussion of the monopolistic stage of capitalism in the twenties. His conclusion was that concentration, mobility barriers to capital, and collusion within or across industries lead not to the abolishment of competition but to oligopolistic groups and to competition and rivalry among them. Monopoly prices and monopoly profit rates above the average are not an overall phenomenon but are related to special cases.

Thus, we can see different streams in the post-Marxian discussion of the monopolistic stage of capitalism. One stream emphasizes the disappearance of competition. Power, especially regarding prices and profits, becomes the dominant force in the economy, bringing about a persistence of a hierarchy of profit rates. The other stream keeps alive the idea that, regardless of the genesis of oligopolies and oligopoly groups, capitalism is regulated by self-expansion of capital, rivalry, and competition. Monopoly profit is related to special cases and, in the long run, threatened by the rivalry of other firms. Moreover, rivalry of large firms is thought to increase the instability of capitalism (see Varga 1969). Many post-Marxian— and also post-Keynesian—writers refer to only one tradition of the literature after Marx by concluding that industrial concentration, large minimum capital requirements in certain industries, and collusion lead to a decreased degree of competition and rivalry, resulting in a persistence of monopoly prices, monopoly profits, and a hierarchy of profit rates. They refer primarily to a certain stream of thought in the post-Marxian tradition and to the theory of imperfect competition, developed since the thirties, when they conclude that the regulating laws for prices and profits are altered in the current form of capitalism and that the "transition from competition to monopoly brings with it an increase of profits and heirarchy of profit rates" instead "of the tendency to an equality of profit rates which is a characteristic feature of competitive capitalism" (Sweezy 1968:272).

Central in the post-Marxian as well as the post-Kenynesian view of the impact of the change in industrial structure on pricing and profits—as elaborated in Kalecki, Lange, Sweezy, Steindl, Dobb, and Sylos-Labini—seems to be the assumption that in modern capitalism the large firms possess "discretionary power" and do not play such a passive role as they were thought to play in the classics and Marx. According to this interpretation of the classics and Marx, the firms are active only to capture the most profitable production opportunities. Competition is seen only as a *movement* of capital according to the differentials of profitability in the different sectors, and thus as equivalent to capital mobility. Since prices are assumed to be given by aggregate laws, the units of capital can only passively either capture higher profits or avoid losses through the mobility of capital. The external environment of the firm cannot be influenced, since input as well as output prices are predetermined by aggregate laws. The market prices will respond only to a change in the aggregate distribution of capital. In modern post-Marxian and post-Keynesian theories, this so-called passive behavior of the firm in the classics and Marx, which itself is subordinated to the aggregate laws and the laws of reproduction, is replaced by the *active behavior* of large firms. In post-Marxian and post-Keynesian theories, large firms set prices and profits and determine their own environment. Especially in post-Keynesian theory since Kalecki, the position has been that large corporations are continuing institutions which set markups and prices in accordance with the degree of their market power, usually measured by the degree of industrial concentration or by firm size. The idea of markup pricing or target rate of return pricing replaces the classical and Marxian ideas of production prices (natural prices, prices of production).

This new idea with respect to pricing and profits is closely related to the new understanding of the capitalist firm. The theory of an active oligopoly firm is best summarized by Levine. The modern firm, he writes,

> so far as it takes its own survival and growth to be primary, considers the price to be governed by the condition of retrieval of the costs incurred in production, and by the degree to which the firm can mark

up those costs by a margin to cover the reproduction and expansion of its capital investment. The price of the product is directly connected to the costs of production which establishes a lower limit consistent with the reproduction and expansion of the firm. It is the incorporation of this condition which alters essentially the conception of the market. . . . Once, however, this condition is grasped as a condition built into its productive apparatus, and into its self-conception and strategic decision-making, the classical theory of markets must be radically revised. (Levine 1980:14)

This idea has been developed in part since the turn of the century in the writings of Hobson, Hilferding, Bukharin, and Lenin and in the theory of organized capitalism in the twenties in Europe, but also in the managerially oriented literature in the United States since the twenties (see Chandler 1962, 1977). Most writers stress the importance of the discretionary power of firms. It is assumed that as a result of the rise of large corporations, the large firms primarily follow the goal of survival and growth and develop a markup pricing procedure to pursue these goals of reproduction and expansion of capital. This active behavior has also been seen as the main reason why the Marxian theory of competition, value, and prices does not hold anymore. However, only when the classical and Marxian theories are interpreted in the light of the theory of perfect competition does the firm appear as a quite passive actor, adjusting toward a given set of prices and market conditions. It has already been discussed, and will be further elaborated on in chapter 6, that in Marx the firm is considered a unit of capital, aiming at its own reproduction and expansion. Competition is seen as a result of this goal of the capitalist firm and thus as a more general concept. This goal of the large firms, rediscovered in post-Marxian and post-Keynesian theory, is already very fundamental in Marx. Moreover, as shown later, the markup pricing developed by the large corporations since the twenties does not contradict the classical and Marxian concept of production prices but can be integrated into it. Markup pricing and target rate-of-return pricing seem to have their origin not in the rise of industrial concentration but in the rise of multiplant and multiproduct corporations in the twenties; they reflect not so much a change in the market structure as a change in production processes and organization of production.

2.5. Summary and Empirical Predictions
of the Different Theories

The classical/Marxian, neoclassical, and post/Marxian/post-Keynesian theories of competition and price have been reviewed in order to be able to spell out their operational predictions about empirical tests on prices and differential profit rates. As mentioned before, the classical theories, especially the Marxian, have developed not a concept of equilibrium price but a center of gravity concept. The center of gravity has the characteristics of a production or reproduction price: only long-run changes in the structure of production and in the level of the reproduction of the labor power (which determines the average profit rate) affect the regulating price. Short-run changes in demand (but also slight and short-run changes in relative input prices and in production coefficients of any industry) do not affect the regulating price. Moreover, scarcity and rent are treated as a special case which does not affect the production price, as in the case of Ricardo, since rent is not a component of price, or which has, as in the case of Marx, limited and predictable effects on the regulating prices. In empirical research on prices and profit rate differentials, we would expect industrial prices that are basically determined by the long-run cost of reproduction of a commodity (including a normal rate of return on capital invested). Since Marx also provides us with a dynamic theory of competition, uniform rates of return for firms and industries are not what would be expected in an actual economic system, but rather differential profit rates for a certain period of time, which are not necessarily due to market power but to those causes that have been discussed in section 2.3.4.

Contrary to the classical and Marxian theories, in neoclassical general equilibrium theory prices for commodity and factors of production are considered an index of scarcity. Under the condition of perfect competition, given resources will be allocated according to the preferences of consumers in such a way that an optimal satisfaction in consumption is achieved. The main difference from the classics and Marx is considered to be the elaboration of the theory of demand and how variations in quantitites influence prices and vice versa. This is the critique of the classics and Marx made by neoclassical authors:

> There is, however, a very important sense in which none of the classical economists had a true general equilibrium theory: None gave an explicit role to demand conditions. . . . A general equilibrium theory is a theory about both the quantities and the prices of all commodities. The classical authors found, however, that prices appeared to be determined by a system of relations, derived from the equal rate of profit condition, into which quantities do not enter. . . . Thus, in a certain definite sense, the classical economists had no true theory of resorce allocation, since the influence of prices on quantities was not studied and the reciprocal influence denied. (Arrow and Hahn 1971:2)

In a perfectly competitive economy, prices would converge toward market-clearing equilibrium prices by the response of supply and demand to actual prices, and profit rate differentials would converge toward an equilibrium profit rate (i.e., the interest rate as the "normal" profit rate). Besides the role of quantity variation and demand in neoclassical economics, another factor, derived from the theory of imperfect competition, would have to play an important role in the empirical determination of prices: industrial concentration. Empirical research would expect a different price determination in highly concentrated industries compared with industries having a low degree of concentration and a high and significantly positive correlation between highly concentrated industries and profit rates.

The post-Marxian and post-Keynesian theories, by stressing the role of industrial concentration and the size of the firm as important determinants for industrial and corporate pricing, would predict that neither the variation in demand, nor scarcity and rent, nor production prices play an important role in empirical price movements. According to the assumed active role of the large oligopolistic firms, one would expect to find a markup or target rate of return pricing in concentrated industries and large firms, which would lead to a strong correlation between differential profit rates and industrial concentration or firm size. Since, as maintained in the theory, this pricing behavior is assumed to be a result of the

structural and institutional change of capitalism since the turn of
the century, one would expect not only a persistence of differential
profit rates due to concentration and firm size, but also strong
empirical evidence for a pricing behavior that contradicts sharply
the classical and Marxian theories on a production price (natural
prices, prices of production). By focusing mainly on empirical
studies on pricing and differential profit rates for manufacturing
production, we neglect commodities with restricted reproducibility,
i.e., the special cases of scarce products or "natural" or "artificial"
monopolies. In this way, we can test the relevance of the three different approaches for an empirically oriented theory of price and
profit determination.

Notes

1. This is a point which has been criticized very often in the writings of Robinson (e.g.,
1974).
2. Of course, there are more general neoclassic economic models which discuss a
general equilibrium by dropping some of the assumptions of the standard model of competition. But in the case of a small number of firms in an industry , oligopolistic competition, increasing returns to scale, entry and exit barriers, and/or the presence of uncertainty and
risk, it is rather difficult to derive a unique equilibrium with a welfare optimum (see Arrow and
Hahn 1971: 129; Negish 1961; Nikaido 1968; Roberts and Sonnenschein 1977). The empirical literature is mainly oriented toward the above-outlined neoclassical *standard* model of
competition. Accordingly, deviations from that standard model are considered causes of
the oligopolization or monopolization of markets.
3. We refer her to neo-Ricardian interpretations of the classical and Marxian theories.
As has been pointed out, it has to be questioned whether the neo-Ricardians have
interpreted the *Marxian* theory of competition correctly by neglecting the difference between the classical and the Marxian theories of competition. The latter theory will be
discussed in section 2.3.
4. The use of linear production models for interpreting classical theory is somewhat
problematic, but at this level of the discussion it may be a useful instrument (see sec. 2.3
and appendix 3.2). Moreover, this interpretation of the classical model is given by most
writers who base their analysis on the Sraffa system (see Garegnani 1981). Also, the assumption of a *given* physical system in this view of the classics is still an unresolved
question.
5. Smith speaks of such centers of gravity when he develops the notion of natural
price:

> The natural price, is the *central price, to which the prices of all commodities are
> continually gravitating.* Different accidents sometimes keep them suspended a

good deal above it, and sometimes may force them down, even somewhat below it. But whatever may be the obstacle which hinders them from setting in this center of repose and its continuance, they are constantly tending towards it. (Smith 1976:75)

6. When the capital/labor ratio is uniform, the prices as formulated in (2.3) will be proportional to labor values (see Schefold 1976).

7. Schefold, who analyzes the properties of (Sraffa) prices as a function of the rate of profit, found two main results: there are n linear independent vectors of prices in terms of the wage rate corresponding to n different rates of profits, which is shown also to be true for joint production systems (see Schefold 1976); and prices in terms of the wage rate are positive even for joint product systems at rates of profit within a bounded interval (see Schefold 1978, 1980; Abraham-Frois and Berrebi 1982). However, in the literature it has not been analyzed properly to what extent relative prices change as a result of a change of the rate of profit or input-coefficients in a *large* economic system. There is another way to estimate the change in relative prices due to a change in the rate of profit, which can be derived from appendix 1. The equation system of (2.3) can be written as $\mathbf{p} = w\mathbf{l}[\mathbf{B}^*(r)]^{-1}$, where $w = 1$ and $[\mathbf{B}^*(r)]^{-1}$ represents $[\mathbf{I} - (1 + r)\mathbf{A}]^{-1}$. In this form, the estimate of change in value due to a change in the structure of production or in the profit rate r, worked out in appendix 1, can be applied.

8. Ricardo assumes a very small disturbance effect due to a change in the income distribution. In his earlier writings he develops the idea that a change in relative prices is much more sensitive to a change in values than to a change in income distribution (see Ricardo 1951, ch. 1, sec. 5).

9. Ricardo and Smith also speak of such differentials of profit rates, when the market price deviates from the natural price for a considerably long time. (see Ricardo 1951, ch. 4; Smith 1976, ch. 7). For stability of natural prices, see Flaschel and Semmler 1984.

10. Differing from the classic and especially from the neoclassic writers, Marx develops a very dynamic notion of competition. Only the Austrian school of economics has a similar dynamic theory of competition (see Schumpeter 1943; Kirzner 1973; and Semmler 1984b). For dynamics of competition see Nikaido 1983.

11. An excellent summary of the Marxian notion of competition can be found in Kuruma 1973.

12. Marx says, "The battle of competition is fought by cheapening commodities" (Marx 1967a:626).

13. As Marx put it, "The assumption that the commodities of the various spheres of production are sold at their value merely implies, of course, that their value is the center of gravity around which their prices fluctuate, and their continual rises and drops tend to equalize" (Marx 1967b:178).

14. Marx considers the social value of a commodity to be determined by the socially necessary labor time, which is a weighted average of the labor time directly and indirectly used up in the multiple production processes in one industry. Assuming, for example, n producers, we can write the social value of a commodity as

$$\overline{\lambda}_i = \sum_{J=1}^{n} \beta_i^j \lambda_i^j,$$

with

$$\beta_i^j = x_i^j \bigg/ \sum_{J=1}^{n} x_i^j$$

We can see that different convex combinations of the individual values can represent the social value or the market value. (See Marx 1967b:182 and sec. 6.2 of this book). Sometimes Marx also assumes the extremes x_i^1 or x_i^n to represent the social value. In any case, the weights, and thus the market shares of the firms, must be considered to be given. (On the other hand, if $\bar{\lambda}_i$ is considered to be given, then different convex combinations of the individual values can represent the social value). A more formal treatment of this problem will be given in section 6.2 (see also Semmler 1984b).

15. Marx is not quite clear on this point. We can find the assumption that the mass of commodities is available in the market and that the market price will be determined by the market interaction of supply and demand. (This, as Deleplace (1981) has shown, is the position of Smith.) However, usually Marx makes the assumption that the investment decisions are oriented toward the market price and the market rate of profit as a guideline for investment and production (see Marx 1967b:190).

16. This adjustment process of the market price toward the market value (or, in Smith, toward the natural price) assumes not only, as mentioned above, that the market value does not change, but also that the market value is known by the buyers. Smith, for example, explicitly stated: "The market price of every particular commodity is regulated between the portion between the quantity which is *actually* brought to the market and the demand of those who are willing to pay the *natural price* of the commodity, or the whole value of the rent, labor and profit which must be payed to bring it thither" (Smith 1976:73) As we can see, already in Smith the assumption was made that the buyers who address their "effectual demand" to the market know the long-run prices (in the case of Smith, the natural prices). But these are obviously very strong assumptions for a market system.

17. Marx (1967b) gives many examples in ch. 10, vol. 3 of *Capital* in which the market value changes during the adjustment process or the fluctuation of the market price around the market value. It might be argued, as it is by Deleplace, that the market value should be considered constant during the adjustment process, since a theory of the change of the market value (the center of gravity) is based on a theory of accumulation and should not be confused with the demonstration of the working of the market processes (see sec. 2.3.3). However, this point is still a matter of dispute in Marxian economics (see also Itoh 1980).

18. The change of the center of gravity however, does not necessarily follow from a changing relation of supply and demand. If there are different types of production processes in one industry, a rise or decline in output could affect the multiple production processes equally.

19. Even in this case, Marx maintains that the "law of value" determines the price movement indirectly. He writes:

> No matter how the prices are regulated, we arrive at the following: 1) the law of value dominates price movements with reductions or increases in required labor time making prices of production fall or rise. . . . 2) the average profit determining the prices of production must always be approximately equal to that quantity of surplus value which falls to the share of individual capital in its capacity of an aliquot part of the total social capital. . . . (Marx 1967b:179)

In the Marxian sense, the natural price or the price of production is the form of the center of gravity "that appears in competition." Therefore, he says,

> We can well understand why the same economists who oppose determining the value of commodities by labor time, i.e., by the quantity of labor contained in them, why they always speak of prices of production as centers around which market prices fluctuate. They afford to do it, because the price of production is an utterly external and prima facie meaningless form of value of commodities, a form as it appears in competition. . . . (p. 198)

20. If we allow for buying and selling at market prices (which imply differences in profitability) and even at different periods of time, which is characteristic for investments, then profit rates in industry above or below the average can prevail even if demand and supply are in balance (see sec. 5.2). On the other hand, the adjustment process does not necessarily have to be stable in the sense that the market price returns to the price of production. See Nikaido 1983; Flaschel and Semmler 1984.

21. Mathematical perturbation analysis can be applied to this problem (see Fox 1965).

22. The possibly sensitive effect on relative values of a change in coefficients does not mean that the values change discontinuously due to a small change in coefficients. Rather, it means that values change with a "different speed."

23. For example, when in one industry a new capital enters or some old capitals become more inefficient, this may change the organic composition in that industry (and also in other industries), and the whole value vector may be affected greatly.

24. It is true that the eigenvalue, and thus the profit rate, is a continuous function of A, but in the case of an ill-conditioned eigenvalue, it can change sensitively in response to a small perturbation of A (see appendix 2 and Ortega 1972:44). Which raises the question, whether the new profit rate and relative prices represent a relevant economic equilibrium.

25. However, it is possible to show that there exists an upper limit for the price change due to a change in the real wage vector d (see appendix 2). The direction in which prices of production—measured in any numeraire—change when income distribution changes still remains a question to be solved. Here, only upper limits are discussed. The question of to what extent prices in a large economic system switch over when the income distribution (the vector d) is altered still has to be discussed in the Marxian as well as in the Sraffian framework. Sraffa (1960, ch. 6) in his example refers only to two labor inputs in different time periods; he does not discuss this problem of switching of prices in a large economic system, where different price effects due to changes in different variables may cancel out to a certain extent. A first attempt to solve this problem has been made by Schefold (1976), who discusses the change of relative prices due to a change in the profit rate within the Sraffian framework, where wages are paid ex post.

26. As mentioned, price change due to technical or structural change is discussed here in a circulating capital model. However the approach developed here can easily be extended when fixed capital is included in the model of production prices (see sec. 3.1.3).

27. For example, concerning supply and demand, Marx maintains that supply and demand are equated only "when the whole is viewed over a certain period, but only as an average of past movements" (Marx 1967b:190). This quotation, as well as the following one, shows that Marx thought of values and prices of production as moving averages and not as an equilibrium solution of a linear system. Concerning the law of value, which regulates prices, Marx says, "Under capitalist production, the general law acts as the prevailing tendency only in a very complicated and approximate manner, as a never ascertainable average of ceaseless fluctuations" (p. 161). Another mathematical concept might have to be worked out to enable the Marxian theory of competition, value, and price to be modeled correctly (see Lange 1963, ch. 3, where he speaks of the "stochastic character" of economic laws). Thus, a price vector may prevail that is not necessarily an equilibrium price vector. Marx speaks about "opposing movements" in regard to coefficients in industries as well as to prices, profits, and wages. He uses this concept to demonstrate their relative stability in a large economic system, in which the different effects of change in different variables tend to cancel each other out in the short run (see Marx 1967b, ch. 10).

28. In Marx, it is capital accumulation and change in productivity which lead to a change in direct and indirect labor requirements as the first good approximation for centers

of gravity. Moveover, it is maintained that the change in values dominates the influence of the change in income distribution on production prices. Marx speaks of an *indirect* regulation of relative prices by the law of value, or the socially necessary labor time (see Marx 1967b:179). This proof of the empirical relevance of the labor theory of value, which maintains that the change in direct and indirect labor requirements is more important for relative price changes than the change in income distribution, was first attacked by Boehm-Bawerk (1949). An exact proof has not been given for this Marxian theorem, but neither has an exact counterproof, since it is very difficult to estimate the change in relative prices (prices of production) due to a simultaneous change in the labor coefficients *and* wages (or income distribution). However, some empirical evidence for the dominance of the change in productivity over the change of other input costs for relative price change can be found (see sec. 3.2.3).

29. The conditions for free competition worked out in the classical theory, however, represent not an assumption of idealized market conditions but preconditions of competition which at that time had not yet been realized. We might argue that with the formation of larger enterprise units, with regional and intersectoral mobility of capital, and with the removal of state-imposed restrictions on competition, competition in the Marxian sense, and thus the tendency toward the formation of an average profit rate, becomes fully effective. (Clifton 1977, 1979). But this does not mean that capitalist market systems got closer to "perfect competition." The assumption of a large number of buyers and sellers on the markets, of market participants who act independently of one another but who are without influence, and of the anonymous regulation of prices and quantities by supply and demand and their convergence toward equilibrium prices and quantities certainly does not have to be made.

30. In Ricardo and in neo-Ricardian literature, it has been denied that an absolute rent, i.e., a rent also on marginal land, exists. Only differential rent exists—differential rent I as a result of different fertility of land (however, it depends on the income distribution) and differential rent II as a result of scarcity and of different methods of production for the same quality of land. Rent in this sense is a result of scarcity; however, since the marginal producer determines the price without paying rent, rent does not enter into the price determination (see Abraham-Frois and Berrebi 1976, sec. 3.4, 1979, 1980; Cartelier 1979; Lipietz 1979).

31. In Marxian literature, it is usually assumed that the marginal producer pays rent (absolute rent) and other producers pay differential rent of type I or II. In Marxian discussion, it has been debated whether the absolute rent has its source in the excess of surplus-value over profit, appropriated by the capitalist farmer due to a lower organic composition of capital in agriculture, or whether the absolute rent has its source in the monopoly power of owners of landed property and therefore is a phenomenon of a monopoly price (see Fine 1979; Murray 1977; Fujimori 1981). As argued above, Marx saw the main source of the phenomenon of absolute rent in the restricted mobility of capital due to the private ownership of natural resources. In neoclassical literature, only the exhaustibility of resources is considered a source for rent (see Gray 1914; Hotelling 1931; Gordon 1967).

32. Marx (1967b:861) mentions the possibility that there is also a rent for the marginal producer even if the organic composition of capital is not below the average for those spheres of production, but due to the interrelation of the extensive and intensive rent, absolute rent as well as its effect on the prices of the commodity and on the overall redistribution is limited and predictable. This point has been worked out by Koshimura (1977) and by Okishio (1956).

33. However, as we will see later, there is a restricted reproducibility not only for agricultural products and exhaustible resources but also, to a certain extent, for products of industrial capitals.

34. Also, the market price does not have to be the same for all producers (see Marx 1967b:193; Arrow 1959). Whereas in the Marxian theory "the general rate of profit is never anything more than a tendency, a movement to equalize specific rates of profit" (Marx 1967b:366), in the neoclassical theory of competition differentials of profit rates are a result of "market imperfections or risk."

35. This may be shown in the following quotation:

. . . the oscillation of market prices, rising now over, sinking now under the . . . natural price, depends on the fluctuations of supply and demand. . . . The average periods during which the fluctuations of market prices compensate each other are different for different kinds of commodities, because with one kind it is easier to adapt supply and demand than with the other (Marx 1970:208)

36. See Marx 1967b, ch. 23. However, here too the size of the absolute rent is rather limited, since any increase in price allows the application of a new technique (intensive rent) or may lead to the discovery of new resources with a different location (extensive rent).

37. Marx says:

This movement of capital is primarily caused by the level of market prices, which lift profits above the general average in one place and depress them below it in the other. Merchant's capital is left out of consideration as it is irrelevant at this point. . . . Yet, with respect to each sphere of actual production—industry, agriculture, mining, etc.—the transfer of capital from one sphere to another offers considerable difficulties, particularly on account of the existing fixed capital. Experience shows, moreover, that if a branch of industry, such as, say, the cotton industry, yields unusually high profits at one period, it makes very little profit, or even suffers losses, at another, so that in a certain cycle of years, the average profit is very much the same as in other industries. (Marx 1967b:208)

But, of course, capital mobility takes place also by using depreciation reserves for new purposes rather than for reinvestment.

38. Marx also refers to the first possible cause of a higher profit rate as "accidental monopoly" (see Marx 1967b:178). The second cause, of course, also includes the possible case of an "artificial or natural monopoly." In any case, however, Marx assumes that these types of monopolies as well as their effects are limited and predictable (p. 861).

Part 2. Empirical Evidence on Industrial and Corporate Pricing and Differential Profit Rates

After working out empirical price equations and defining the main variables which are relevant for the determination of relative prices and their changes in the different theories, I present a review of numerous empirical studies on pricing and differential profit rates. This review will help us to evaluate the contributions of the different approaches toward a theory of the empirical determinants of industrial and corporate prices and profit differentials.

3. EMPIRICAL EVIDENCE ON INDUSTRIAL AND CORPORATE PRICING

In this chapter I want to give a review of econometric studies on industrial and corporate pricing and confront the three different approaches with the empirical evidence. Three points are discussed here. In section 3.1, I attempt to work out empirical price equations used in the literature for the three approaches. This requires a discussion of the empirically relevant variables for the so-called competitive prices (neoclassic), oligopoly prices (post-Marxian/post-Keynesian), and production prices (classic/Marxian). In section 3.2, I will examine whether there is any clear empirical evidence for the competitive pricing mechanism, for oligopolistic pricing due to market power, or for classical and Marxian production prices. In this section, I will summarize econometric studies which could give an answer on these positions. Even if there are "higher prices" in industries where firms have market power and profit rates are above the average, does this necessarily mean that prices in those industries increase faster than prices in other industries? One important aspect of section 3.3 will be a discussion of the timing and magnitude of price change in so-called oligopolistic industries vis-à-vis timing and magnitude of price change in competitive industries.

3.1. Price Equations for the Competitive Mechanism, Oligopolistic Pricing, and Production Prices

3.1.1. COMPETITIVE MECHANISM AND SUPPLY AND DEMAND—NEOCLASSICAL THEORY

According to the neoclassical theory, prices respond to the disequilibrium of supply and demand in competitive markets. This theorem usually is expressed in the so-called excess demand function: $z_i(\mathbf{p}^*) = D_i(\mathbf{p}^*) - S_i(\mathbf{p}^*)$; i.e., prices respond to the difference between demand (D) and supply (S) in each market, and the excess demand ($\mathbf{z}$) depends continuously on actual prices ($\mathbf{p}^*$) (see appendix 5). Using a Euclidean distance measure, we can say that if there is any arbitrary price vector $\mathbf{p}^*_t$ prevailing in the markets that is not the equilibrium price vector $\mathbf{p}^\circ$, then supply and demand, enforced by competitive forces, will change such that the differences between supply and demand $\| \mathbf{D}^*_{t+1} - \mathbf{S}^*_{t+1} \|$ and between the actual price vector and the equilibrium price vector $\| \mathbf{p}^*_{t+1} - \mathbf{p}^\circ \|$ become smaller and smaller. Thus, $\| \mathbf{D}^*_{t+1} - \mathbf{S}^*_{t+1} \| < \| \mathbf{D}^*_t - \mathbf{S}^*_t \|$ and $\| \mathbf{p}^*_{t+1} - \mathbf{p}^\circ \| < \| \mathbf{p}^*_t - \mathbf{p}^\circ \|$. These differences decrease in a dynamic adjustment process and ultimately converge toward zero (where $\| \; \|$ is the Euclidean vector norm). In the neoclassical theory it is assumed that the adjustment mechanism is such that, once the possible production technique, the initial endowment of the individuals, and the taste of the consumers are given, actual prices and quantities will converge toward equilibrium prices and quantities, a convergence caused by competitive forces on the side of sellers and buyers. $\mathbf{D}^\circ$ will become identical with $\mathbf{S}^\circ$ and $\mathbf{p}^*$ with $\mathbf{p}^\circ$. Thus, in equilibrium we get for each market: $z_i(\mathbf{p}^\circ) = D_i(\mathbf{p}^\circ) - S_i(\mathbf{p}^\circ) = 0$. The necessary assumptions for such a clearing process of the market are shown in section 2.1.

For the most part it is admitted that this process of convergence and continuous clearing of the market is a result of the competitive mechanism only in situations where the costs of changing prices and quantities are negligible. But in reality the costs of continuous price and quantity change are pretty high and the transactions are taking place amid uncertainty. Thus even the neoclassical theory has to concede that the "continuous clearing case, where production equals supply and supply equals demand, is probably an exception. Disequilibrium is the more common situation" (Eckstein and Fromm 1968:1160). Neoclassical economists are aware of the adjustment cost and uncertainty as obstacles to a continuous adjustment process toward an equilibrium. Nevertheless, they assume that, in principle, prices will respond to disequilibria of the markets and that prices are ultimately determined to supply and demand, i.e., by the competitive mechanism.

Setting aside the causes of the disequilibria in the markets, the firms, by following marginalist principles, will maximize profits, as given by the following expression: $\Pi = px - wL(x) - p_m mx$, where Π is the profit, p the output price, x the level of output, w the wage rate, $L(x)$ the man-hours, p_m the material price, and m the material inputs per unit of output (see Eckstein and Fromm 1968:1162).

Profit maximization of competitive firms requires

$$p = w(dL/dx) + p_m m, \qquad (3.1)$$

where the price p is given by supply and demand of the product x_i on the market,

$$\delta p / \delta w = dL/dx, \text{ and } \delta p / \delta m = m.$$

For discrete price change when the change in marginal costs equals the change in variable cost (VC) (fixed costs may be omitted at the moment), we delete the second-order interactions to get

$$\Delta p = w \, \Delta(L/x) + (L/x) \, \Delta w + p_m \, \Delta m + m \, \Delta p_m. \qquad (3.2)$$

Hence the change in price is equal to the change in unit labor cost, which is the sum of the change in the wage rate and the unit labor requirement, plus the change in material cost, which itself is dependent on change in material prices and unit material requirements (see Eckstein 1972 and Beal 1975).

Thus, we may write the expression above in the following form:

$$\Delta p = \Delta ULC + \Delta UMC = \Delta VC, \qquad (3.2a)$$

where ULC and UMC are the unit labor and unit material costs.

If we assume monopolies in the markets or monopolistic competition based on product differentiation, we get the following expression:

$$p = MR \frac{1}{1 - 1/e} = MC \frac{1}{1 - 1/e}, \qquad (3.3)$$

where MR is marginal revenue, MC marginal cost, and e the elasticity of demand. Since $(p - MC)/p = 1/e$, we get $(p - MC)/p = 1/e = \pi^m$. π^m is the monopoly price-cost margin. According to Lerner (1933), the price-cost margins for monopolies are a function of the elasticity of demand. Within the framework of the neoclassical theory of monopoly, the profit for a monopoly is determined by the elasticity of demand. This is also fundamental in the treatment of monopolies in a general equilibrium framework (see Negishi 1961; Arrow and Hahn 1971, ch. 6). Thus, in the case of monopoly power in the market, we get the following modified formula for price changes:

$$p = VC \frac{1}{1 - 1/e}. \qquad (3.3a)$$

But we have to bear in mind that fixed capital and thus fixed costs are omitted and that changes of prices are only a function of changes in variable costs. In empirically oriented neoclassical literature it is taken for granted that prices respond to two things: factors influencing marginal cost, especially costs such as unit labor cost and unit material cost, and disequilibria on the markets, such as unfilled orders, disequilibria in inventories, and the industrial operating level (which are indicators of changes in demand). A number of neoclassically oriented studies have been conducted to test the competitive market mechanism. I shall come back to this point later.

3.1.2. MARKET POWER AND OLIGOPOLISTIC PRICING—POST-KEYNESIAN THEORY

In more critically oriented theories, it is assumed that concentration, entry barriers, and collusion within or across industries have broken down the competitive mechanism. Theories of monopolistic or oligopolistic markets were developed according to which prices do not respond to disequilibria in supply and demand.[1] In this school of thought, the "law of supply and demand" of neoclassical economics is rejected, price reaction functions do not exist and prices do not converge toward equilibrium prices. This position is taken especially by post-Keynesian writers like Kalecki (1971), Dobb (1973), Robinson (1965, 1971), Steindl (1952), Sylos-Labini (1969), Harcourt and Kenyon (1976), Eichner (1973, 1976, 1980), Kregel (1973), Wood (1975), Asimakopulos (1975), Hazledine (1974), and Robinson and Eatwell (1973). According to these authors, prices do not react in the short run to quantity disequilibria in the market. Prices are constituted by the cost of production (at a normal rate of capacity utilization) and a markup determined by the degree of monopoly. In referring to the theoretical framework of Sraffa, Dobb (1973:268) writes:

> We have seen that Kalecki provided an explanation of distribution of this very type, and with the situation of modern capitalism evidently in mind. According to this the share of profits in (gross) output was determined by the degree of monopoly, which gave the firm or entrepreneur the power to exact a mark-up on prime cost by price raising. Whatever the level of money-wages, the ratio of prices to it (and hence the real wage and profit-margin) will be dependent upon the price-raising power with which firms are endowed—something that varies in inverse relation to the amount of effective competition.

Accordingly, prices respond only to changes in the variable or fixed costs. In the neoclassical theory, even in cases where monopolistic or oligopolistic firms dominate the market, prices react to supply and demand. The degree of monopolization of the markets is itself determined by the elasticity of demand e. In post-Keynesian theory, monopolistic or oligopolistic firms do not react to a disequilibrium in the market by price adjustment, at least in the short run. According to post-Keynesian authors, in oligopolistic industries the price decisions are subject to great uncertainty because of interdependent reaction. These authors argue that the big companies are likely to view pricing decisions in a longer run. Increases in costs are passed along in discretionary fashion. The management of big firms is likely to expand the firm in the longer run and therefore is less likely to attempt to equilibrate supply and demand in the short run. It will not change prices frequently. When demand falls, the adjustment will be made by lowering production and less by cutting prices. See the original contributions by Steindl (1952) and Sylos-Labini (1969).

Within the post-Keynesian school of thinking several variants of oligopolistic pricing can be found.

According to one version of oligopolistic long-term pricing, prices are set to earn a target rate of return on capital at a standard volume of output. Prices are changed if the cost of production for the standard output changes, either because of changes in prices of inputs or because of technical progress. The method of target return prices can be expressed as follows:

$$p = ULC^N + UMC^N + \frac{\pi K}{x^N}, \qquad (3.4)$$

where π is the target rate of return on capital, K the capital stock, x^N the normal output, and ULC^N the unit labor cost, and UMC^N the unit material cost at normal output x^N.

Another variant of oligopolistic pricing is markup pricing. This can be expressed by the following formula:

$$p = (1 + \mu)(ULC^N + UMC^N), \qquad (3.5)$$

where μ is the markup factor, which covers the capital cost $(\pi K/x^N)$. But the capital/output ratio and the profit rate do not enter the price equation. Since

$$(1 + \mu)(ULC^N + UMC^N) = ULC^N + UMC^N + \frac{\pi K}{x^N}$$

$$\mu VC = \frac{\pi K}{x^N}, \qquad (3.6)$$

the markup over variable cost must change if the capital output ratio or the target rate of return changes. Thus, these expressions of oligopolistic pricing are highly correlated with each other. Moreover, if we assume a certain rate of depreciation as the main part of fixed cost in the price equation, the markup over variable cost has to vary with this part of fixed cost even if the capital/output ratio and the profit rate do not alter. Since in this case the markup must cover the depreciation as well, we get the following relation:

$$\mu(ULC^N + UMC^N) = \frac{dK}{x^N} + \frac{\pi K}{x^N}.$$ (3.6a)

If the fixed cost dK/x^N is increasing, when the demand declines the markup has to rise. Many empirical studies do not consider this interrelation of fixed cost and markup size. I shall come back to this point in the empirical part of this chapter.

Several theories exist to explain the size of the target rate of return or the markup over variable cost in oligopolistic markets. One of the earliest positions on this question was taken by Kalecki (1971). In his view the markup over variable cost in different industries is determined by the different degrees of industrial concentration, and the different markups within one industry are determined by the distribution of power among the firms in that industry. He uses the following expression for markup pricing:

$$p = mu + n\bar{p}.$$ (3.7)

In this equation, u is the variable cost, $\bar{p}$ the weighted average price of all firms in the industry, and m and n positive coefficients, with n less than 1. The variables m and n can be regarded as coefficients which indicate the firm's position within one industry. On the other hand, the weighted average of m and n determine the markup for the industry, depending on the degree of industrial concentration. Thus, we can write Kalecki's markup pricing formula for the average price in an industry in the following way:[2]

$$\bar{p} = (1 + \bar{\mu})\bar{u},$$ (3.7a)

where $1 + \bar{\mu} = \bar{m}/(1 - \bar{n})$, $\bar{m}$ and $\bar{n}$ are the weighted averages of the coefficients m and n, $\bar{\mu}$ is the markup, and $\bar{u}$ is the weighted average of the variable costs of the firms.

For other authors, like Bain (1956), Sylos-Labini (1969), Modigliani (1958), and Baron (1973), the target return on capital or the markup factor is determined by potential competition, i.e., by barriers to entry into markets of already established firms. This version of oligopolistic pricing is called limit pricing or entry-preventing pricing. According to this theory oligopolistic firms set prices above their costs but below prices at which potential competitors could enter the market and earn positive profits. If this pricing method is assumed, markups, and thus prices, depend on many factors, like the degree of concentration, economies of scale, product differentiation, absolute cost advantages of already established firms, capital requirements, elasticity of demand, substitution, and internal interdependence of oligopolistic firms. The markup and the prices seem to become arbitrary within the framework of this approach. However, this seems to be a very good starting point for analyzing differentials of profit rates between firms and industries. I shall deal with this problem in chapter 4.

Modern literature on large corporations has taken a new position regarding the size of the target return or the markup. According to the majority of this literature (see Baumol 1962; Morris 1964), the aim of the companies is not short-run profit maximization but maximization of sales, expansion of the market share, and expansion of the firm in the long run. Authors like Lanzilotti (1958; see also Kaplan, Dirlam, and Lanzilotti 1958), Wood (1975), Harcourt and Kenyon (1976), Hazledine (1974), and Eichner (1973, 1976, 1980) take the position that the leading corporations in the market, which are also the price leaders in the markets, calculate target rates of return and set prices so that they are able to finance the internal expansion of the firm. As Eichner (1976:x) formulates it, "The idea is that the pricing decision, when some degree of market power exists, is ultimately linked to the investment decision: that, indeed under the circumstances, prices are likely to be set so as to assure the internally generated funds necessary to finance a firm's desired rate of capital expansion." As mentioned above, short-run profit maximization is not the goal of the firm: "The broadest generalization that can be made about the goal or goals of megacorp is that it will seek to maximize its own long-run rate of growth" (p. 23). Taking this goal of the big corporation for granted, the price *level* in an oligopolistic industry can be analyzed in terms of the following formula:

$$ p = VC + \frac{FC + CL}{CU^N}, \qquad (3.8) $$

where VC is variable cost, FC fixed cost, CL corporate levy (the desired internal funds to finance the investment expenditure) and CU^N normal degree of capacity utilization. A change in the price level of the oligopolistic industries, if the variable and fixed costs are held constant, reflects a change in the required internal funds of the corporations (pp. 57, 65). Also, in this theory the markup and the target rate of return on capital represented by the factor $(FC + CL)/CU^N$ seem to be arbitrary for each firm and each industry. Only the possibility of substitution, the entry of new firms, and "government intervention" (p. 77) appear to be limiting factors for the target rate of return.

On the whole, in this modern literature on oligopolistic pricing the size of the target rate of return and the corresponding size of the markup are determined by numerous factors, such as the market structure (industrial concentration), entry barriers, international trade barriers, long-run elasticity of demand, possibility of substitution, degree of interdependent reactions among oligopolistic firms, government intervention, and so on. Different theories stress different factors, but this common ground is that price changes are due only to a change in cost of production and not to supply and demand. Accordingly, discrete price change can be expressed as follows:

$$\Delta p = \Delta ULC^N + \Delta UMC^N + \pi\Delta \left(\frac{K}{x^N}\right). \qquad (3.9)$$

The target rate of return or markup theory suggests that the following variables are important for price changes: changes in standard unit labor cost, changes in standard unit material cost, changes in standard capital output ratio, and changes in the target rate of return (or markup) and the standard volume of output.

3.1.3. PRODUCTION PRICES—CLASSICAL AND MARXIAN THEORIES

I have stated before that the classics and Marx have developed concepts of production prices which provide a simple and transparent idea of how prices of reproducible products are determined. In the context of this theory, it can also be shown how the target rates of return on investments or markups are determined. The classical concept of production prices can develop target rates of return and markups which are not arbitrary but determined by the structure of production and the cost of reproduction of labor power. By referring mainly to the Marxian concept of prices of production, I want to present a simple model and an example of how the rate of return on capital in a theory of industrial pricing can be derived. In order to keep the model simple and transparent, I want to assume that firms calculate a return only on fixed capital advanced, not on total capital advanced. After reviewing the empirical evidence on pricing and profits, I will present a more complex model, which discusses industrial and corporate prices which include profit on total capital advanced and derives not only the target rate of return but also the markups for each line of business. In addition, the impact of differential profit rate on prices will be discussed, and I will also discuss the notations in more detail. As shown in chapter 2, the classical/Marxian production prices, which include a profit on fixed capital (see equation [2.4]), can be written as[3]

$$\mathbf{p} = \mathbf{pdl} + \mathbf{pA} + \mathbf{pB'} + r\mathbf{p\tilde{B}}. \tag{3.10}$$

Or, combining **pdl**, which is equal to the unit wage cost (assuming homogeneous labor), and **pA**, representing the material cost, into the expression $\mathbf{p\overline{A}}$, we can write

$$\mathbf{p} = \mathbf{p\overline{A}} + \mathbf{pB'} + r\mathbf{p\tilde{B}}. \tag{3.10a}$$

$\mathbf{\tilde{B}}$ represents the capital stock matrix, which will be explained in more detail in section 5.3. We assume that a fraction of the fixed capital has been depreciated during the period of production, and therefore circulating capital and a fraction of fixed capital have to be replaced. Since we want to include the role of fixed capital for pricing, we do not assume that all capital goods are circulating capital goods. The elements of the matrix $\mathbf{B'}$ can be derived as follows: $b'_{ij} = \tilde{b}_{ij}/t_{ij}$, where t_{ij} represents the turnover time in years for fixed capital. For such a treatment of fixed capital, also see Pasinetti (1973) and Brody (1970, ch. 1.2). Thus, $\mathbf{B'}$ represents the replacement matrix, $r\mathbf{p\tilde{B}}$ the vector of profit per unit of output, and r the profit rate, which can be considered the rate of return on fixed capital advanced and will be interpreted later as the target rate of return. Markup pricing can also be derived from this approach. The details will be discussed in section 5.3. Brody (1970:81) developed types of price equations for socialist planning which are equivalent to markup prices. In order to determine the target rate of return on fixed capital advanced, the equation above can be written as follows:

$$r\mathbf{p}\tilde{\mathbf{B}} = \mathbf{p}(\mathbf{I} - \mathbf{A}^+), \tag{3.10b}$$

where $\mathbf{A}^+$ represents $\overline{\mathbf{A}} + \mathbf{B}'$. Rewriting the equation by multiplying both sides by $(\mathbf{I} - \mathbf{A}^+)^{-1}$, we get the following expression:

$$\mathbf{p} = r\mathbf{p}\tilde{\mathbf{B}}(\mathbf{I} - \mathbf{A}^+)^{-1}, \tag{3.10c}$$

or

$$\mathbf{p}\lambda = \mathbf{p}\tilde{\mathbf{B}}(\mathbf{I} - \mathbf{A}^+)^{-1}, \tag{3.11}$$

where $\lambda = 1/r$. If the matrix $\tilde{\mathbf{B}}(\mathbf{I} - \mathbf{A}^+)^{-1}$ is nonnegative and indecomposable, Frobenius' theorem provides that λ is the maximum, real, and nonnegative eigenvalue of the matrix $\tilde{\mathbf{B}}(\mathbf{I} - \mathbf{A}^+)^{-1}$ and $\mathbf{p}$ the corresponding left-hand eigenvector, which is positive (see appendix 3). The value of λ, and thus the profit rate r or the target rate of return on fixed capital, as well as the production prices, is completely determined by the structure of production, the turnover time, and the level of reproduction of labor power. If we assume that the turnover time will not change much over time, then the main determinants will be the structure of production and the cost of reproduction of labor power. Assuming for reasons of simplicity, that the rate of return, or the profit rate, is uniform in all industries—this assumption will be relaxed later—this approach tells us how big the maximum profit rate, the target rate of return, and the markups will be. As will be shown later, the markups cannot be arbitrary.

I want to illustrate how the target rate of return can be derived from the structure of production and the cost of reproduction of labor power by presenting an example of three industries. In order to keep the example very simple, I will assume that the first and the third industries produce goods that can be used both as intermediate goods and as consumption goods (columns). The second industry produces replacements for fixed capital goods, for example machines of a certain type, that are used up annually. Machines have a constant efficiency, and when those machines that are used up during the period of production are replaced, the depreciation enters the cost price of the product. The following matrices are assumed:[4] a transaction matrix of intermediate goods

$$A = \begin{bmatrix} 0.413 & 2.571 & 0.5 \\ 0 & 0 & 0 \\ 0.02 & 0.286 & 0.25 \end{bmatrix},$$

a matrix of consumption goods for the reproduction of labor power

$$dl = \begin{bmatrix} 2 \\ 0 \\ 0.166 \end{bmatrix} [0.04 \quad 0.5715 \quad 0.5] = \begin{bmatrix} 0.08 & 1.143 & 1 \\ 0 & 0 & 0 \\ 0.007 & 0.095 & 0.083 \end{bmatrix},$$

a replacement matrix for fixed capital

$$B' = \begin{bmatrix} 0 & 0 & 0 \\ 0.027 & 0.286 & 0.05 \\ 0 & 0 & 0 \end{bmatrix},$$

and a matrix of capital coefficients

$$\tilde{B} = \begin{bmatrix} 0 & 0 & 0 \\ 0.266 & 2.857 & 0.5 \\ 0 & 0 & 0 \end{bmatrix},$$

where $b'_{ij} = \tilde{b}_{ij}/t_{ij}$. The turnover time t_{ij} is ten years. The price system for which we assume a target rate of return on investment can be rearranged such that we can calculate the eigenvalue according to equation (3.11):

$$p\lambda = p \begin{bmatrix} 0 & 0 & 0 \\ 0.266 & 2.857 & 0.5 \\ 0 & 0 & 0 \end{bmatrix} \begin{bmatrix} 0.507 & -3.714 & -1.5 \\ -0.027 & 0.714 & -0.05 \\ -0.027 & -0.381 & 0.667 \end{bmatrix}^{-1}.$$

Calculating the maximum eigenvalue λ and prices, we get $\lambda = 15.6$ and therefore $r = 6.4\%$, $p_1 = 0.0716$, $p_2 = 0.6821$, and $p_3 = 0.2462$ (prices are normalized such that $\Sigma p = 1$). The labor values can also be calculated for the given example (see Pasinetti 1977:144), where $\tilde{A} = A + B'$,

$$\Lambda = 1 \, (I - \tilde{A})^{-1},$$

with $\lambda_1 = 0.1818$, $\lambda_2 = 1.818$, $\lambda_3 = 0.90909$.

As we can see, the relative labor values differ from the production prices, calculated according to equation 3.11. As we can also see from this example, for a uniform rate of return or a uniform profit rate for fixed capital advanced, this approach determines the size of the target rate of return, which cannot be arbitrary. As we will later see, the markup over prime cost cannot be arbitrary either. However, if we assume that the rates of return are different for firms and industries, we do not get as easily the determinants for the rates of return and prices. I shall come back to this question in sections 5.3 and 6.3. The approach discussed here also allows a discussion of the empirical determinants of price change. As shown, the classical and Marxian positions assume that price changes—taking the turnover time as constant—are regulated basically by the change in the structure of production and the cost of reproduction of labor power.

The mathematical procedure to estimate the change in labor values and prices of production due to a change in the matrices or the labor vector was discussed in chapter 2.3.3.[5] Empirical measures for testing relative prices and price change can be derived directly from equation (3.10). The main determinants for price change can be isolated. From (3.10), by substituting w (the wage rate) for **pd**, we get (see Carter 1970; Shaikh 1982)

$$\mathbf{p} = w\mathbf{lQ} + r\mathbf{p}\tilde{B}\mathbf{Q}, \tag{3.12}$$

or

$$p_i = \left\{ w\mathbf{lQ} \left(\mathbf{I} + \frac{r}{w}\frac{\mathbf{p}\tilde{B}\mathbf{Q}}{\mathbf{lQ}} \right) \right\}_i, \tag{3.12a}$$

where $\mathbf{Q} = (\mathbf{I} - \tilde{A})^{-1}$ and $\tilde{A} = A + B'$, $r\mathbf{p}\tilde{B}\mathbf{Q}$ is the vertically integrated profits, $w\mathbf{l}\mathbf{Q}$ the vertically integrated wages, $\mathbf{l}\mathbf{Q}$ the direct and indirect labor requirements, and $\tilde{\mathbf{B}}\mathbf{Q}$ the direct and indirect capital requirements. Thus, price change over the time period from 0 to t can be written in the following form

$$
\frac{p_i^t}{p_i^0} = \frac{\left\{ w^t \mathbf{l}^t \mathbf{Q}^t \left(\mathbf{I} + \frac{r^t}{w^t} \frac{\mathbf{p}^t \tilde{\mathbf{B}}^t \mathbf{Q}^t}{\mathbf{l}^t \mathbf{Q}^t} \right) \right\}_i}{\left\{ w^0 \mathbf{l}^0 \mathbf{Q}^0 \left(\mathbf{I} + \frac{r^0}{w^0} \frac{\mathbf{p}^0 \tilde{\mathbf{B}}^0 \mathbf{Q}^0}{\mathbf{l}^0 \mathbf{Q}^0} \right) \right\}_i}, \tag{3.13}
$$

or, setting $\mathbf{p}\tilde{\mathbf{B}} = \mathbf{b}$ and keeping the wage rate and the rate of profit constant, we can write:

$$
\frac{p_i^t}{p_i^0} = \frac{\{ (w^0 \mathbf{l}^t + r^0 \mathbf{b}^t) \mathbf{Q}^t \}_i}{\{ (w^0 \mathbf{l}^0 + r^0 \mathbf{b}^0) \mathbf{Q}^0 \}_i} . \tag{3.13a}
$$

As can be seen from these forms, the simplest definition of the determinants of price change could refer to the direct labor requirements $\mathbf{l}$ or to the inverse relation, productivity.[6] Ricardo and Marx sometimes refer to this determinant of price change; however, in the main they refer to the direct and indirect labor requirements $\Lambda = \mathbf{l}\mathbf{Q}$ as a good proxy for price determination. For Marx, the direct and indirect labor requirements "dominate the price movement" (1967b:178). Moreover, taking wages and rate of profit as given, price change can be tested according to equation (3.13a), where only the change in the structure of production determines the price change. In section 3.2.3. I will discuss some studies which have performed empirical tests with such price equations.

In the next section I want to give a survey of econometric studies concerning the determinants of industrial prices. Are the industrial prices regulated by the mechanism of perfect competition and supply and demand or by market power and oligopolistic pricing? To what degree are prices determined by production prices, independent of the forces of supply and demand, market power, and other random events? How strong is the empirical evidence for each of those positions?

3.2. Empirical Evidence on Determinants of Industrial and Corporate Pricing

In empirical literature we find numerous econometric price tests, which at least attempt to give an answer to the first two questions raised above. However, there are only a few studies that ask the third.

3.2.1. SUPPLY AND DEMAND AND COMPETITIVE PRICES

Several econometric price equations, based on neoclassical theory, consider cost and demand to regulate market prices. Eckstein and Fromm (1968) worked out a typical neoclassical price equation, which can be tested empirically. They tested the following price equation for the price level:

$$p = \alpha + \beta_1 ULC^N + \beta_2 ULC^N_{-1} + \beta_3(ULC - ULC^N) + \beta_4 p_m$$
$$+ \beta_5 x/x_K + \beta_6(O_u/S)_{-1} + p_{-1} + u,$$

where x/x_K and O_u/S represent the utilization of capacity and the ratio of unfilled orders to sales. Both variables are proxies for the influence of demand on prices. The prices p that are tested are wholesale prices from 1953 to 1965 for all manufacturing industries of the United States. Accordingly, the price equation for *discrete price change* is:

$$\Delta p = \alpha + \beta_1 \Delta ULC^N + \beta_2 \Delta ULC^N_{-1} + \beta_3 \Delta(ULC - ULC^N)$$
$$+ \beta_4 \Delta p_m + V_5 \Delta(x/x_K) + B^6 D(O_u/S) + \beta_7 \Delta p_{-1} + u.$$

Another equation can be written which considers *percentage price change* as a function of percentage change of the cost and demand variables (see Eckstein and Fromm 1968:1176). First the standard unit cost ULC^N has to be calculated. In order to get ULC^N, the actual unit labor cost has to be corrected for short-run swings in productivity.

The results for *price level* show high beta coefficients for the cost variables, especially for the standard unit wage cost ($\beta_1 = 0.491$, $\beta_2 = 0.543$, $\beta_3 = 0.267$, and $\beta_4 = 0.186$). Similar results are obtained for discrete price changes and for percentage over four quarters, "giving some preliminary support to the target return hypothesis as a part of the pricing process" (p. 1171). The two demand factors in the price equation—the industrial operating rate and the change in the ratio of unfilled orders to sales—are also significant, but viewed in terms of beta coefficients, they explain a smaller part of the price level. The influence of the demand variables becomes greater in the price equations for discrete price change and percentage price change. Here the beta coefficients are almost as large as the coefficients for the cost factors. The lagged variables show high beta coefficients, especially in the equation for the price level. In the equations for price change the lagged variables do not reveal such large beta coefficients. That means that *prices respond rather promptly to cost and demand changes.* In another test a variable (π) was included, which refers to the target return approach. "The profit rate (π) is statistically significant and has a negative sign, which is evidence in support of the target-return pricing hypothesis" (p. 1174). Within the demand factors, the industrial operating rate, which reflects the relation between production and capacity, plays a greater role than the ratio of unfilled orders to sales. Because the beta coefficients for cost variables are in all three types of equations greater than the coefficients for the demand variables, they can speak only of a "relative significance of different demand variables" (p. 1177), but they assume that "price change appears to be a coincident and slightly lagging indicator for the business cycle. The excess demand measures are leading indicators, and thus even though they may presage price changes their immediate mechanical correlation with price changes may be weaker. . ." (p. 1179).

In their studies, Nordhaus and Godley (1972) and Coutts et al. (1978) tested a markup pricing hypothesis for English manufacturing industries (excluding food, drink, and tobacco) for the period 1955 to 1970. According to their hypothesis, prices do not react to temporary changes in demand or cost but rather change with long-run normal costs. (Normal cost in this concept comes close to the classical and Marxian notions of cost of production.) As mentioned above, target return pricing, markup pricing, or normal cost pricing is considered an oligopolistic pricing method in post-Keynesian theory; i.e., "output price is set by taking a constant percentage over average normal historical current cost" (Nordhaus and Godley

1972:854). To get the normal cost from the average cost variables (like average earnings), the effect of cyclical changes in output has to be removed. Other costs, like material cost, fuel service, and direct tax, were taken into account by Nordhaus and Godley. A time lag between cost changes and price changes was also considered. The final price equation for predicting markup prices took the form

$$p_t = (\text{markup } 1963) \times (\text{historical normal unit cost}).$$

The predicted prices were always near the actual price, except for the period after 1961, when the predicted prices were higher than the actual prices. Thus, a remarkable decline in markup after 1961 was noticed. "If this theory of profits were precisely correct, the ratio of predicted price to actual price would remain constant. In fact external evidence shows that profit margins have declined substantially over the period" (p. 866). By introducing a demand variable, a price equation of the following type was tested:

$$\Delta\ln \hat{p}_t = a + \beta_1\Delta\ln p_t + \beta_2\Delta \ln (x/x^N) + u,$$

where $\hat{p}$ was the predicted price and p the actual price. The hypothesis was tested that the difference between predicted prices and actual prices can be explained by demand variables. The result was that the coefficients for the demand variables were mostly insignificant and very small—0.000238 for $\ln(x/x^N)$. After testing a series of other demand variables, Nordhaus and Godley concluded that "the effect of demand on prices over a normal cycle is uncertain but small" (p. 872). Furthermore, they concluded "that for non-food manufacturing industry the normal price hypothesis is correct" (p. 873).

Ripley and Segal (1973) provided a cross-sectional study for 395 U.S. manufacturing industries for the time 1959 to 1969. They used the following econometric price equation to test the theory of markup pricing:

$$\Delta p_t = \alpha + \beta_1\Delta ULC_t + \beta_2\Delta M_t + \beta_3\Delta x_t + u,$$

where Δp_t is the rate of change of price index, ΔM_t the rate of change of material cost and Δx_t the rate of change of output (value added). The equation can be derived from a markup pricing theory according to which prices include a markup over variable cost: $p = \beta_1 ULC + \beta_2 UMC$. The differentiation of this price equation leads to the abovementioned formula for percentage price change. The results of Ripley and Segal are (t statistics in parentheses)

$$\Delta p = 1.22 + 0.36 \, \Delta \, ULC + 0.17 \, \Delta \, M - 0.20 \Delta x$$
$$\quad (12) \qquad (9.9) \qquad\quad (7.3) \qquad\quad (8.0)$$

$$R^2 = 0.57.$$

Capital costs are not considered in this model. Although the result is significant and the coefficients are high, this model does not give a clear proof of markup pricing in industries. This simple equation is also consistent with the competitive mechanism, according to which prices may also rise in response to cost increase when supply falls and/or some firms leave the industry.

The last term in the equation above is included to capture the effects on prices of decreasing fixed costs. (This effect could have been made much more obvious if Ripley and Segal had taken into account a variable for fixed cost, like the capital/output ratio.) But this study too seems to show that prices are determined by costs and a markup over variable costs. However, since capital cost, market power, and demand variables are not specified, this study cannot conclusively prove the theory of markup and target return pricing. It shows only that prices respond to cost changes.

3.2.2. MARKET POWER AND OLIGOPOLISTIC PRICING

Whereas the econometric studies mentioned above do not use any market power variable to test the competitive mechanism or the oligopolistic pricing hypothesis, the following articles consider the *degree of industrial concentration* as a market power variable.

Yordon (1961) provide a study that investigated the price response to cost and demand change over the period 1947 to 1958 for fourteen U.S. industries. Half of them were classified as concentrated and half as nonconcentrated industries. He tested the following expression for quarterly changes in cost and demand conditions:

$$p_t - p_{t-3} = \alpha + \beta_1(L_t - L_{t-3}) + \beta_2(M_t - M_{t-3}) + \beta_3(M_t - M_{t-3})$$
$$+ \beta_4(U_t - U_{t-3}) + \beta_5(U_t - U_{t-3}) + u,$$

where L is the input coefficient for labor times wage rate, M is material cost per unit of output, and U is an index of utilization of capacity, a measure of demand change. The first term in both $M_t - M_{t-3}$ and $U_t - U_{t-3}$ is positive, the second negative. The econometric test for concentrated and nonconcentrated industries revealed that the coefficients for the change in utilization index (the measure of demand change) were very low and only slightly different in concentrated and nonconcentrated industries (Yordon 1961:292). (Industries with a concentration ratio for eight firms greater than 50 percent were considered concentrated industries.) Yordon concluded, "The insensitivity of price to demand change in concentrated industries is striking" (p. 291). Little difference was found between the two groups of industries. "In the concentrated group price response to demand change did not appear at all; in the unconcentrated group such response was quite limited, explaining only two percent of the variation in price change. . . . The findings suggest that insensitivity of prices to demand change is not confined to highly oligopolistic industries, but is characteristic of most manufacturing industries. . . . Prices were insensitive to demand changes, but were rapidly and fully responsive to cost change" (p. 287). But this study also shows some shortcomings: weights for the cost variables are not used, and capital cost variables are not introduced. Moreover, the demand variables are not specified enough. An increasing demand (indicated by an increase in the utilization of capacity) may also lead to a decreasing price, since fixed costs per unit of output are decreasing. This might be true until the normal utilization of capacity is reached. This ambiguous result of the change in demand must be specified when the determinants for the competitive mechanism or oligopolistic pricing are proven.

Phlips (1969) made a study of concentration and prices for three EEC countries (Belgium, the Netherlands, and France) for the period 1958 to 1964. Taking demand, cost change and industrial concentration ratios into account, he ran a multiple regression between those variables and the price change from 1958 to 1964 for the three countries. He tested the following linear regression:

$$\frac{p_{64}}{p_{58}} = \alpha + \beta_1 CR_4 + \beta_2 \frac{w_{64}}{w_{58}} + \beta_3 \frac{m_{64}}{m_{58}} + \beta_4 \frac{Q_{64}}{Q_{58}} + u,$$

where w is the wage share in output, m the material cost share in output, CR_4 the concentration ratios for four firms, and Q the level of output. The results for all three countries are similar. The beta coefficients for the concentration ratios are negative for the Netherlands and Belgium and positive but not significant for France. (The demand variable Q was tested only for Belgium and had a significant negative sign.) Whereas the beta coefficients for the concentration ratios are very low, the coefficient for the demand variable (in the case of Belgium) is almost half the size of the highest beta coefficient. The results of Phlips can be interpreted in such a way that prices respond positively to cost change and negatively to demand change. The oligopolistic pricing theory, according to which different price responses to cost and demand changes are supposed to be found in competitive and oligopolistic industries, cannot be proven by the results of Phlips. All industries increased their prices in response to cost increase regardless of the degree of concentration. The equations do not show a difference concerning changes in demand in concentrated and nonconcentrated industries, and the sign for the demand variable is negative. Thus, the empirical results do not support the competitive mechanism, according to which prices should go up when demand increases, or at least go up after the firms reach the point of full-capacity utilization. Neither the oligopolistic nor the competitive pricing mechanism is proven by the findings of Phlips. But it has to be mentioned that his methodology is not very precise. He compares only two periods, the demand variable is tested only for Belgium, cost variables are not weighted by the proportion of each cost factor in output, and capital costs are not considered.

Recently a study was conducted by Lustgarden (1975a, 1975b), who tried to avoid all these shortcomings. He used a target return approach to test the oligopolistic pricing theory. In contrast to the majority of the other studied, he also included weights for his cost variables. His reason was that unit cost variables influence the price only in proportion to their importance in total cost. For a price change between two different points in time he used the following equation:

$$\frac{p_1}{p_0} = \frac{\pi_1 K_1/Q_1}{\pi_0 K_0/Q_0} \frac{\pi_0 K_0}{VS_0} + \frac{SW_1/Q_1}{SW_0/Q_0} \frac{SW_0}{VS_0} + \frac{MC_1/Q_1}{MC_0/Q_0} \frac{MC_0}{VS_0} + u,$$

where $\pi_0 K_0 / V S_0$, $S W_0 / V S_0$, and $M C_0 / V S_0$ are the weights for capital cost, salary and wage cost, and material cost.

The target rate of return approach assumes that prices in oligopolistic industries—indicated by high concentration ratios— are determined by variable cost and rate of return on capital. Thus, when demand declines prices go up or remain stable in concentrated industries, whereas in industries with low concentration ratios prices go down when demand falls. When demand increases, prices go up faster in competitive industries than in oligopolistic industries. Because of this assumption, derived from the theory of oligopolistic pricing, Lustgarden substituted π_1 / π_0 for the concentration ratios in his regression equation. The time period chosen was 1958 to 1970; the concentration ratios are the concentration ratios for four firms, adjusted for regional and local markets. The empirical results of Lustgarden, however, fail to correspond to the theoretical assumptions of oligopolistic pricing. In a stage of decreasing demand, i.e., in a recessionary period, the coefficients of the concentration ratios were insignificant or negatively significant, whereas, according to the theory of oligopolistic pricing, positive coefficients were expected. The beta coefficients for the concentration ratios for periods of recession in the U.S. economy, like 1960–1961 and 1969– 1970, were very low and did not exceed 0.01 for his different calculations (see Lustgarden 1975a:200). Lustgarden concluded that there is no empirical support for the oligopolistic pricing method (p. 202).

Because increases in cost, price change, and demand change are interrelated, Lustgarden did not use in his extended econometric price equation the output variable Q as a proxy for demand, but a demand variable that is derived directly from an input-output table. The results are as follows:

$$\frac{p_1}{p_0} = 0.559 + 0.416 \; DC + 0.342 \; OH + 0.047 \; \frac{D_1 DM_1}{DM_0}$$
$$\text{(0.017)} \qquad \text{(0.019)} \qquad \text{(0.021)}$$

$$+ \; 0.046 \; \frac{D_2 DM_1}{DM_0} + 0.046 \; \frac{D_3 DM_1}{DM_0},$$
$$\text{(0.021)} \qquad \text{(0.021)}$$

$$R^2 = 0.342.$$

where $DC = (VC_1 / VS_0)/(Q_1 / Q_0)$ (VC is the variable costs, Q the output level, and VS the value of shipments); OH = overhead cost = $(1 - VC_0 / VS_0)(K_1 / K_0)/(Q_1 / Q_0)$; DM represents demand variables; and $D_1 = 1$ when $CR_4 > 60\%$, $D_2 = 1$ when $30\% < CR_4 < 60\%$, $D_3 = 1$ when $CR_4 < 30\%$, and all three are zero otherwise. The standard error is given in parentheses.

According to this test, conducted for the period 1958 to 1970, the demand variable does not seem to be an important variable in explaining prices. The beta coefficients are very low in comparison with the coefficients for the cost variables. On the other hand, the demand variables tend to have equal impact on prices regardless of the level of industry concentration.

Another recently discussed study was prepared by Stigler and Kindahl (1970), who tried to prove that in general, prices move in the same direction as aggregate demand. After they studied a whole series of new transaction prices (buyer prices for manufacturing industries of the United States), from 1957 to 1966, their main finding was that the new calculated transaction prices (from the National Bureau of Economic Research) showed a "predominant tendency to . . . move in response to movement of general business" (Stigler and Kindahl 1970:9). They compared the price series of the Bureau of Labor Statistics (BLS) with their new price series (NB) and found that the majority of NB prices decreased as follows in the contractions of 1957–1958 and 1960–1961, when the demand was going down:

	All Prices		Excluding Steel Products	
Price changes	BLS	NB	BLS	NB
Decrease	23	40	23	40
No change (±0.5 % per month)	19	10	16	7
Increase	26	18	18	10

But these findings were heavily attacked by Means and other representatives of the oligopolistic pricing hypothesis. I will elaborate on this point in section 3.3.3., when I discuss price behavior in business cycles.

3.2.3. PRODUCTION PRICES AS CENTERS OF GRAVITY
FOR MARKET PRICES

In section 3.1.3 price equations were developed that allow for an empirical examination of the classical and Marxian approaches to the theory of industrial price. Few empirical studies can be seen as supporting the concept of production prices as centers of gravity for market prices. As mentioned before, the idea of this price concept is that neither the perfect competitive mechanism and demand nor industrial concentration and oligopoly pricing play an important role for industrial prices, but that the long-run structure of production, i.e., the direct and indirect labor requirements, determines the labor values, and the structure of production and cost of reproduction of labor power determine the prices of production as centers of gravity for market prices. For change in relative prices a very simple version of this concept can be formulated by referring only to the direct labor requirements. Average annual price change can be taken as a dependent and average annual change in productivity as an independent variable. A simple time-series regression test can then be performed. In the following test, the deflated gross value added per person-hour (Y/L) was taken as a meassure of productivity and the gross product deflator as a measure of price change. The relation of the rate of change of direct labor requirements to price change can be tested in the following form:

$$\Delta p = \alpha + \beta \Delta (Y/L) + u.$$

Using the data provided by Houthakker (1979) gave the following results for the time period from 1947 to 1977 and for 84 sectors of the U.S. economy:

$$\Delta p = 5.22 - 0.707 \, \Delta(Y/L)$$
$$(0.056)$$

$$R^2 = 0.74.$$

It can be concluded that at a 1 percent significance level a highly significant negative relation of the rate of change in productivity—an inverse index of the change in direct labor requirements—to price change was revealed. This, however, as already stated by Boehm-

Bawerk (1949), is only a very incomplete test of the positions of Ricardo and Marx. Tests should be performed that examine to what extent actual prices are determined by direct and indirect labor requirements.

According to Shaikh (1982), by assuming a uniform wage rate in all industries, we can write equation (3.12a) for relative prices as follows:

$$\frac{p_i}{p_j} = \frac{\lambda_i \,(1 + \Pi'_i/w'_i)}{\lambda_j \,(1 + \Pi'_j/w'_j)},$$

where Π'_i and Π'_j represent the vertically integrated profit, λ_i and λ_j the vertically integrated labor requirements, w'_i and w'_j the vertically integrated wages. The dependence of relative prices $p_i/p_j = p_{ij}$ on direct and indirect labor requirements can be tested by formulating the following long-linear cross-sectional regression test:

$$\ln p_{ij} = \alpha + \beta \ln \lambda_{ij} + u_{ij},$$

where p_{ij} is the relative actual prices and u_{ij} a disturbance term representing the second part of the price equation:

$$(1 + \Pi'_i/w'_i)/(1 + \Pi'_j/w'_j).$$

Moreover, the price change over time can be tested in the following way:

$$\ln (p_{ij})_{\Delta t} = \alpha + \beta \ln (\lambda_{ij})_{\Delta t} + u_{ij},$$

where Δt means the change in relative actual prices and in relative values over time. The results of the cross-sectional regression test performed by Shaikh using input-output tables for the United States in 1947 and 1963 are as follows:

for 1947 (190 sectors):

$$\ln p_{ij} = 0.005 + 0.96809 \ln \lambda_{ij}$$
$$(0.01498)$$

$$R^2 = 0.958.$$

for 1963 (83 sectors):

$$\ln p_{ij} = 0.0138 + 0.9907 \ln \lambda_{ij}$$
$$(0.026)$$

$$R^2 = 0.948.$$

An intertemporal test for the United States has not been performed, since the sizes of the two input-output tables are not comparable. However, a test for the Italian economy, using the data of Marzi and Varri (1977) shows a strong correlation between change in relative values and change in relative prices of production. Another test has been performed by Carter (1970), which could also be considered an examination of the classical/Marxian position on price determination. Carter examines the influence of the change of the structure of production on price change. She basically tests the concept of natural price in Smith or the prices of production concept in Marx. According to our discussion in section 3.1.3 the price change can also be written as equation (3.13a):

$$\frac{p_i^t}{p_i^0} = \frac{\{(w^0 \mathbf{1}^t + r^0 \mathbf{b}^t)\mathbf{Q}^t\}_i}{\{(w^0 \mathbf{1}^0 + r^0 \mathbf{b}^0)\mathbf{Q}^0\}_i}.$$

Taking w^0 and r^0 of the period 0 as unaltered factor costs for the period t as well, the price change from 0 to t can be considered to be determined by the direct and indirect labor requirements $\mathbf{lQ}$ and the direct and indirect capital requirements $\mathbf{bQ}$ (where $\mathbf{b}$ is the vector of the money expression of direct capital requirements). In Carter's test, 1947 is taken as period 0 and 1958 as period t. Figure 3.1 shows the relation between the change in the structure of production, measured as change in vertically integrated labor and capital requirements, and the change in relative actual prices. As can be seen, the computed prices are close to the actual prices, except for some industries.

The difference between the computed and actual prices can be explained to a great extent by the change in the wage rate and the profit rate, which were assumed to be constant in order to measure solely the impact of structural change on prices. Carter's main conclusion is: "On the whole, prices rose least for the products with greatest structural improvement, and most for those where total factor economies were smallest. . . . Price changes are at least rough indicators for changing primary factor content" (p. 163). Since her approach measures the impact of structural change on prices— omitting the change in the wage rate and the rate of profit—Carter indeed measures the influence of production prices as formulated in section 3.1.3 on actual prices.

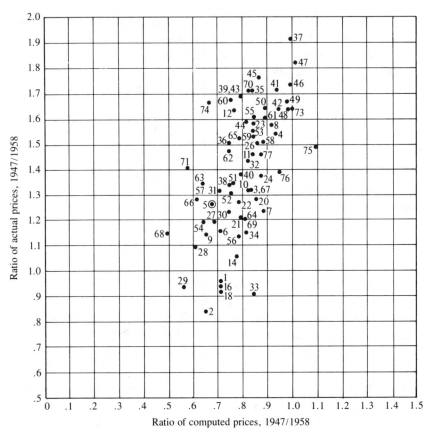

Figure 3.1. Computed Prices and Actual Prices, 1947–1948. Source: Carter 1970:160.

Brody (1970) develops another approach to testing the determination of actual prices by production prices. However, he takes into account not only the structure of production but also the cost of reproduction of labor power. His price equation is an extension of the price equation (3.10a), since he considers a rate of return on *total* capital advanced. For the economy of Hungary, he computes the prices of production for five highly aggregated sectors, by using the following price equation:

$$p = p(A^+ + rB^+),$$

where A^+ is the flow matrix, including the consumption goods for the reproduction of labor power and the replacement matrix $\mathbf{B}'$. The coefficients of the stock matrix $\mathbf{B}^+$, representing total capital advanced, are calculated in the following way: $\mathbf{B}^+ = \mathbf{T}\mathbf{A}^+$, where $\mathbf{T}$ is the diagonal matrix of turnover time. The rate of return on total capital advanced is not considered to be arbitrarily determined—as in the case of Carter, where the interest rate is taken as the rate of return on investment—but is calculated from the maximum eigenvalue of the matrix $\mathbf{B}^+(\mathbf{I} - \mathbf{A}^+)^{-1}$. The computed prices deviate from the actual prices as follows (see Brody 1970:157):

	Industry	Agriculture	Other production	Foreign trade	Manpower
p_i/p_i^o	0.84	0.85	1.05	1.11	1.14

The expression p_i/p_i^o is the ratio of production price to actual price. As can be seen from the table, the products of industry and agriculture are overpriced, indicating higher rates of return on total capital advanced. The approaches discussed here that test the concept of production prices are based on the assumption of the existence of *uniform* profit rates; differential profit rates are not considered yet.

3.2.4. SUMMARY AND CONCLUSIONS

The empirical studies discussed above do not reveal any unambiguous proof for either the competitive mechanism and prices determined by supply and demand or the oligopolistic pricing method based on a certain degree of concentration or other market power variables. In most industrial areas pricing responds only slightly to the discrepancy of supply and demand (at least as far as downward price movement is concerned), but the data coefficients for the demand variables are generally very low. In some studies a slight relevance of the demand variable to price level was shown (see Eckstein and Fromm 1968; Lustgarden 1975a, 1975b), but the demand variables are usually not specified enough to give a unique proof of their importance. Demand changes seem to have a slight influence on both concentrated and nonconcentrated industries Cost variables are usually not weighted. Some other variables, like capital cost, are also frequently missing in these studies; therefore the response of prices to change in capital cost could not be taken into account. The other cost variables, unit wage rate and unit material cost, reveal an unambiguous influence on prices, although a time lag between cost change and price change has to be considered. Thus, in the long run prices seem to be regulated by cost of production and some kind of target return on capital (markup). Other influences on actual prices (like random events, such as speculation) are not specified in the econometric studies. The other influences also may cause the fluctuation of actual prices, but empirical regression tests did not show that they did. But the determination of prices by "cost of production" does not prove the markup theory of pricing, according to which the markup differs among industries depending on the degree of market power in each industry.

On the other hand, the concept of production prices as centers of gravity of market prices seems to be supported by the empirical price tests as well. According to this concept, prices are regulated by cost of production and some kind of average profit rate. But this concept cannot be proven completely by the empirical results discussed above. The concept assumes that for pricing, an *average* profit rate is determining the markup (target return) in all industries. Since the studies do not specify the size of the markup or target rate of return, they cannot completely prove the production price concept. It will be possible to pursue this problem further after presenting the empirical evidence on an *average* profit rate or on *differentials* of profit rates.

3.3. Supply and Demand, Market Power, Production Prices, and Price Change

In discussing the relation of market power to price change, I shall not deal with Marxian, post-Keynesian, or neoclassical theories of inflation. In recent years, especially since the end of the sixties, when the rate of inflation increased, many empirical studies were conducted testing the hypothesis that the rate of price change in manufacturing industries was caused by a high degree of industrial concentration. In the empirically oriented literature we find three positions concerning market power (industrial concentration) and price change. (Since there are no studies that test price changes in the framework of the production price concept, except those mentioned in section 3.2.3, I will mostly refer here to the other two approaches). The first position, that of neoclassical theory, is that the degree of concentration really does not matter. Price increases in the manufacturing industries are independent of the degree of concentration. Only the *change* in the degree of industrial concentration influences the price change. A second position claims that concentration and market power do not *cause* inflation but transmit inflationary pressure and influence the timing and magnitude of price change in the industries. In this context, the question is raised whether industrial concentration dampens or enforces the price increase. The third approach proclaims that prices in concentrated and nonconcentrated industries behave differently when the aggregate demand rises or falls. This is the discussion about the behavior of so-called administered prices, or rigid prices in concentrated industries. (Especially this last position discusses relative price change in the business cycle.)

3.3.1. NEUTRAL EFFECT OF CONCENTRATION ON PRICE CHANGE

In empirical research some writers take the position that price change is not caused by market power, and neither has the dispersion of market power or the dispersion of concentration ratios between industries any special impact on timing and magnitude of price change. Phlips (1969), for example, tried to show, in his above-mentioned study, "Business Pricing Policy and Inflation," that for the period of 1958 to 1964 the high degree of concentration had no effect or negative effects on price increase. He ran a simple linear regression between price increase and concentration ratios for four firms (CR_4) for countries of the European Community. His result for Belgium, for example, was

$$\frac{p_{64}}{p_{58}} = \underset{(6.81)}{125.51} - \underset{(0.132)}{0.31} \ CR_4.$$

But these results are not very significant from the viewpoint of economic theory, because cost and demand variables have to be included in the price equation. After including cost variables like wage cost and material cost and a demand variable Q (level of output), the coefficient for CR_4 became smaller but was still negative. When cost variables were weighted the coefficients were below 0.05. The coefficients were not significantly "different from zero in the best regressions" (Phlips 1969:10). (The reason that the unweighted cost variable revealed a higher correlation between concentration and price change was the negative relation between concentration and labor intensity.) Phlips's main conclusion concerning the EEC countries he studied was that "concentrated industries appear to behave in the same way as unconcentrated industries as far as upward price flexibility is concerned. Prices tend to follow increase in unit costs, while market structure does not appear to have any particular influence" (p. 14).

A similar position was taken by Yordon in his 1961 article. In an econometric price equation he measured the influence of cost and demand change on prices separately in the concentrated and the nonconcentrated industries. His results concerning competitive or oligopolistic pricing have been presented above. But regarding the question of market power and the *rate of price change*, his findings were that concentrated industries neither increased the rate of inflation nor dampened it. "On the whole, inflationary pressures seemed to be transmitted through the two groups of industries in a similar manner: prices were insensitive to demand changes, but were rapidly and fully responsive to cost increase" (p. 287). The empirical results of these authors seem to support the neoclassical view of monopoly power, according to which monopoly power cannot influence the *rate* of inflation. Once their market power has increased, monopolies or oligopolies set prices (with joint profit maximization) and adjust output so that they maximize profit. In equilibrium, monopolies or oligopolies will have exercised the full power of their uncompetitive advantage. As a result the rate of inflation will not be influenced by an *unchanged* level of monopoly power (see also Phelps 1970:126; Cagan 1975). The rate of inflation will be influenced only by macroeconomic factors like aggregate demand or the quantity of money (see Cagan 1974, 1975).

3.3.2. CONCENTRATION, DAMPENING OR ENFORCING PRICE INCREASE

A number of empirical studies examine the impact of the degree of industrial concentration on timing and magnitude of price increase. The question has been raised whether concentrated industries pass a higher or lower proportion of cost increase on into prices than nonconcentrated industries do.

The study of Ripley and Segal (1973) tries to reply to that question. They applied their econometric equation

$$\Delta p = \alpha + \beta_1 \Delta ULC + \beta_2 \Delta M + \beta_3 \Delta x + u$$

to two groups of industries, industries with $CR_8 > 50\%$ and industries with $CR_8 < 50\%$. For the concentrated industries they used a dummy variable with a value of 1 for concentrated industries and 0 for nonconcentrated ones. The result was, "In general the response of price changes to materials costs and output changes is not affected by concentration, but in concentrated industries only 30 per cent of unit labor cost changes is passed on in higher prices, while in nonconcentrated closer to 50 per cent of unit labor cost changes is passed on in higher prices" (p. 268). The coefficients are (t statistics in parentheses)

$$\Delta p = 1.15 + 0.5\Delta ULC + 0.17\Delta M - 0.19\Delta x - 0.22\Delta ULC^*.$$
$$\quad\; (11.5) \quad\;\; (10.5) \qquad\quad (7.3) \qquad\quad (7.9) \qquad\quad (4.4)$$

The relatively high coefficient for the cost variable ULC^*, which is weighted by the concentration dummy, seems to indicate that price changes are negatively correlated with unit labor cost. Industries with higher concentrations seem to pass on a lower percentage of increasing wage cost. But it must be mentioned that Ripley and Segal could have improved their results by testing the correlation, not only between wages and price increase in concentrated and nonconcetrated industries, but also between capital intensity, unit wage cost, and price change in concentrated and nonconcentrated industries. If the concentrated industries are more capital intensive then the nonconcentrated, a given percentage wage increase would automatically lead to lower price increase. If they had taken into account the variable capital intensity, their results would have become clearer.

Lustgarden (1975a) has calculated the wage rate per person-hour, the output per production worker person-hour (productivity), and the total labor cost per unit of output for four groups of industries. The group of industries are $CR_4 < 25\%$, $25\% < CR_4 < 50\%$, $50\% < CR_4 < 75\%$, and $CR_4 > 75\%$. He got the results that the wage rate increased at a high rate in the concentrated industries, $50\% < CR_4 < 75\%$ and $CR_4 > 75\%$, but that the growth rate of productivity exceeds the growth rate of hourly earnings in those industries. Since those groups of concentrated industries also reveal a lower rate of price increase, he concluded, "Relatively greater productivity in concentrated industries led to relatively lower unit labor costs and relatively lower prices" (p. 32). He also concluded that, in spite of industrial concentration, the concentrated industries were forced by competition to lower prices relative to nonconcentrated industries.

Wilder et al. (1977) got a similar result concerning the magnitude of price increase in concentrated industries. Their study covered the period 1959 to 1972. They tested a markup pricing equation with a cost variable VC (unit wage cost plus unit material cost), a demand variable IS (inventory-to-sales ratio), and a market power variable CR_8. They examined the following multiple regression for percentage rates of change of industrial wholesale prices:

$$\Delta p = \alpha + \beta_1 \Delta VC + \beta_2 \Delta IS + \beta_3 CR_8 + u.$$

They undertook a cross-sectional year-to-year test for 357 U.S. industries. In their results the coefficients for the concentration ratios are insignificant or significant negatively for fourteen periods. The coefficients for the variable cost are all significant positively; for the proxy of demand change the coefficients are mostly insignificant. According to these results, a greater price change is not positively correlated with a higher degree of concentration. Interaction variables between concentration, variable cost, and the demand variable were introduced. The additional interaction variables were variable cost change, $CR_8 \Delta VC$, and demand change, $CR_8 \Delta IS$. The statistical test over all fourteen years revealed that the interaction between industry concentration and unit variable cost change ($CR_8 \Delta VC$) was negative and statistically significant. Thus, Wilder et al., by using the change in variable cost, only got the same result as

Ripley and Segal and Lustgarden, i.e., that concentrated industries pass on a smaller proportion of unit variable cost than do less concentrated industries. They concluded, "Given a rate of cost increase, the effect of concentration on the rate of price increase is weakly negative" (p. 739). But because they did not differentiate between increase in wage cost, productivity, material cost, and increase in fixed costs, they could not differentiate different causes of cost increases, and thus price increases in concentrated and unconcentrated industries. Moreover, since they did not use weighted variables, they did not even know whether the fact that concentrated industries have a more capital-intensive production method might have caused their results.[7]

Concentrated industries not only show a more capital-intensive production (see Weston and Ornstein 1973a; Ornstein et al. 1973) but also might reveal a higher growth rate of capital intensity than nonconcentrated industries. Thus the results of price equations which use only variable costs would be heavily influenced by the dispersion of capital intensity among industries. The hypothesis that concentrated industries pass on a lower proportion of a given percentage of wage increase and thus dampen inflation was tested by quite biased price equations in all three studies. Because of this, the results are not very reliable. A production price concept, which takes into account a profit rate on capital (and thus a variable for capital costs), would have avoided such a bias. (Moreover, even the result that concentrated industries pass on a lower percentage of cost increase because of their higher growth rate of productivity is in accordance with the production price concept, according to which price *change* is dependent on a change in productivity in the industries). On the other side, these results contradict other econometric studies which give the opposite result.

As mentioned above, the study of Yordon (1961) has shown that the degree of concentration does not affect the rate of price increase in response to cost change. According to his data, which cover the time period from 1947 to 1958, there is no evidence that "the mechanism of price change in concentrated industries provides a dampening effect . . . on inflation" (p. 292).

There also exist some studies which clearly reveal a significant positive correlation between the degree of concentration and the rate of price increase. Weiss (1966) tested a linear equation of the form

$$\Delta p = \alpha + \beta_1 CR_4 + \beta_2 \Delta Q + \beta_3 \Delta(MC/Q)$$
$$+ \beta_4 \Delta(W/Q) + \text{loc Reg.} + u,$$

where Δp is the percentage increase in prices and loc Reg. represents an adjustment for geographic character of the market. His data covered the periods 1953 to 1959 and 1959 to 1963. Whereas industrial concentration had a significant positive effect on price changes during the period 1953 to 1959, concentration was not significantly related to price changes during the period 1959 to 1963. In Weiss's 1971 study, concentration and price changes were negatively and significantly related during the interval 1967 to 1968 but not significantly related for 1963 to 1968.

Dalton (1973) reexamined the data of Weiss for the period 1958 to 1963, using the methodology of Weiss, but weighted the cost variables by the ratio of unit labor cost to value of shipment and the unit material cost by the ratio of material cost to value of shipment. Whereas Weiss in his study got a significant positive sign only for the period 1953 to 1959, Dalton revealed a significant positive correlation between concentration and price increase for 1958 to 1963 and for 1967 to 1969 after using weighted cost variables.

The discrepancy in the results of Phlips, Ripley and Segal, Lustgarden, and Wilder et al. on one side and Weiss (1966, 1971) and Dalton (1973) on the other may be due to different time periods observed by the authors or to a bias in the applied methodology. Empirical price equations, without using a variable for capital cost $(\pi K/x)$ and without using weights for the cost variables, are heavily biased in favor of a lower price increase in higher-concentrated industries. Under the assumption of markup pricing, a given percentage of wage or material cost increase shows up as a lower increase in prices in industries where the ratio of labor input to output and/or the ratio of material input to output is below the average and the ratio of capital to output (capital output ratio) is above the average. But these are only the direct effects of wage or material cost increases in industries with different input-output relations. Indirect effects of products from industries with input-output relations which deviate from the average may produce a distortion of the original effect of wage or material cost increase in the next industry and change its rate of price increase. These effects are well known in Sraffa's theory of prices of production. These different effects can be calculated only by using the concept of vertically integrated cost of production (see part 2).

On the other side, the empirical evidence on higher price increase in response to wage or material cost increase in concentrated industries is not very strong. This also would mean that differentials of profit rates would increase in the course of time between concentrated and nonconcentrated industries. Since neither position discussed above seems to be reasonable concerning cost and price increases in concentrated and nonconcentrated industries in the long run, we have to look for differences in price movements in concentrated and nonconcentrated industries in different stages of the business cycle.

3.3.3. CONCENTRATION, PRICE RIGIDITY, AND BUSINESS CYCLES

In this section I want to address the question of whether the timing and magnitude of price changes are different in concentrated and nonconcentrated industries in the typical stages of the *business cycle*, especially in a *recession*, when the aggregate demand is declining, and in an *upswing*, when aggregate demand is increasing. Means (1935) already raised this question in the thirties, when he showed empirical data which revealed a strong tendency of prices not to fall during the Great Depression. He called these prices administered prices. They did not fall, or at least remained relatively inflexible, when the aggregate demand was declining. He classified prices into four groups: those that did not change in four months but change at least once in ten months (administered prices), those that changed one to three times in four months (intermediate prices), and those that changed more than three times in four months (market-dominated prices). In the original discussion initiated by Means, concentration and market power did not play a direct role in the administered price hypothesis. He wrote, "Administered prices should not be confused with monopoly. The presence of administered prices does not indicate the presence of monopoly, nor do market prices indicate the absence of monopoly. In many highly competitive industries, such as the automobile industry, prices are made administratively and held for fairly long periods of time. . . . In general monopolized industries have administered prices but so also do a great number of vigorously competitive industries in which the number of competitors are few" (p. 78).

This broad definition of administered prices was challenged by Stigler and Kindahl (1970) and Stigler (1975), who published newly collected data obtained from buyers on industrial commodities. In their book they tested the administered price hypothesis "that contraction in business and the recession lead to no systematic reduction of industrial prices and expansion in business may only tardily lead to price increase" (p. 7). As mentioned before, they found that the new price index moved in response to "general business activity, and there is no evidence here to suggest that price rigidity or administration is a significant phenomenon" (p. 9).

Means (1972) responded to that challenge in an article, showing that in fact the new price series (called NB series) did not contradict the administered price hypothesis once this hypothesis was made more clear. Means rejected the definition given by Stigler and Kindahl and wanted to make sure that administered prices meant "relative inflexibility, not price rigidity or contra-cyclical behavior" (p. 293). By rearranging price groups he could show that the majority of the so-called administered prices did "not move in response to the cyclical movements of business" (p. 304). Having started that new discussion, Stigler and Kindahl replied to the response of Means, trying to show that Means had arbitrarily redefined fifteen of their price series as not market dominated and had redefined the business cycle turning points as well. His definition of administered prices and market-dominated prices assumed that the four-firm concentration ratio is low; the market is worldwide; and the industry is raw-material dominated. Some articles (Stigler and Kindahl 1973; Weston et al. 1974; Bohi and Scully 1975) were published in order to make the definitions more clear and to test the new price series collected by Stigler and Kindahl. But most of these articles did not consider the degree of concentration a determinant for the administered pricing method in a recession.

I will now summarize those articles which tested the administered price hypothesis by including industrial concentration as a determinant for administered pricing. Table 3.1 shows the regression studies on the administered price hypothesis for periods of *recession* and periods of *expansion*. For the different studies, the regression coefficients for concentration ratios are listed in Table 3.1. A significant positive coefficient in recessionary periods means that prices in concentrated industries grow faster than in nonconcentrated industries (or at least remain more inflexible), whereas in prosperity significant negative coefficients mean that prices grow more slowly in concentrated than in nonconcentrated industries. These regression results would confirm the administered price hypothesis.

Of course, the studies use different methodologies; some studies use weighted cost variables, some do not. But, despite the different methodologies, we may compare and summarize the results. Table 3.1 shows the variables tested in different studies and the results of the beta coefficients for the concentration ratios. I will start with the regression tests for the recessionary periods. The coefficients for the concentration ratios in recessionary periods are sometimes positively significant and sometimes insignificant at a 5- or 10-percent level.

As mentioned above, the study of Lustgarden (1975a, 1975b) shows that the coefficients for the concentration ratio in his several different equations are insignificant for the recessionary periods 1960–1961 and 1969–1970. The beta coefficients for the concentration ratios in the study of Wilder et al. (1977) are not significant at a 5-percent level for either the recession period 1960–1961 or for 1969–1970. Weiss's study (1971) also shows no significant beta coefficients for the concentration ratios. Only Sellekaerts and Lesage (1973) got positive beta coefficients for their study concerning the recessonary period in Canada from 1957 to 1959. They used different concentration measures. The concentration ratios for both establishments and enterprises were significantly positive. These are the only empirical results which seem to confirm the administered price hypothesis.

On the other side, the expansionary periods of the business

Table 3.1. Regression Studies on Administered Prices for Periods of Recession and Expansion

Author	Country	Time Period	Regression Coefficient for Concentration Ratios	Independent Variables
Lustgarden 1975a, 1975b	United States	*recession*		
		1960–1961	−0.010[a]	weighted ULC, UMC, CR_4
			−0.010[a]	weighted UVC, 1 − UVC, CR_4
			−0.006[a]	log (K_1/K_0), log (Q_1/Q_0), log (1 − UVC), log CR_4
		1969–1970	−0.009[a]	weighted ULC, UMC, CR_4
			−0.007[a]	weighted UVC, 1 − UVC, CR_4
			−0.002[a]	log (K_1/K_0), log (Q_1/Q_0), log (1 − UVC), log CR_4
		expansion		
		1958–1959	0.010[a]	weighted ULC, UVC, CR_4
			0.011[a]	weighted UVC, 1 − UVC, CR_4
			−0.046[a]	log (K_1/K_0), log (Q_1/Q_0), log (1 − UVC), log CR_4
		1968–1969	−0.027[b]	weighted ULC, UMC, CR_4
			−0.017[a]	weighted UVC, 1 − UVC, CR_4
			−0.043[b]	log (K_1/K_0), log (Q_1/Q_0), log (1 − UVC), log CR_4
Weiss 1971	United States	*recession*		
		1957–1958	0.089[a]	CR_4
			0.198[a,c]	CR_4
		1960–1961	−0.156[a]	CR_4
			−0.037[a,c]	CR_4
		expansion		
		1961–1962	0.149[a]	CR_4
			0.034[a,c]	CR_4
		1964–1966	−0.012[a]	CR_4
			−0.078[a,c]	CR_4

Study	Country	Period	Coefficient	Description
Sellekaerts and Lesage 1973	Canada	*recession*		
		1957–1959	0.161[b,d]	unweighted ULC, UNC, Q, CR
		1960–1961	0.119[b,e]	unweighted ULC, UMC, Q, CR
		expansion		
		1963–1966	−0.139[a]	unweighted ULC, UMC, Q, CR
Dalton 1973	United States	*expansion*		
		1967–1969	0.053[f]	weighted ULC, UMC, CR_4, corrected for local markets
			0.053[g]	
Wilder et al. 1977	United States	*recession*		
		1960–1961	−0.06[a]	unweighted VC, inventory/sales ratio, VC_{-1}, p_{-1}, CR_8
		1969–1970	−0.01[a]	unweighted VC, inventory/sales ratio, VC_{-1}, p_{-1}, CR_8
		expansion		
		1959–1960	−0.04[a]	unweighted VC, inventory/sales ratio, VC_{-1}, p_{-1}, CR_8
		1963–1964	−0.01[a]	unweighted VC, inventory/sales ratio, VC_{-1}, p_{-1}, CR_8
		1967–1968	−0.01[b]	unweighted VC, inventory/sales ratio, VC_{-1}, p_{-1}, CR_8
		1968–1969	−0.01[b]	unweighted VC, inventory/sales ratio, VC_{-1}, p_{-1}, CR_8

[a]Not significant.
[b]Significant at 0.05 level.
[c]Corrected concentration ratios for local markets.
[d]Establishment concentration measures (Herfindahl-index); VC includes only wages.
[e]Enterprise concentration ratios (Herfindahl-index); VC includes wages and salary.
[f]ULC with wages and salary, not significant.
[g]ULC with wages only, not significant.

cycle, during which the prices in concentrated industries are supposed to increase more slowly than those in nonconcentrated industries, generally show no significant beta coefficients either, as is clear in the results of the regression studies of Lustgarden (1975a, 1975b), Weiss (1966, 1971), and Dalton (1973). The administered price theory is confirmed only in the study of Wilder et al. (1977) for the expansionary periods 1967–1968 and 1968–1969, where the coefficients of the concentration ratios are significantly negative, i.e., prices increase more slowly in concentrated industries than in nonconcentrated industries in periods of expansion. The study of Sellekaerts and Lesage (1973) does not confirm the administered price hypothesis for the expansion period 1963 to 1968 in Canada. The coefficients are insignificant.

In sum, most studies reveal a very low beta coefficient for the concentration ratios; some of them are insignificant, some are significantly negative, and one study shows significantly positive coefficients in the recessionary period. In expansion most coefficients are insignificant: some of them are significantly negative (Wilder et al. 1977). According to the administered price theory, the coefficients for the concentration ratios have to be significantly positive in a recession and significantly negative in an expansionary period. Although there is a slight tendency to confirm the administered price theory, the regression studies discussed above do not show a clear-cut proof for this theory. Especially for the recessions of 1957–1958 and 1969–1970, there seemed to be a slight tendency toward inflexibility of prices in concentrated industries (see also Cagan 1975:89). For the recession of 1974–1975 there are no similar regression studies available.

Weston et al. (1974) got a similar result by observing only the price movements in recessionary and expansionary periods in the U.S. economy. Relating the percentage price increase to three groups of concentration levels, they obtained the results presented in Table 3.2 concerning timing and magnitude of price increase in concentrated and nonconcentrated industries. Only the contraction of 1960–1961 showed deviating results.

A similar result was presented by Wachtel and Adelsheim (1977), who calculated the price-cost difference for three groups of industries, i.e., $CR_4 > 50\%$, $25\% < CR_4 < 50\%$, and $CR_4 < 25\%$.

Table 3.2. Tests of the Administered Price Hypothesis

	Concentration Level[a]		
	Less Than 40%	40% to 60%	Over 60%
	n = 16	n = 29	n = 18
Contraction, 7/57–4/58			
Increase or No Change	37.5%	58.6%	66.7%
Decrease	62.5	41.4	33.3
Expansion, 4/58–6/59			
Decrease or No Change	56.2	62.1	38.9
Increase	43.8	37.9	61.1
Contraction, 1/60–1/61			
Increase or No Change	50.0	44.8	38.9
Decrease	50.0	55.2	61.1
Expansion, 1/61–3/62			
Decrease or No Change	75.0	79.3	88.9
Increase	25.0	20.7	11.1
Contraction, 11/69–11/70			
Increase or No Change	81.6[b]	85.2[c]	84.0[d]
Decrease	18.4	14.8	16.0

NOTE: The price indexes from July 1957 to March 1962 are the 63 price indexes of the National Bureau of Economic Research, used in Stigler and Kindahl 1970. From November 1969 to November 1970 the 90 Industry Wholesale Price Indexes of the Bureau of Labor Statistics are used.
[a]Four-firm concentration index for 5-digit SIC product classes.
[b]n = 38.
[c]n = 27.
[d]n = 25.
SOURCE: Weston et al. 1974:233.

In recessionary periods the difference between price and cost (variable cost) was growing in highly concentrated industries, whereas in expansionary periods the difference was declining. Since $p - VC$ is equal to μVC (μ is the factor that determines the markup over variable cost), it was shown that in concentrated industries the markup in $(1 + \mu)VC = p$ was increasing faster during recessions than in periods of expansion. Only the recession of 1969–1970 seemed to be an exception to their theory. According to their analysis, in that period international competition was increasing; therefore the oligopolistic firms in concentrated industries could not raise the markup (p. 13). (These results support the administered price hypothesis only indirectly, because the differentials in price increase in concentrated and nonconcentrated industries are corre-

Table 3.3. Price Change in Concentrated and Nonconcentrated Industries

CR_4	Number of Products	Change (percent)
Over 50%	137	5.9
25–50%	110	−1.0
Less than 25%	49	−6.1
Total	296	1.6

lated, not with cost change in those industries, but with the markup over variable costs.)

Another empirical work also seemed to confirm the administered price theory. The recently published study by Blair (1974) also shows a tendency of prices to increase in concentrated industries in recessionary periods. Table 3.3 shows the number of products for which prices increased and decreased during the recession of 1969–1970 (p. 485). His main conclusion concerning that recession was, "All [products] but one [were] characterized by either a price increase for the concentrated items accompanied by a decrease in the less concentrated products or by a greater increase in the concentrated than in less concentrated products" (p. 458). On the other side, the period of expansion from December 1970 to December 1971 shows the opposite picture. During the expansion the weighted average price for concentrated products rose only 2.7 percent, while for the nonconcentrated products the increase was nearly three times as great (7.8 percent). The change for the intermediate category was 6.0 percent (p. 465).

In sum, the administered price theory seems to be slightly supported both by econometric tests and by price change and concentration statistics. But it is not so clear what are the underlying causes of that different price behavior in concentrated and nonconcentrated industries.

3.4. Summary and an Alternative Explanation for Price Change in the Business Cycle

Since the statistics discussed above only compare price change and concentration ratios and the econometric price equations summarized in this part only test the correlation of variable cost and concentration ratios (or groups of concentrated industries) and price change, the results of these studies are ambiguous. As mentioned above, the oligopolistic pricing method can be written in two ways (see equations [3.4] and [3.5]).

$$p = ULC^N + UMC^N + \frac{dK}{x^N} + \frac{\pi K}{x^N} \qquad (3.14)$$

$$p = (1 + \mu)(ULC^N + UMC^N) \qquad (3.14a)$$

Equation (3.14a) refers to markup pricing, usually tested in the above-mentioned linear regressions; equation (3.14), which now includes fixed cost dK/x^N, refers to the target return pricing method. If we assume that prices are set to cover wage cost, material cost, depreciation per unit of output, and an average profit rate per unit of output, the markup over variable cost has to go up in a recession, when the depreciation per unit of output (or other parts of fixed costs, which may be hidden in wage or material cost) and the capital output ratio increase. But why do prices apparently not behave in the same way in nonconcentrated industries, i.e., why do prices apparently respond differently in concentrated and nonconcentrated industries, when demand is declining?

The reason for these differences in price movements in concentrated and nonconcentrated industries may lie in the empirically well-established fact that concentrated industries are on the average more capital intensive than other industries (see Ornstein et al. 1973 and sec. 4.3).[8] If this is true, then fixed cost is increasing much faster in concentrated industries when demand and the utilization of capacity is declining.[9] Thus, concentrated industries, or industries with a high proportion of fixed costs to total costs (measured at a normal rate of capacity utilization), will suffer losses in profit per unit of output unless the markup[10] and the price are going up in those industries. The opposite effect will appear in a period with increasing demand. Fixed cost per unit of output is decreasing rapidly when the utilization of capacity is rising.[11] Since the administered price hypothesis refers only to variable cost and concentration ratios (as indicators for market power), this theory mostly neglects the role of fixed costs as a possible cause of different price changes for different industries in different periods of time.

To what extent there is pressure to prevent a downward price change in a recession in industries with a high proportion of fixed costs is illustrated in Blair 1974. As shown by Blair, decreasing utilization of capacity leads to an increase of fixed costs per unit of output. If the prices do not change, the profit margin or the target rate of return will decrease. As mentioned before, part of the labor costs can also be considered fixed costs, as well as other operating costs besides depreciation. In such industries the target rate of return can be kept constant when prices are increased.

By referring to the target rate of return pricing we can show to what extent prices must move upward in order to cover fixed costs and keep the rate of return constant. (In the following model, fixed costs represent only the depreciation charge.) From equation (3.14) we can derive the discrete price change for the target rate of return approach. We get approximately

$$\Delta p = \Delta ULC^N + \Delta UMC^N + \frac{\Delta dK}{x^N} + \frac{d\Delta K}{x^N} + \frac{\Delta \pi K}{x^N} + \frac{\pi \Delta K}{x^N}. \quad (3.15)$$

Since we assume that the potential capital/output ratio K/x^N and the target rate of return π do not change, we get

$$\Delta p = \Delta ULC^N + \Delta UMC^N + \frac{\Delta dK}{x^N}. \quad (3.15a)$$

The depreciation charge per unit of output at the normal level of utilization of capacity is

$$\frac{D}{x^N} = \frac{dK}{x^N},$$

with D the total annual depreciation. The depreciation charge per unit of actual output (x^0) is $D/x^0 > D/x^N$ for $x^0 < x^N$. Thus, for a given K/x^N the depreciation charge has to increase, since we have

$$\frac{D}{x^0} = \frac{(d + \Delta d)K}{x^N} = \frac{dK}{x^0}.$$

Assuming a linear relation between the change in depreciation $\Delta dK/x^N$ and K/x^0 or D/x^0, we can formulate two very simple multiple regressions to test the relative importance of fixed costs and industrial concentration for price changes in periods of recession and expansion. From the formula above, by leaving out wage and material costs,[12] we get

$$\Delta p = \alpha + \beta_1 \frac{K}{x^0} + \beta_2 CR_6 + u \qquad (3.16)$$

or

$$\Delta p = \alpha + \beta_1 \frac{D}{x^0} + \beta_2 CR_6 + u. \qquad (3.16a)$$

Variables K/x^0 and D/x^0 can both be considered proxies for dK/x^0. These specifications allow us to test Blair's approach. A similar analysis has already been conducted by Neal (1942). By referring to the theory of markup pricing, he shows that the price-cost margin $(p - c)/p$ is significantly related to price change in the recessionary years 1931–1933.[13] Since the price-cost margin contains profit and the change in fixed costs per unit of output, it is reasonable to expect that prices will be less flexible downward where the price-cost margin is higher. A multiple regression test for 83 industries (three-digit level) in the U.S. economy, with actual gross or net capital/output ratio and concentration ratios for the six largest firms, performed for equations (3.16) and (3.16a). We get the following results for the periods of expansion and recession for (3.16). 1970–1972 was chosen as the period of expansion and 1973–1975 as the recessionary period. The average price change was taken as the independent variable (standard error in parentheses).[14]

Expansion:
For net capital/output ratio

$$\Delta p = 9.75 + 0.494 \, NK/x^0 - 0.86 \, CR_6,$$
$$ (1.85) (0.03)$$

$$R^2 = 0.094.$$

Only β_2 is significant at the 1-percent level.

For gross capital/output ratio

$$\Delta p = 8.37 + 1.96 \; GK/x^0 - 0.75 \; CR_6,$$
$$\quad\quad\quad\quad (0.72) \quad\quad\quad\quad (0.029)$$

$$R^2 = 0.172.$$

Here, β_1 and β_2 are significant at the 1-percent level.

Recession:

For net capital/output ratio

$$\Delta p = 17.1 + 14.39 \; NK/x^0 + 0.116 \; CR_6,$$
$$\quad\quad\quad\quad (5.64) \quad\quad\quad\quad (0.11)$$

$$R^2 = 0.172.$$

Only β_1 is significant at the 1-percent level.

For gross capital/output ratio

$$\Delta p = 17 + 18.58 \; GK/x^0 + 0.903 \; CR_6,$$
$$\quad\quad\quad\quad (4.38) \quad\quad\quad\quad (0.11)$$

$$R^2 = 0.19.$$

Only β_1 is significant at the 1-percent level.

By using D/x^0 (the difference between the actual net and actual gross capital/output ratios) as a proxy for the change in the percentage depreciation charge in equation (3.15a), we get the following results for equation (3.16a):

$$\Delta p = 18.3 + 67.8 \; D/x^0 + 0.9 \; CR_6,$$
$$\quad\quad\quad\quad (18.35) \quad\quad\quad (0.11)$$

$$R^2 = 0.15.$$

Only β_1 is significant at the 1-percent level.

In the expansionary period, we see different results for net and gross capital/output ratio. But in both cases, the coefficient for the concentration ratio is negative. In the recessionary period, for which we assumed, in accordance with Blair, a positive correlation between the capital/output ratio and price change, the hypothesis is confirmed that the actual net or gross capital/output ratios are more important for price change than the concentration ratios. A similar result is obtained for D/x^0 as proxy for the increased depreciation cost per unit of output in a recessionary period.[15]

These regression tests stress the role that investment in fixed capital and the restricted mobility of capital in industries with a high proportion of fixed capital play in price change in the recessionary period of the business cycle. However, they do not give an explanation of the long-run trend in price changes, nor do they answer the question of why prices—especially since the Second World War—respond less and less to the business cycle (see Cagan 1974, 1975). These considerations can explain only the dispersion of the price change in the recessionary period of the business cycle. Moreover, the assumptions under which industries with a high proportion of fixed costs may experience a greater price change than others have to be pointed out. These assumptions are that

changes in prices are made only in *discrete intervals* by firms in industries with capital-intensive production, and those firms try to attain a target rate of return not only over the long run but also in discrete intervals (for example, in a period of recession).

there are no *substitution effects* in the short run; thus, the elasticity of demand with respect to prices is very low in the short run in those sectors (see Blair 1972:518).

there are *restrictions on the mobility of capital*, i.e., on the inflow and outflow of capital, in those industries in the short run.

interdependent reaction does prevent oligopolistic firms from deviating behavior concerning prices when demand declines, and rivalry between firms is not directed toward price competition during such a period.

Since these assumptions are very strong, especially the last, more elaborate regression tests on the dispersion of price change in a recessionary period would have to use additional variables to account for those other influences, which are neglected here.

In sum, I have shown in this chapter that neither variations in demand nor in industrial concentration can be considered important determinants of industrial pricing. The first variable is important in the theory of perfectly competitive economy, the second in the theory of imperfect competition. Moreover, cost-determined pricing and markup pricing procedures, which are usually regarded as the post-Marxian/post-Keynesian contribution to a theory of industrial and corporate pricing, are not limited to concentrated and oligopolized industries but seem to be widespread procedures and can be found in concentrated and nonconcentrated industries. Although not many empirical studies have been performed to test classical and Marxian concepts of production prices, and although a theory of short-run changes in relative prices has not been developed sufficiently for this approach, it still represents a first good and transparent approximation of an empirically oriented theory of industrial pricing, one which should be pursued further. Moreover, there is not sufficient empirical evidence to prove that price changes and their dispersion between industries in a recessionary or expansionary period of the business cycle are caused either by short-run changes in demand, by industrial concentration, or by an increase of the markups or target rates of return due to exercised market power of oligopoly firms. With regard to price changes and their dispersion in the business cycle, an alternative to the explanations that attribute them to industrial concentration has been expressed. There is indeed strong evidence for uneven price changes between industries in recessionary and expansionary periods (see Cagan 1974). The idea expressed here refers more to the classical and Marxian concepts of long-run prices (production price) and stresses the importance of the change in relative cost structure caused by a different relative dependence of industry prices on labor input, material input, and fixed capital. As discussed, the relative dependence of industries on fixed capital and thus on capital costs—which usually correlates positively with the degree of concentration—is considered here an especially important cause of certain dispersion of price changes between industries in the business cycle.[16] However, the question of whether the price level in industries that show a different price movement is too "high" and firms earn profits above the average due to higher markups is not examined in this context. This is the question of causes of differentials of profit rates and markups between industries and firms in the long run. After the empirical evidence on profitability differences has been presented, the problem of the compatibility or incompatibility of the markup pricing and the production price concept will be pursued further.

Notes

1. Since in the post-Marxian and the post-Keynesian theories monopoly and oligopoly prices usually are used synonymously, I will use the expression *oligopoly prices*.

2. Depreciation is regarded here as part of the gross profit.

3. For deriving target rates of return and markups, I refer here to a linear system with constant coefficients. However, as mentioned before, we must be aware of the possibility of sensitive changes of values as regulating centers for market values and prices of production as regulating prices for market prices due to small changes in coefficients in certain types of matrices (see appendixes 1 and 2). As mentioned before, in the classics and Marx short-run changes of input coefficients and relative market prices were considered negligible for production prices as centers of gravity for market prices.

4. The following example is adapted from an examlpe used by Pasinetti (1977:144), for which he has calculated the labor values. Brody (1970, sec. 1.2.2) works out another example where he calculates prices that include target rates of return or markups.

5. According to appendix 2, the change of relative prices of production as centers of gravity for market prices can be estimated from the following form:

$$(\mathbf{A}' + \delta\mathbf{A}')(\mathbf{p}^r + \delta\mathbf{p}^r) = (\lambda_r + \delta\lambda_r)(\mathbf{p}^r + \delta\mathbf{p}^r),$$

where $\mathbf{A}'$ is $\{\tilde{\mathbf{B}}(\mathbf{I} - \mathbf{A}^+)^{-1}\}'$, the index r refers to the rth eigenvalue and corresponding eigenvector, and $\delta\mathbf{p}$ is the change in prices of production, as defined above. Thus, the classical and Marxian concepts of production prices also provide us with a theory of price change for a model with fixed capital, where the price includes a rate of return on capital invested.

6. The price equation (3.12) can be written as

$$\mathbf{p} = w\mathbf{l} + w\sum_{i=1}^{\infty} \mathbf{l}\tilde{\mathbf{A}}^i + r\mathbf{p}\tilde{\mathbf{B}}(\mathbf{I} - \tilde{\mathbf{A}})^{-1}$$

or

$$\mathbf{p} = w\mathbf{l} + w\sum_{i=1}^{\infty} \mathbf{l}\tilde{\mathbf{A}}^i + \Pi'.$$

The relative prices are

$$
\frac{p_i}{p_j} = \frac{wl_i \left[1 + \dfrac{\left\{ \displaystyle\sum_{i=1}^{\infty} \mathrm{l\tilde{A}}^i \right\}_i}{wl_i} + \dfrac{\Pi_i'}{wl_i} \right]}{wl_j \left[1 + \dfrac{\left\{ \displaystyle\sum_{i=1}^{\infty} \mathrm{l\tilde{A}}^i \right\}_j}{wl_j} + \dfrac{\Pi_j'}{wl_j} \right]}.
$$

Assuming that the relative wages do not change, the relative prices are determined by the relative direct labor requirements l_i / l_j and another term, represented by the second part of the equation. An empirical test for this approach will be performed below.

7. For a further debate on the price test of Wilder, Williams, and Singh, see DeRosa and Goldstein 1982.

8. Historically, it also seems to be true that the phenomenon of rigid prices is very much related to the increase of fixed investment. This will be shown in ch. 6, where I will discuss the generation of large corporations and the new type of industrial pricing they introduce. As also shown in sec. 2.4, the role of fixed capital for pricing and profits has been heavily stressed in the Marxian tradition since Hilferding.

9. The role of fixed cost for changing average cost and changing profit per unit of output is nicely illustrated by Blair (1974:469; see also Kalecki 1968:17).

10. Also, whether or not the markup has to go up when demand falls depends on the relation of variable cost to fixed cost in the industries.

11. But this does not mean that prices in those industries go down during the expansionary period of the business cycle, since variable costs have usually risen sharply in this stage of the business cycle.

12. Since we are focusing in the following test more on the recessionary period of the industrial cycle, we can justify leaving out the wage and material costs, which mostly do not increase significantly in a recessionary period. Moreover, the relative dependence of industries on wage and material costs does not increase in a recessionary period, since the wage or material cost per unit of output will not change much if the demand falls and the utilization of capacity decreases. Industries with a higher relative dependence on fixed capital investments will experience a greater change in the relative cost structure when the utilization of capacity decreases.

13. Most of the econometric studies that test the relation of price change and the price-cost margin do not consider this problem; only Neal (1942) has discussed it.

14. The following data sources were used for the test: The data on output and price change are taken from U.S. Department of Labor (1979a), the data for the gross and net capital stock from U.S. Department of Labor (1979b), and the concentration ratios from U.S. Bureau of Census (1975).

15. Lustgarden (1975a) has developed another regression test for percentage price change which takes into account not only changes in capital costs but also changes in prime costs. However, for recessionary periods the coefficients for the concentration ratios remain negative, or positive but insignificant (p. 42).

16. It should be clear that the approach presented here cannot explain the long-run trend in the price level, especially the upward trend in most advanced capitalist coun-

tries since the twenties and the increasing time lag between the decline of demand and the downward flexibility of prices in recessionary periods since the Second World War (see Cagan 1974, 1975). This requires a theory of money and inflation, which cannot be discussed here. The approach presented here allows us to explain only the dispersion of price change for industries in the business cycle.

4. EMPIRICAL EVIDENCE ON DIFFERENTIAL PROFIT RATES FOR INDUSTRIES AND FIRMS

4.1. Methodological Remarks

Both the neoclassical theory of imperfect competition and the post-Marxian/post-Keynesian theory provide us with an empirical concept to measure monopoly power as a possible cause for profitability differences. It is assumed that the degree of monopolization of an industry is determined by

  the degree of concentration in the seller market, which is a measure of independent firms in the market and their capacity to influence the market price of the commodities

  the extent of entry barriers to industries, which is a measure of the mobility of capital between industries

  the degree of collusion between the firms within one industry or across industries, which is a direct measure of eliminated competition and the influence of oligopolies on prices and quantities.

This argument holds that the degree of concentration determines the possibility of colluding within one industry, whereas high entry barriers decrease the potential competition from outside the industry. Thus, high entry barriers are deterrent to new competition. The general conclusion is that high concentration ratios, high entry barriers, or a high degree of collusion in industries results in prices which are above competitive prices and profit rates which are above the average profit rate.

In empirical research all these measures must be well defined. For the measurements of profits in industries or for firms we find three types of measure in empirical studies. (The measure for each study is specified further in table 4.1.) The first is price-cost margin, $(p - c)/p$, where p is the price of the commodities and c is either average variable cost or competitive cost (average variable cost plus a competitive profit rate). Another measure is profit margin: $(p - c)/c$. This is the relation of profits to average variable cost or competitive cost. The third possible measure of the performance of firms is the profit rate, $(\Pi - T)/A$ or $(\Pi - T)/E$, where Π is the mass of profit, T is tax, A is assets, and E is equity. All three types of profit measures are nonetheless highly problematic. The profit margin or the price-cost margin does not measure the profit rate.

Even if the profit margins are everywhere the same, the profit rates might be different because of different capital/output ratios in different industries (see sec. 5.1.4). However, the profit rate is also a very ambiguous measure of the monopolization of industries. On the one hand, the cost of maintaining a monopolistic position (such as excess capacity of oligopolistic firms) may increase the cost of production. Thus, the empirically measured profits do not show the real profits of oligopolized industries. On the other hand, if monopoly profits in the course of time are capitalized by the firms, this has an effect on assets. Thus, the profit rates of monopoly firms may converge toward an average rate, if there is a persistence in monopoly profits over the course of time. Moreover, as shown in section 5.2, if buying and selling is not taking place at equilibrium prices and uniform profit rates, the profit is affected by the structure of inputs and input costs, and a profit rate above the average does not indicate a monopoly profit.[1]

The *concentration ratios* published by the U.S. Department of Commerce as an approximation of oligopolization in industries are too rough to measure any monopolization. These concentration ratios are therefore generally adjusted for industry groups, for regional markets, for firm size distribution in industries, and for import and export shares of industries. (see Shepherd 1970). Yet, after all these adjustments, industry concentration ratios remain a very rough measure of monopolization.

Other kinds of concentration (vertical or conglomerate) which might increase the market power within one industry are usually not taken into account. The degree of international integration of the economy is also generally neglected.

The concept of *entry barriers* was introduced by Bain in the fifties. In the literature we find four types of entry barriers: product differentiation, economies of scale, absolute cost advantages of established firms in comparison with new competitors, and heavy capital requirements in industries to produce competitively in an industry. Product differentiation as an entry barrier is measured by the advertising expenditures of the firms; economies of scale are measured by the minimum efficient scale of production (the smallest production scale at which economies of scale are realized); and absolute cost advantages can be calculated by comparing the costs for credits, raw materials, and patents to firms or industries. Capital requirements in industries are mostly measured by the absolute amount of investment in the industries or by the capital/output ratios.

The most difficult task is the *measurement of collusion*, i.e., the cooperative behavior of capitalists inside the industries or across the industries. Since collusion means all kinds of formal and informal agreements among firms, data on cooperative behavior of firms are in the main unavailable. Some authors try to measure the degree of collusion by the number of prosecuted firms found guilty according to the Sherman Act, but these cases, officially known as cooperative conduct of firms, by their nature cannot reveal the real extent of collusion among firms.

In empirical literature we find five types of econometric studies testing the relation of market power or other industry or firm variables and differential profit rates. These regressions are mostly linear. In older empirical analyses a very simple type of regression is used to measure the dependence of differentials of profit rates on market power. It is assumed that if the concentration ratios of four or eight firms are greater than a critical value, concentration has a significant influence on prices and profit rates. Thus, we find the following simple linear regression:

$$\pi = \alpha + \beta CR_8 + u, \qquad (4.1)$$

where CR_8 is the concentration ratio for eight firms. Since the correlations mostly turn out to be very poor, concentration ratios of industry groups are related to profit differentials. For example, in Bain's study (1951), industry groups for which CR_8 is between 30 and 70 percent have the lowest profit rates, whereas industry groups with CR_8 between 0 and 30 percent or between 70 and 100 percent reveal higher profit rates. Bain assumes that if the concentration ratio for eight firms exceeds 70 percent the influence of market power on prices will be significant. Stigler (1963) assumes a critical value of 60 percent for a four-firm concentration ratio. Sometimes other direct market power variables, like large firm shares, degree of protection in industries, and import shares, are used to run linear regressions between market power and differentials of profit rates (see Shepherd 1970:286). In some of the recent studies the concentration ratios for the United States are corrected for regional markets, firm size distribution within industries, and sometimes import and export shares in industries.

When a multiple regression approach is used to measure the dependence of differentials of profit rates on barriers to entry we get the following regression equation:

$$\pi = \alpha + \beta_1 X_1 + \beta_2 X_2 + \beta_3 X_3 + \beta_4 X_4 + u, \qquad (4.2)$$

where X_1 measures product differentiation, X_2 economies of scale, X_3 absolute cost advantages, and X_4 the capital requirement in industries. Regressions are calculated for industry groups with high concentration and for groups with low concentration. Thus, the interconnection between entry barriers and concentration, and their influence on industrial profit rates can be measured. (see Bain 1956; Mann 1966; Qualls 1972; Stonebraker 1976). Another concept for considering concentration *and* entry barriers in regard to their influence on industry profit rates is introduced by Pugil (1976). He weights the entry barrier variables with concentration ratios; he is thus considering the interrelation of concentration and entry barriers. His study is one of the few that consider the influence of the degree of foreign competition on the profit rates of industries.

Another type of regression measures the interrelation of collusion and differentials of profit rates. Since it is assumed that other industry variables have an influence on industry performance, these influences have to be controlled for. Thus, we get the following multiple regression:

$$\pi = \alpha + \beta_1 CR + B_2 \dot{X}/X + \beta_3 \text{Coll.} + \dot{u}. \qquad (4.3)$$

where CR represents the concentration, $\dot{X}/X$ is the industry growth rate, and Coll. is an indicator for the degree of collusion in industries (see Ash and Seneca 1976).[2]

In reality, not only market power variables (like the concentration ratio) but also other industry variables (such as productivity $[Y/L]$, capital/output ratio $[K/Y]$, wage rate or wage share $[W/Y]$, share of exports in industries $[E/S]$, and growth rates in industries $[\dot{X}/X]$) might influence the profit rates significantly. We find in the literature a fourth type of multiple regression:

$$\pi = \alpha + \beta_1 CR + \beta_2 Y/L + \beta_3 K/Y + \beta_4 W/Y + \beta_5 E/S \ldots$$
$$+ \beta_n \dot{X}/X + u. \qquad (4.4)$$

This kind of regression tests the influence of concentration and industry supply and demand conditions on differentials of profit rates. Also, entry barriers can be included in multiple regression equations. For the most part, the hypothesis being tested is that the conditions of production and demand have a greater influence on profit rates than do concentration and entry barriers (see Bodoff 1973; Winn and Leabo 1974; Ornstein 1973). But, as will be seen, a long adjustment time to equalize supply and demand and to overcome mobility barriers of capital must be expected if the conditions of supply and demand should turn out to have a significant influence on profit rate differentials.

A fifth type of study examines the interfirm profitability differences. Size classes of firms, growth rates, and/or the market share of firms, which usually are taken as proxies for market power or economies of scale, are correlated with differences of profit rates. Numerous other firm or industry variables are taken into account in some studies (see Marcus 1969; Ornstein 1973; Mancke 1974; Singh and Whittington 1968; B. Gale 1972; Bruzzel et al. 1975; Gale and Branch 1982).

4.2. Empirical Results on Differential Profit Rates

The following is a summary of the major results of empirical studies on differential profit rates. Most of the studies cited were conducted for U.S. manufacturing industries. The period of observation is from the 1930s to the 1970s. Table 4.1 summarizes the different studies on the market power/differential profit rate hypothesis, their methodological approaches, and the specific results.

4.2.1. SUMMARY OF STUDIES ON MARKET POWER
AND DIFFERENTIAL PROFIT RATES

The main controversy in the studies is over the problem of evidence on the *persistence* of differential profit rates due to market power variables. Therefore, table 4.1 mainly refers to the first three types of studies introduced above, because they are dealing with the relation of industry structure, market power, and profit rate differentials. I have listed the studies that originally put forward the market power/differential profit rate hypothesis, those that presented the main critique of this hypothesis, and those that represent a reply to the criticism of the hypothesis by referring to entry barriers as an additional variable for market power (for a more detailed listing of the studies, see Weiss 1974). However, table 4.1. lists only studies that concentrate on market power variables as causes of differential profit rates. In the following more detailed discussion I present the main empirical results of studies on industry supply and demand conditions and on firm size classes as well. An evaluation of the empirical results in light of the classical, and especially Marxian, theory will be postponed to chapter 5.

4.2.2. CONCENTRATION AND INTERINDUSTRY
AND INTERFIRM PROFITABILITY DIFFERENCES

The results of the main empirical studies may be summarized with a few points:
1. Older cross-sectional and time series studies of the thirties,

Table 4.1. Studies on Market Power and Differential Profit Rates

1. MARKET POWER/DIFFERENTIAL PROFIT RATE HYPOTHESIS

Study	Concentration	Entry Barrier	Other Variables	Profit Measure	Country	Period	Influence of Concentration on Profits	Influence of Other Variables on Profits	Comment
Bain 1951	8 firms 4 digit CR > 70% CR < 70%			$\dfrac{\Pi - T}{E}$	U.S.	1936–40	positive significant ($r^2 = 0.109$)		at CR > 70% r^2 is significant
Levinson 1960	8 firms 2 digit			$\dfrac{\Pi - T}{E}$	U.S.	1947–58	positive significant ($r^2 = 0.005$, $r^2 = 0.57$, $r^2 = 0.278$)		
Fuchs 1961	4 firms 3 digit			$\dfrac{\Pi - T + i}{A}$	U.S.	1953–54	positive significant ($r^2 = 0.08$)		
Weiss 1963	4 firms 2 digit			$\dfrac{\Pi - T}{E}$	U.S.	1949–58	positive significant ($r^2 = 0.533$)		
Schwartzman 1959	4 firms 4 digit		export import	$\dfrac{p}{c}$	U.S. Canada	1954	positive significant	export share has a negative influence on PRD	results are significant for all digit levels

Author / Year	Sample	Measure	Country	Period / Result	Notes
Stigler 1963	4 firms CR > 60% CR < 60%	$\dfrac{\Pi - T + i}{A}$	U.S.	1938–41 } no influence 1942–44 } on PRD 1945–47 } 1948–50 } positive 1951–54 } influence on 1955–57 } PRD	at CR > 60% r^2 is significant
Collins and Preston 1970	4 firms 4 digit	$\dfrac{p - c - T}{p}$	U.S.	1958 positive significant ($r^2 = 0.34$)	results are significant for all digit levels; profit measures are highly correlated; profit margin is highly correlated with capital/output ratio
		$\dfrac{\Pi - T + i}{A}$		1958 positive significant ($r^2 = 0.41$)	
		$\dfrac{\Pi - T}{E}$		1958 positive significant ($r^2 = 0.43$)	
		$\dfrac{p - c - T}{p}$		1956–60 positive significant ($r^2 = 0.18$)	
		$\dfrac{\Pi - T + i}{A}$		1956–60 positive significant ($r^2 = 0.37$)	
		$\dfrac{\Pi - T}{E}$		1956–60 positive significant ($r^2 = 0.49$)	
Shepherd 1972	4 firms (weighted average)	$\dfrac{\Pi - T}{E}$ firm sales growth log of asset size advertising-sales ratio	U.S.	1960–69 positive significant	

continued on next page

Table 4.1 (continued)

Study	Concentration	Entry Barrier	Other Variables	Profit Measure	Country	Period	Influence of Concentration on Profits	Influence of Other Variables on Profits	Comment
Sherman 1968	4 and 8 firms 4 digit			$\frac{\Pi}{E}, \frac{\Pi-T}{E}$	U.S.	1955 and 1959	positive significant for both periods	PRDs are correlated with firm size and concentration	
Bain 1956	8 firms 4 digit CR > 70% CR < 70%	economies of scale, product differentiation, absolute cost advantage, capital requirements		$\frac{\Pi-T}{E}$	U.S.	1936–40	positive significant for all entry barriers	PRDs are correlated with concentration only in industry groups with high entry barriers	
Comanor and Wilson 1967	4 and 8 firms 4 digit	average firm size, capital requirements advertising		$\frac{\Pi-T}{E}$	U.S.	1954–57	positive significant	influence not significant if firm size and capital requirements are considered	

Study	Concentration measure	Entry barrier	Variable	Formula	Country	Period	Result	Comments
Hall and Weiss 1967	4 firms (corrected)	capital requirements	capital stock growth of output	$\dfrac{\Pi - T}{E}$ $\dfrac{\Pi - T}{A}$		1956–62	positive significant	capital requirements as entry barrier are significantly correlated with PRD
Ash and Seneca 1976			collusion in violation of the Sherman Act	$\dfrac{\Pi}{E}$	U.S.	1958–67		collusion shows a negative significant correlation with PRD

2. CRITIQUE OF THE MARKET POWER/DIFFERENTIAL PROFIT RATE HYPOTHESIS

Study	Concentration measure	Variable	Formula	Country	Period	Result	Comments
Demsetz 1973a	4 firms 4 digit	capital stock	$\dfrac{\Pi + i}{E}$	U.S.	1963	positive significant only for firms with capital stock above $50 million	Demsetz' hypothesis is that the greater efficiency of bigger firms causes differentials of profit rates; thus, only bigger firms in concentrated industries show profit rates above the average
Demsetz 1973b	4 firms 4 digit	capital stock	$\dfrac{\Pi + i}{E}$	U.S.	1969	positive significant for firms above $35 million	

continued on next page

Table 4.1. (continued)

Study	Concentration	Entry Barrier	Other Variables	Profit Measure	Country	Period	Influence of Concentration on Profits	Influence of Other Variables on Profits	Comment
Brozen 1971a	$\dfrac{4\ \text{firms}}{4\ \text{digit}}$			$\dfrac{\Pi - T}{E}$	U.S.	1939 1940	no significant correlation		Brozen shows no significant correlation between concentration and profit rates by using other industry samples and time series than Bain uses
Ornstein 1973	$\dfrac{4\ \text{firms}}{4\ \text{digit}}$	economies of scale capital requirements	firm size capital intensity unit wage cost demand growth	$\dfrac{\Pi - T}{E}$	U.S.	1949–50 1954–55 1959–60	no significant correlation of PRD with concentration and firm size	positive influence of growth rate of demand and economies of scale but no significant influence of firm size, capital require-	positive significant correlation between concentration and economies of scale and capital requirements

Study	Sample	Variables	PRD measure	Country	Period	Results	Results	Interpretation
								ments, and unit wage cost on PRD
Bodoff 1973	4 firms 4 digit	wage cost capital intensity productivity scale of production growth of demand	$\dfrac{p}{c}$	U.S. Canada	1958 1963 1967	no significant correlation of price-cost margin with concentration	positive significant correlation of price-cost margin with productivity and capital intensity	
Winn and Leabo 1974	4 firms 4 digit	capital intensity assets growth sales growth	$\dfrac{\Pi - i}{A}$	U.S.	1960–68	positive significant correlation of PRD with concentration	negative correlation of capital intensity and sales growth with PRD, positive correlation with assets growth	greater efficiency in supply-demand response in highly concentrated industries causes PRD
Caves and Porter 1976	4 firms 4 digit	exit barriers capital/output ratio depreciation and fixed costs	$\dfrac{\Pi}{A}$	U.S.	1970–73		exit barriers are negatively correlated with PRD	exit barriers are mobility barriers and thus are negatively correlated with PRD

continued on next page

Table 4.1 (continued)

Study	Concentration	Entry Barrier	Other Variables	Profit Measure	Country	Period	Influence of Concentration on Profits	Influence of Other Variables on Profits	Comment
			advertising						
			R & D expenditure						
			skilled labor						
			joint input						
Brozen 1973, 1971b	8 firms 4 digit			$\dfrac{\Pi - T}{E}$	U.S.	1936–40 1953–57 1962–66	positive but not significant		Brozen shows that in the course of time the profit rate above the average (measured by Bain, Stigler, Mann) tends toward an average profit rate

Weston 1973		target rate of return		U.S.	1968–70 1965–70	Weston reveals that high rates of return of big firms in the course of time converge toward an average profit rate; remaining PRDs are due to higher efficiency

3. REPLY TO THE CRITICISM—THE ROLE OF ENTRY BARRIERS

MacAvoy et al. 1971	4 firms 4 digit CR > 70%		$\dfrac{\Pi - T}{E}$	U.S.	1936–40 1953–57 1962–66	positive significant correlation of PRD with concentration	industries with high and stable concentration ($CR_4 > 80\%$) show a profit rate persistently above the average
Winn 1977	4 firms 4 digit	capital stock capital/output ratio	$\dfrac{\Pi}{A}$ (profit rate deviation from	U.S.	1960–68	positive significant correlation of PRD with concentration	concentration increases profit rate but also in-

continued on next page

Table 4.1 (continued)

Study	Concentration	Entry Barrier	Other Variables	Profit Measure	Country	Period	Influence of Concentration on Profits	Influence of Other Variables on Profits	Comment
				the average)					creases its variability, whereas in industries with high capital requirements and high capital/output ratios variability of profit rate is low
McEnally 1976		economies of scale		$\dfrac{\Pi - T}{A}$	U.S.	1950–65			high entry barriers are positive significantly related to high dispersion of profit rates among and within industries
		product differentiation							
		absolute cost advantage							
		capital requirements							

Mann 1966	8 firms 4 digit CR > 70% CR < 70%	economies of scale product differentiation absolute cost advantage capital requirements	$\dfrac{\Pi - T}{E}$	U.S.	1950–60	positive significant for all entry barriers	PRDs are correlated with concentration only in industry groups with high entry barriers
Qualls 1972	4 firms 4 digit CR > 70%	economies of scale product differentiation absolute cost advantage capital requirements	$\dfrac{p - c^* - T}{p}$	U.S.	1950–60	positive significant correlation of price-cost margin with concentration	positive significant correlation of price-cost margin with entry barriers	high concentration has an influence on price-cost margin only in connection with high entry barriers
Qualls 1974	4 firms 4 digit CR > 70%	economies of scale product differentiation	$\dfrac{p - c^* - T}{p}$	U.S.	1950–60 1960–65	positive significant correlation of price-cost margin with concentration	positive significant correlation of price-cost margins with entry barriers	concentration increases the price-cost margin only in relation to

continued on next page

Table 4.1 (continued)

Study	Concentration	Entry Barrier	Other Variables	Profit Measure	Country	Period	Influence of Concentration on Profits	Influence of Other Variables on Profits	Comment
		absolute cost advantage capital requirements					in industries with high entry barriers		high entry barriers. Qualls uses price-cost margins instead of profit rates (entry barrier data are from Mann); differences in capital/output ratios are not considered
Stonebraker 1976		advertising R & D expenditure economies of scale minimum firm size	growth rate of industries	$\dfrac{\text{II} - \text{T}}{\text{E}}$	U.S.	1955–68		entry barriers and growth rates are significantly correlated with PRD	

KEY: A = assets; E = equity; PRD = profit rate differentials; T = tax; II = reported profits; CR = concentration ratios; c = average variable cost; c* = competitive cost (average variable cost plus a competitive profit rate on assets); i = interest rate; p = price.

forties, and fifties concerning concentration and profit rates usually reveal a significant positive relation between concentration and profit rates (see Bain 1951; Mann 1966; Stigler 1963; Collins and Preston 1970), although the correlation coefficients are sometimes very low (see Bain 1951). The hypothesis is that concentration leads to collusion and collusion to higher profit margins or profit rates. Concentration leads to higher profits according to Bain's results when $CR_8 > 70\%$, and according to Stigler's results (1963) when $CR_4 > 60\%$. But their methodologies and data bases are in the main very weak. Moreover, these studies can not explain the possible persistence of higher profits due to concentration in the seller's market (see Brozen 1971; Demsetz 1973a, 1973b). It has been argued that competition and rivalry, even among the big companies, made the profit rates of oligopolies converge toward a normal one. This is the main argument used by Weston, Ornstein, Demsetz, and Brozen. Indeed, they showed, once the concentration ratio, cross-sectional, and time series data of Bain, Mann, and Stigler were reexamined by including more industries and extending the time period, that differential profit rates due to concentration were no longer shown (see Brozen 1971a, 1971b, 1973). Moreover, a persistence of profit rates among industries, according to Demsetz (1973a, 1973b), results not from market power as measured by concentration but, on the contrary, from higher productivity of firms in concentrated industries. In his numerous studies Demsetz showed a significant relation of profit rates to concentration ratios only for large firms, i.e., firms with assets greater than $50 million. Hence, he concluded that differentials of profit rates reflect not market power but the efficiency of large corporations in concentrated industries.

2. Using Bain's method, a number of studies presented in the sixties and seventies revealed a significant positive relation between high profits (profit margins or profit rates) and entry barriers (see Bain 1956; Mann 1966; Comanor and Wilson 1967; Stonebraker 1976; Ornstein 1973; Qualls 1972, 1974). They also demonstrated that high concentration ratios have an effect on prices and profits over time only if at the same time there are high barriers to entry. Otherwise there would be potential competitors, who could enter

the market and bring down the profit rate to the average (limit pricing). In this approach, it is conceded that if the market barriers are low and hence allow the threat of new competition, concentration ratios do not show any significant positive relation to differentials of profit rates. On the other hand, if high entry barriers exist, high concentration ratios have a significant effect on profit rates. This hypothesis seems to have a strong empirical basis, and recently a number of empirical studies have supported it (see Qualls 1972; Mann 1966; Stonebraker 1976). It has also been shown that, across industry groups with high entry barriers, the dispersion of profit rates is very great, as it is between firms in the same industry (see McEnally 1976).

This concept of entry barriers was also extended to other possible cases. First, it was assumed that oligopoly groups also developed strategies against new competition (for example, they could maintain underutilized capacities in oligopolistic industries as an impediment to entry). Barriers to entry are thus no longer to be seen as structural determinants of the oligopolistic markets (like economies of scale, heavy capital requirements, and concentration) but as an outcome of the activities of the oligopolistic firms themselves. Economists like Harrod, Modigliani, Sylos-Labini, and Lombardini have argued in this manner since the fifties, and Caves and Porter (1977) recently came back to this concept of the entry-preventing strategies of oligopolistic groups. But, since the measurement of these activities and strategies of large firms is quite difficult, no empirical study of the subject is available. Second, it was shown that not only entry barriers but also exit barriers cause differentials in profit rates. Firms will stay in industries with profit rates below the average if there are exit barriers like high investments in selling costs, high expenditures for research and development, a high minimum efficient scale of production, or heavy capital requirements. In an empirical paper, Caves and Porter (1976) showed a significant negative correlation between exit barriers and profit rates. Since the measured exit barriers are almost the same as the entry barriers used in the former conception, the concept of entry barriers became very ambiguous. This meant that firms could not leave an industry, even if the profit rates were low. In a period of stagnation and declining demand, entry barriers may turn out to be exit barriers and profit rates may be, over a certain length of time, below the average rather than above it. (This had already been pointed out in Hilferding's book in 1910 [modern edition 1968].) These results do not contradict the earlier findings, since those findings were related to the prosperity of the fifties and sixties. Heavy capital requirements and high capital/output ratios may be such barriers. Weston and Ornstein (1973a), for example, found a high correlation between concentrated industries and capital intensity. Thus, these barriers are in fact barriers to mobility of capital. (Capital requirements functioning as a mobility barrier to capital are illustrated in the steel and car industries in the eighties.)

3. Other studies have been conceived concerning cooperative activities of oligopoly firms and collusion among firms. Ash and Seneca (1976) found that if other factors which may cause differentials of profit rates (such as concentration, or growth rates of industries) are excluded, collusion shows a significant negative effect on profits. Therefore, collusion may be a result of low profits and not a cause of high profits. But since most cooperative activities of firms are secret and may be seldom uncovered, the results of the Ash and Seneca study may not be very convincing (see also Fraas and Greer 1977).

4. Other studies do not refer to the concept of monopoly power as measured by concentration, entry barriers, and collusion. Instead, they demonstrate that the differentials of profit rates are significantly related to the productivity, capital/output ratios, and unit wage costs of each industry (see Bodoff 1973; Schwartzman 1959) and to growth and demand conditions (see Ornstein 1973; Hall and Weiss 1967; Winn and Leabo 1974). Most of these studies reveal that differentials of profit rates are strongly related to supply and demand conditions of commodities. When investigators have taken into account the effect of concentration and sometimes even of entry barriers in multiple regression equations, it has been shown that the conditions of production and demand have a strong effect on differentials in profit rates (see Ornstein 1973; Winn and Leabo 1974). Studies for other countries also have demonstrated these results (for France see Deleplace 1974; for West Germany see Sass

1975; Semmler 1980). However, the results are convincing only if we assume barriers to mobility of capital, i.e., barriers to moving from industries with low profit rates to industries with high profit rates.

5. The last type of study examines the *interfirm profitability differences* due to firm size, growth rate of firms, market share as proxy for market power or economies of scale, and other industry or firm variables (see Marcus 1969; Ornstein 1973; Mancke 1974). There are a few studies which inequivocally reveal a dependence of profit rates on firm size. It is usually demonstrated that medium-sized firms or groups of firms smaller than the largest have the highest profit rates (and growth rates; see Stekler 1963). However, studies have been conceived that reveal not a difference in profit rates and growth rates among firms but differences in the variance and stability of profit rates and growth among groups of firms of different sizes. Smaller firms may have the same profit rates as big firms, but their profit rates are more unstable and vary strongly in the course of the business cycle (see Singh and Whittington 1968; Eatwell 1971). Moreover, it has been found that the dispersion of profit rates is usually greater among small firms than among big firms. In regard to the market share of firms (a more refined measure of the position of a firm in an industry or line of business than the concentration ratio), there have been positive correlations with profit rates, especially for diversified and vertically integrated firms. However, other industry and firm variables, such as capacity utilization, industry growth, exports, and minimum efficient scale, are also very important for interfirm profitability differences (see Ravenscraft 1981). As shown before, Ravenscraft (1981) and Scott (1981), who conducted new studies based on recently published data on lines of business by the U.S. Federal Trade Commission, found that market shares have some importance for diversified firms with multimarket contacts. However, other variables are important as well, and moreover it is not clear in these studies whether the positive correlation of market shares with profit rates stems from economies of scale and efficiency or from market power and higher prices.

Some recently published studies have elaborated on whether industrial concentration and oligopolistic coordination lead to higher prices and higher profitability for larger firms or whether their higher market shares are an indicator of economies of scale and lower costs for larger firms. Articles by B. Gale (1972), Bruzzel et al. (1975), Caves et al. (1977), and Gale and Branch (1982) show that market share (indicating scale economies and lower costs) has greater explanatory power for interfirm profitability than concentration ratios have. Using the market share (MS) of firms and four-firm concentration ratios (CR_4) as independent variables and rate of return on investment as the dependent variable, the results for 2,000 firms over the time period 1970–1979 are as follows (see Gale and Branch 1982):

$$\pi = 11.5 + 0.499 MS - 0.019 CR_4,$$
$$(0.027)(0.019)$$

$$R^2 = 0.199.$$

The coefficient for the concentration ratio is insignificant. Tests performed with profit margins and price-cost margins as measures of profitability show similar results. We can conclude that even though larger firms in industries may show a higher profitability, this is not necessarily a result of market power but may be due to size and cost advantages of firms with a higher market share. This position has been debated in Ravenscraft 1981 and in Caves et al. 1977.

As mentioned in chapter 4.1, three of the five types of studies refer to market power variables (concentration, entry barriers, and collusion), the other two to supply and demand conditions for industries and to the size of firms as causes of differential profit rates. From the review of the studies and recent discussion among scholars in the field, we can draw three preliminary conclusions. First, there does not seem to be overwhelming evidence that industrial concentration by itself leads to persistence of higher profit rates. Entry barriers seem to be a necessary condition for profit rate differentials.[3] Second, entry barriers can turn into exit barriers, leading to profit rates for industries and firms below the average. Therefore, in accordance with the more recent publications, it might be more appropriate to speak not of entry barriers but of *mobility barriers* causing differential profit rates. Third, there are few studies which reveal unequivocally that firm size is the dominant variable for interfirm profitability differences. Higher profitability corresponding to firm size and larger market share in product lines may be the result of market power *or* of economies of scale and cost advantages, yet recent studies have shown that economies of scale and cost advantages influence the profitability of firms more than industrial concentration. Before evaluating these studies from the classical and Marxian perspective again, I want to present a short empirical test on industrial concentration, mobility of capital, and profitability differences in West German industry.

4.3. Concentration, Mobility Barriers, and Differential Profit Rates: A Simple Test for West Germany

While there are a large number of econometric studies on differential profit rates for U.S. industries, very few studies have been done for West Germany. Sass (1975) provides such an analysis for 1953–1960 and reports a significant negative correlation between concentration and profit rates (see also Semmler 1980). Using the recently published data of Krengel et al. (1977) and those of the monopoly report (Monopolkommission 1976), I will provide a cross-sectional analysis for the year 1973.

This year was chosen for two reasons: it is the year for which the most recent data on concentration ratios are available and it is the year before the recession of the mid-seventies, a year when utilization of capacity was quite high. Most of the above-mentioned studies restrict themselves to the market effects of concentration. Here the question posed will be expanded to include an analysis of the effects of concentration on conditions of production in the various industries.

The following questions will be examined: first, what is the correlation between concentration and conditions of production in the various industries? Second, can differential profit rates be explained by variations in concentration ratios? Finally, do barriers to capital mobility influence profit rate differentials?

4.3.1. CONCENTRATION AND SUPPLY CONDITIONS

In this section, the correlation of the capital/labor ratio, the capital/output ratio, the wage share, and the wage rate with industrial concentration will be examined. The market shares of the ten, six, and three biggest firms were taken as independent variables.

An equation specifying the relation between the capital/labor ratio (K/L) and the concentration ratio is

$$(K/L)_i = \alpha_i + \beta_i CR_i + u_i.$$

The empirical results are as follows:

	α	β	r^2
CR_{10}	21,487.5	801.7	0.19
	(16,899.2)	(330.5)	
CR_6	55,544.9	0.388	0.0
	(113,254)	(41.2)	
CR_3	35,735.6	770.8	0.10
	(15,330.4)	(455.4)	

In this table, α and β are the estimated regression coefficients. The standard errors of the estimated regression coefficients are in parentheses. r^2 gives the correlation coefficient. The test shows a significant positive correlation of the capital/labor ratio with CR_{10} and CR_3. There is not a significant correlation with CR_6 at the 5-percent significance level.

A similar pattern of correlation emerges with the regression of the capital/output ratio on the concentration ratio.

$$(K/Y)_i = \alpha_i + \beta_i CR_i + u_i$$

shows the following results:

	α	β	r^2
CR_{10}	1.156	0.0691	0.18
	(0.153)	(0.03)	
CR_6	1.45	0.000	0.004
	(0.10)	(0.0037)	
CR_3	0.1282	0.065	0.09
	(0.138)	(0.004)	

Significant positive correlation is evident only for CR_{10}, while CR_3 shows only a slight correlation. Hence it is only with the 10-firm concentration index that one can posit a high correlation between concentration and capital/output ratios.

The test of the correlation between wage shares and concentration ratios specified by

$$w_i = \alpha_i + \beta_i CR_i + u_i$$

shows the following results:

	α	β	r^2
CR_{10}	0.572 (0.071)	−0.001 (0.001)	0.04
CR_6	0.534 (0.034)	−0.002 (10.001)	0.06
CR_3	0.551 (0.062)	−0.001 (0.002)	0.034

The empirical results show no significant correlation with any of the three concentration indices. Therefore we must reject the frequently supported thesis that the wage share is higher in concentrated industries than in less concentrated ones (e.g., because of more powerful unions). The reason this empirical correlation does not exist for West Germany seems to be that in concentrated sectors the capital/labor ratio is significantly higher than in nonconcentrated sectors. This hypothesis is further supported by the additional test

$$(W/L)_i = \alpha_i + \beta_i CR_i + u_i,$$

in which W/L stands for the average wage rate per worker in the industries. The results are as follows:

	α	β	r^2
CR_{10}	17,195.0 (995.4)	57.95 (19.5)	0.26
CR_6	20,075.9 (663.4)	3.98 (2.4)	0.09
CR_3	18,017.5 (901.0)	63.8 (26.8)	0.185

Significant positive correlations exist between the average wage rate per worker and CR_{10}, as well as CR_3. For these two concentration indices, the wage rate per worker increases with concentration. Thus, in concentrated sectors, the wage rate per worker is higher than average but the share of wages is not, since capital intensity and productivity are also above average. A further regression test between the utilization of capacity and CR_6 showed the following results:

$$UC_i = 91.99 - 0.18 CR_6,$$

$$r^2 = 0.0026,$$

where $UC = (Y^* - Y)/Y$. Y^* stands for the potential and Y for the actual net output. The results are not significant at the 5-percent level.

It can be concluded that capacity utilization (and the profit rate influenced by it) does not depend on the concentration ratio. A high concentration does not necessarily entail increased underutilization of capacity, as suggested by the concentration/market power hypothesis.

In summary, concentrated industries are characterized by above-average capital/labor ratios, especially when measured against the 10-firm index—and an above-average capital/output ratio. Concentrated sectors are not as labor intensive as less concentrated sectors. Industrial concentration tends to have negative effects on the overall level of employment. Moreover, the correlation between the capital/output ratio and industrial concentration seems to support the argument about price rigidity in concentrated industries in the recessionary period of the business cycle that was presented in section 3.4.

4.3.2. CONCENTRATION AND DIFFERENTIAL PROFIT RATES

The "concentration/profit rate" hypothesis proposes that a high concentration ratio enables oligopolies to establish a hierarchy of profit rates between highly concentrated and less concentrated sectors. The data on industry profit rates are taken from Altvater et al. (1979) and those on concentration ratios from the Monopolkommission (1976). The test year is again 1973, and the data cover twenty-seven industries.

Sass (1975:29) has already tested the correlation between concentration and profit rates for twenty-six industries in the 1953–1960 period. He used the concentration ratio given in German Bundestag (1969). A single concentration index, the 10-firm index, was used. Sass obtained a significant negative correlation between concentration ratios and sectoral profit rates. Sass's correlation coefficient is $r = -0.41$. The correlation test of changes in concentration ratios and sectoral profits is also negative ($r = -0.47$).

Since Sass's data are based on less recent time series and allow for only one concentration ratio (CR_{10}), we shall investigate this problem with more recent data (1973) and three concentration indices. There is a slight difference between the profit rate calculated by Sass and that used here, since Sass based his calculations on nominal figures. The regression equation

$$\pi_i = \alpha_i + \beta_i CR_i + u_i$$

showed the following results:

	α	β	r^2
CR_{10}	0.401	−0.003	0.002
	(0.063)	(0.001)	
CR_6	0.406	0.001	0.004
	(0.066)	(0.001)	
CR_3	0.389	−0.001	0.001
	(0.054)	(0.002)	

At a significance level of 5 percent this leads to acceptance of the null hypothesis H_0: $\beta = 0$ and rejection of the alternate hypothesis H_0: $\beta \neq 0$. This was the same for all three concentration indices. We may conclude that for West German industry, insofar as the year 1973 can be taken as representative, differences in sectoral profit rates are not influenced by differences in concentration ratios.

Both the linear regression and the calculation of the average profit rate for industries with a concentration ratio CR_6 of more than 60 percent—which in U.S. studies is generally viewed as the critical limit for the development of market power—show that the concentration ratios do not provide an explanation for the dispersion of profit rates in the industries. Concentration and the chance for cooperative action by big firms in one industry did not lead to higher profit rates.

There are no apparent profit rate hierarchies due to concentration; but admittedly the test used here does not enable us to determine whether or not the profit rates of individual dominating firms or firms of certain sizes are raised, e.g., by high efficiency or lower production costs. To do this a study would require the use of company data. Such a study—like that of Sass—should be qualified, in that the concentration ratio used represents a high level of industry aggregation. This usually leads to a bias against the influence of the concentration ratio, since a high aggregation makes the concentration ratio for a line of business smaller (Weiss 1974). A further, more detailed classification of industries might bring different results, but no other concentration surveys for West Germany nor data for regional markets are available for this purpose.

On the other hand, the calculation of concentration ratios does not take into account the degree of integration of West Germany in the world market. Since the import and export shares in manufacturing are very high, this is an important consideration. Taking the degree of world market integration into account generally leads to a reduction in the actual concentration ratio, which in turn tends to diminish any correlation between concentration and profit rate (Pugil 1976). Hence we can take it that both Sass's and my calculations presented here offer a refutation of the "concentration/ profit rate hierarchy" hypothesis—although the results are still subject to methodological difficulties. Apparently concentration in itself is not a means of increasing market power or raising the profit rate. It still remains to be explored to what extent differential profit rates are correlated with other industry variables.

4.3.3. MOBILITY BARRIERS AND DIFFERENTIAL PROFIT RATES

Having eliminated concentration ratios as explanatory variables for differential profit rates, the question remains whether differences in industry supply and demand conditions—which are effective only if there are mobility barriers—or other structural mobility barriers of capital can cause differential profit rates. As discussed earlier, Marxian theory indeed assumed restricted mobility for industrial capital and high mobility for merchant and money capital. Since a number of tests on the relation of demand variables and differential profit rates have been conducted with positive results (see Ornstein 1973; Hall and Weiss 1967; Winn and Leabo 1974), I will focus on the supply side, pursuing the question of to what extent supply variables lead to restricted mobility of capital and thus to differential profit rates.

In the following test the relation of the capital/output ratio K/Y (the ratio of gross capital stock to actual net output) to the profit share Π/Y is used as an indirect measure of the mobility barriers of capital.[4] Under the neoclassical assumptions of non-indivisibility of resources and perfect mobility of firms, we would not expect the capital/output ratio to cause differential profit rates. The profit rate can be written as

$$\Pi/K = (Y/K)(1 - w) = (\Pi/Y)(Y/K),$$

or, as a log linear relation:

$$\ln(\Pi/K) = \ln(\Pi/Y) + \ln(Y/K),$$

where Π/Y represents the actual profit share and Y/K the inverse of the actual capital output ratio. Since there is a collinearity between the independent variables, in the case of perfect mobility of capital we would expect a high correlation and a slope of -1 for the beta coefficient in the following regression test:

$$\ln(\Pi_i/Y_i) = \alpha + \beta \ln(Y_i/K_i) + u_i.$$

Deviations of the slope from -1 can be interpreted as a sign of the existence of differential profit rates. This can be illustrated by figure 4.1. If the results show a regression line like (a), we can conclude that the inverse of the capital/output ratio, Y/K, does not cause profit rate differentials. A nonlinear curve like (b) indicates that a higher capital/output ratio (or lower $\ln(Y/K)$) does not correspond to a proportional increase in $\ln(\Pi/Y)$, which leads to a below-average profit rate (in recessionary periods one may expect such a relation). A nonlinear curve like (c) indicates that a higher capital/output

Test of Capital Mobility

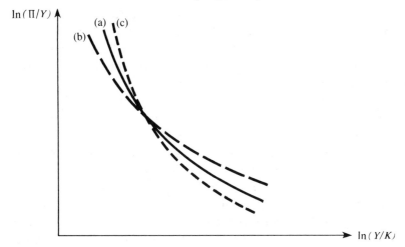

Figure 4.1. Test of Capital Mobility

ratio, or a lower $\ln(Y/K)$, corresponds to a more-than-proportional increase in $\ln(\Pi/Y)$, which will lead to an above-average profit rate (this is expected in periods of high demand and high growth rates).

The regression test performed for the log linear relation shows results that are not significant (standard errors are given in parentheses):

$$\ln(\Pi/Y) = -0.91 - 0.28 \ln(Y/K),$$
$$(0.28)$$

$$R^2 = 0.03.$$

The regression tests performed for nonlinear functions showed the following results:

$$\ln(\Pi/Y) = -0.91 + 0.57 \ln\left(\frac{1}{\sqrt{Y/K}}\right),$$
$$(0.57)$$

$$R^2 = 0.03,$$

and

$$\ln(\Pi/Y) = -0.91 - 0.14 \ln(Y/K)^2,$$
$$(0.14)$$

$$R^2 = 0.03.$$

The results of both regression tests were not significant.

The first regression test indicates that there is restricted mobility of capital that prevents $\ln(Y/K)$ from being correlated with $\ln(\Pi/Y)$. However, the tests for the nonlinear regression functions provide no evidence of a correlation of (high) capital/output ratios with (proportionally) lower profit shares, indicating, e.g., a lower profit rate, or vice versa. Yet it must be mentioned that the lack of significance shown by the regression tests may have been caused by the use of the *actual* capital/output ratios, which are determined not only by the long-run trend of the capital/output ratios in industries but also by changes in the capacity utilization in the course of the business cycle. However, in the test year, 1973, the overall utilization of capacity was quite normal (94 percent) and the actual and potential capital/output ratios did not deviate significantly. Moreover, since restricted capital mobility may lead to differential profit rates more clearly during the upswings and downswings of the business cycle, it would have been preferable to test curve (c) during an upswing year and curve (b) in a downswing. The lack of evidence for curves (c) and (b) as well may have been a result of the test period. In sum, empirical analysis of West German industry has shown that concentration ratios neither significantly nor persistently affect the level of the profit rate. Recently published U.S. studies also point to highly questionable empirical findings as the basis for the concentration/differential profit rate thesis. Consonant with the more recent U.S. studies, I conclude that profit rate differentials seem to be attributable more to mobility barriers than to the degree of concentration as a market power variable.

Notes

1. Among scholars in the field the idea has been expressed very often that accounting profits will most likely differ from "true" profits due to loss accounts, capitalization of monopoly profit, excess capacity, excess payments to managers, etc. This might be true, although most likely only within a certain range, since the reported profitability of a firm is still very important for the flow of investable funds. Moreover, because of the measurement problem of "true" profits, the studies of the defenders of the concentration/profit rate

hypothesis as well as those of their critics overwhelmingly refer only to accounting profits. There are only a few studies that try to account for a possible difference between "understated reported profits" and "true profits" (see Cowling and Mueller 1978).

2. Ash and Seneca used a sample of fifty-one firms out of the Fortune 500 list for the period 1958–1967 that were found guilty of Sherman Act conspiracy charges during that period. They are compared with fifty noncollusive firms.

3. Alfred Eichner, in a comment on an earlier version of this section of the book, agreed with the results showing that entry barriers are necessary conditions for higher profit rates but made the suggestion that it might be preferable to make the distinction between "natural" barriers to entry (economies of scale) and "firm-made" barriers to entry. This distinction might be an important one in further research, but as shown above, while it has been made in theoretical studies, empirical studies are not available yet. This distinction will be discussed further in section 5.2. Moreover, as shown later, even "firm-made" barriers to entry can become "barriers to exit."

4. Such mobility barriers are given with the time required to build up new capacity, for production and circulation of the product, and for hiring and firing of workers with specific qualification levels. There are other barriers to market entry and exit, such as ownership of and limited access to production resources, favorable access to capital markets, product differentiation, absolute cost advantages for established firms, economies of scale, and absolute capital requirements. Joint market strategies of industrial groups are entry barriers for potential competitors. Above-average profit rates can be the temporary result, especially in periods of high growth rates of those industries. However, there are also exit barriers. Such exit barriers include high capital requirements in industries, an above-average capital/output ratio, joint inputs for different production processes and nonseparable joint production, a hoarded stock of qualified personnel, high degree of unionization of industries or plants, R & D and sales expenditure for product differentiation, and other long-term production or sales costs and contracts for the firm. Such direct variables as those mentioned here would have to be included if a test for capital mobility were to be performed (see Caves and Porter 1976). However, since the data for such a test are not available, we can only perform an indirect test for capital mobility. For pointing out the possibility of such a test, I thank Duncan Foley.

Part 3. Empirical Studies and the Classical and Marxian Theories

Returning to the question of whether the results of the empirical studies on industrial and corporate pricing and differential profit rates contradict the classical and Marxian theories. I mainly want to focus on an attempt to reconcile the empirical evidence on prices and differential profit rates with the dynamic notion of competition and the concept of production prices. In chapter 5 I discuss these problems by referring only to a model of single-product firms and industrial pricing and profit differentials. In this case, firms are considered to be active in only one industry or line of business. The compatibility of empirically observable differential profit rates and markup pricing with the Marxian concept of prices of production will be discussed. In chapter 6 I will extend the framework and consider the pricing procedure of large, vertically integrated and diversified corporations. Since large corporations nowadays have many production processes at their disposal and operate in many industries, I will make use of the concept of joint production by pursuing the questions already raised. The last chapter will cover the difference between market, or monopoly, power and corporate power.

5. PRODUCTION PRICES, SINGLE-PRODUCT INDUSTRIES, AND INDUSTRIAL PRICING

By referring initially to single-product firms, industrial pricing, and differential profit rates, I plan to evaluate the empirical findings on pricing and profits. By discussing the compatibility of differential profit rates, markups, and target rates of return with the afore-mentioned concept of production prices I will introduce a new interpretation of markup and target rate of return pricing, developed by large firms since the twenties.

5.1. Evaluation of Empirical Studies on Differential Profit Rates

In this section I focus only on the empirical studies on differential profit rates, since only the *persistence* of differential profit rates or markups as maintained in the post-Marxian/post-Keynesian tradition can be taken as a measure of market or monopoly power. On the other hand, the classics and Marx had theories of differential profit rates which might also be consistent with the empirical evidence (see also Semmler 1982a and 1982b).

5.1.1. SUPPLY AND DEMAND CONDITIONS AND DIFFERENTIAL PROFIT RATES

As shown above, one type of empirical study was concerned with differentials in industry supply and demand conditions and their consequences for prices and profit rate differentials. Studies available from the United States, France, Canada, and Germany revealed that the conditions of production, such as capital/output ratio, wage rates, etc., and the conditions of demand and markets, such as share of exports to sales and growth rates, can have a remarkable influence on profit rate differentials. Those differentials can be explained easily by the theory of competition elaborated in chapter 2, in which supply and demand are equal only by accident. Firms are not assumed to be perfectly mobile. Differences in profit rates caused by differences in capital/output ratio, wage rates, and growth rates of industries may be explained by differences in time to adjust supply to demand, that is to say, the time to build up new capacity, to produce and circulate commodities where profit rates are high, and to reduce capacity and withdraw capital from industries with low profit rates. The production and selling of products requires a period of time which varies among industries. When empirical tests reveal this relation between supply and demand conditions and differential profit rates, it seems to be consistent with a dynamic theory of competition, according to which there are always disequilibria of supply and demand, and restrictions—which are different for each industry—prevent supply from being equalized with demand for a certain period of time (see sec. 2.3.4).

5.1.2. MARKET POWER VARIABLES AND DIFFERENTIAL PROFIT RATES

Other kinds of studies refer, not to those causes, but to market power variables (concentration, entry barriers, and collusion) as the main reasons for profit rate differentials. As shown, most of the recent studies have revealed that there is no persistence of profit rate differentials that is due only to concentration. High entry barriers (product differentiation, large-scale production, absolute cost advantages, heavy capital requirements, high capital/output ratios, and entry-preventing strategies of oligopoly groups), which deter new competitors and allow entry-preventing pricing, are a necessary precondition for decreasing competition within industries. High profits are revealed only when high concentration is correlated with high entry barriers, which might facilitate collusion within or across industries. Hence, the question arises of to what extent these empirical findings support the hypothesis of the dominance of market power variables over profit rate differentials. An attempt to use these empirical studies in support of this hypothesis can be questioned on the basis of three considerations.

First, these empirical results do not mean that there is a stable and persistent hierarchy of profit rates in the long run. Studies for the seventies have revealed that entry barriers turn out to be exit barriers in periods of stagnation and declining demand. Large-scale production, high capital requirements, and high capital/output ratios are inseparable from a high proportion of fixed capital in industries. Large capital losses will result if capacity has to be adjusted to declining demand. The profit rate can decrease without firms' being able to adjust at once by moving out of the industry. Not concentration and entry barriers but mobility barriers to capital seem to be the reason for differentials of profit rates. Mobility barriers are different in all industries. The time it takes to provide new capacity in the presence of entry barriers or to withdraw capital from industries with large-scale production, heavy capital requirements, and high capital/output ratios might be much longer than in industries with numerous capitals, low capital requirements, and easy entry. Thus, for industries where the period of adjustment is longer, we can assume that the profit rate will stay above or below the average much longer. The mobility of capital and the period of adjustment toward an average profit rate are different for each industry. This fact is revealed by the empirical tests on concentration and entry barriers. The empirical data can be interpreted in such a way that the profit rates in industries with heavy capital requirements are seen to fluctuate much more slowly than they do in so-called competitive industries. Industries with fewer suppliers and high entry barriers might take a longer time to develop an average rate of profit than other industries. This conclusion can also be drawn from the empirical observations of price movements in those industries, which show, in the short run, less flexibilty in prices than competitive industries do (see sec. 3.4. and also Eichner 1976).

Second, fewer firms on the market, high entry barriers, and the possibility of collusion do not mean that competition of firms as understood in chapter 2 is abolished. As Marx and the major part of the post-Marxian literature assume, regardless of the concentration and centralization of capital, growth, self-expansion, and accumulation of capital remain the goals of the firm. Competition and rivalry among firms are not abolished by concentration and entry barriers. In production, the aim of the capitalist firm is to produce surplus profit by inventing new methods of production, increasing productivity of labor, and decreasing the costs of production. This point has been elaborated in Shaikh (1978, 1980) and Semmler (1984b). In circulation, the purpose is to improve the conditions for realization of profit by extending the market share. Intersectoral competition, carried out on the level of investments, aims at capturing extra profits (or avoiding losses) due to profitability differences. Fewer units of capital and heavy capital requirements might facilitate collusion within an industry, but they also can mean an increasing interdependence and severe rivalry among firms. (Modern game theory illustrates the ambiguity of the effects of increasing concentration on competition among firms.)

Third, the erection of entry and exit barriers, as indicators of less mobility of physical capital, do not necessarily mean that the mobility of money capital will decrease. The mobility of physical resources may have decreased due to an increase in fixed capital in certain industries. However, the rise of large multiplant and multiproduct corporations was accompanied by the creation of large pools of money capital. Historically, as the units of capital have become larger, the mobility of money capital has increased. Large units of capital, i.e., large concentrated capitals and conglomerates, are independent centers of financial power. They can shift money capital quite easily (see Clifton 1977) from region to region and from industry to industry when the competitive strategy of firms make such actions necessary. For example, it is well documented that the international mobility of the money capital of large corporations has increased tremendously in the postwar period. This increase, a result of the generation of large-scale capitals, was overlooked in Hilferding's (1968), as well as in the post-Marxian, discussions of the genesis of monopoly. In these writings monopoly was presented as a result of concentration and increasing immobility of physical capital; the impact of the creation of large financial pools and the increase in the mobility of money capital on the competition of capitals was neglected.

In sum, concentration and entry barriers may lead to a decrease of market competition within (and / or among) industries, a rise in prices, and a delay in the formation of a uniform profit rate. This was considered to be a special case, related to special conditions, and the effects of which are limited and predictable (see sec. 2.4). However, in the main, a decreasing number of firms within an industry does not necessarily entail a decline of competition and rivalry. Entry barriers are also exit barriers and, in fact, barriers to the mobility of industrial capital. The increasing immobility of physical capital may be accompanied by an increasing mobility of money capital. Persistence of profit rate differentials due only to market power variables has been shown to be very unlikely. Yet differential profit rates over a certain period of time due to mobility barriers to capital are likely to exist.

5.1.3. FIRM SIZE, MARKET SHARE, AND DIFFERENTIAL PROFIT RATES

How should the findings on the relation of firm size and market share to differential profit rates be evaluated in light of the classical and Marxian theories? As shown above, differentials in profit rates among firms are to be found in many studies. But there are no empirical studies that can support the hypothesis that the profit rate varies only with firm size and market share. Rather, studies demonstrate differences in the variance and stability of profit rates among small firms and big firms. These findings are consistent with other empirical results concerning price changes in so-called oligopolistic and competitive sectors during the business cycle. The smaller dispersion of the profit rates of big corporations in comparison with small firms may only be an expression of the fact that the profit rates of the big firms are much closer to the average rate of profit (see Clifton 1977). Moreover, differentials in profit rates among firms of different sizes, between firms in concentrated and unconcentrated industries, or between firms with different market shares are

consistent with the theory presented in section 2.4. Within industries, there are always firms of different sizes and with different
market shares, firms with different techniques and lower or higher
costs of production. At the same market price or production price,
the firms have different cost prices and thus different profit rates.
This is even in accord with the empirical fact that in concentrated
industries smaller firms have lower profit rates (see Mueller 1981)
and firms with large market shares show a higher profitability (see
Gale and Branch 1982). Thus, different rates of profit among firms is
not necessarily a sign of monopoly power[1] but appears to be
consistent with the theory of competition presented before.

5.1.4. CAUSES OF DIFFERENTIALS IN PROFIT MARGINS

Empirical findings often reveal a strong correlation between
concentration, entry barriers, and profit margin. These studies show
differences in price-cost margins, $(p - c)/p$; in profit margins,
$(p - c)/c$; or in markups, $(MC + WC)(1 + \mu)$, among industries or
firms (d = depreciation, MC = material cost, WC = wage cost,
μ = markup). In linear regressions, concentration and entry barriers are correlated with price/cost margins, profit margins, and
markups (see Qualls 1972, 1974). Nevertheless, significant positive
results are not equivalent to differentials of profit rates due to
concentration and entry barriers. Since

$$\frac{p - c}{p} = \frac{(d + r)K}{px}$$

or

$$\frac{p - c}{c} = \frac{(d + r)K}{cx}$$

and

$$(MC + WC)(1 + \mu) = MC + WC + \frac{(d + r)K}{x}$$

where K/x is the capital/output ratio, differences in price-cost
margins, profit margins, and markups might only reflect differences
in capital/output ratios or in the organic composition of capital

among industries or firms. Since in concentrated industries or industries with high entry barriers the capital/output ratios are generally higher (see Ornstein et al. 1973), the firms or industries with identical profit rates might have very different price-cost margins, profit margins, or markups. The markup over prime cost—in Kalecki's theory, a measure of the degree of monopoly power—might be only another short-run measure for the uniform profit rate. The markup over prime cost is

$$\mu = \frac{d + r}{(MC + WC)} \cdot \frac{K}{x}.$$

This markup must be different in industries whose capital/output ratios K/x or depreciation d are different, whereas the profit rate r may be the same in all industries. The markup is equal to the profit rate only if a one-year turnover is assumed, thus equating stocks and flows (see also Brody 1970:89). Thus, we can conclude that empirical observations about different markups in so-called oligopolized and nonoligopolized industries and about different changes in markups in the long run or in the course of the business cycle also do not confirm increasing market power or profit rates in so-called oligopolized sectors. Differential markups, as will be shown in more detail in section 5.3, are even consistent with uniform profit rates.

5.2. Production Prices and Differential Profit Rates

After having presented the empirical evidence on differential profit rates and shown that they too are explicable on the basis of a dynamic theory of competition as conceptualized in chapter 2, in the next step I attempt to reconcile the existence of differential profit rates with the theory of production prices. It is assumed here that production takes place in single-product industries and that firms are only single-product firms. Moreover, it is assumed that uniform profit rates do not exist; rather there are individual profit rates for firms and industries. Thus, for a certain length of time, we may have profit rates in industries above or below the average. As shown by the presentation of the studies on differential profit rates in section 4.2, the empirical evidence can be used in support of such a hypothesis. However, assuming the existence of differential profit rates, the concepts of production price, average rate of profit, and cost of production must be modified. To discuss these problems, the concept of vertical integration can be used again.

As shown above, it is quite reasonable to assume the existence of differential profit rates due to shortages or gluts for a short or long period, barriers to the mobility of capital and productivity, and cost differentials of firms. If we take for granted, not uniform profit rates, but differential profit rates for industries due to the causes discussed above, and for reasons of simplicity, uniform techniques of firms within an industry then we can write modified production prices by referring to slightly changed forms of equations (3.10) and (3.12). Production prices which include differential profit rates can be written as:

$$\bar{p} = w\mathbf{l} + \bar{p}\tilde{A} + \bar{p}\tilde{B}\langle \bar{r} \rangle \qquad (5.1)$$

or as

$$\bar{p}[I - (A^+ + \tilde{B}\langle \bar{r} \rangle)] = 0. \qquad (5.1a)$$

The conditions under which we get a positive price vector $\bar{p}$ are discussed in appendix 4. $\langle \bar{r} \rangle$ is here the diagonal matrix of differential profit rates. Moreover, using the concept of vertical integration, introduced in chapters 2 and 3, we can write the modified production prices as new centers of gravity in the following way:

$$\bar{p}_j = w'_j + \overline{\Pi}'_j \qquad (5.2)$$

with

$$\overline{\Pi}'_j = \{\bar{p}\tilde{B}\langle \bar{r} \rangle Q\}_j,$$

where w'_j represents the vertically integrated wages and $\overline{\Pi}'_j$ the vertically integrated profits for differential profit rates in industries. Under the condition of the existence of differential profit rates, we also can formulate a social average rate of profit $\bar{r}^0$:

$$\bar{r}^0 = \frac{\bar{p}x - w'x}{\bar{p}\tilde{B}Qx} \qquad (5.3)$$

$$\bar{r}^0 = \frac{\overline{\Pi}'\mathbf{x}}{\overline{\mathbf{p}}\tilde{\mathbf{B}}\mathbf{Q}\mathbf{x}}, \tag{5.3a}$$

where $\overline{\Pi}' = \overline{\mathbf{p}}\tilde{\mathbf{B}}\langle\bar{\mathbf{r}}\rangle\mathbf{Q}$, $\overline{\mathbf{p}}$ represents the modified prices of production, $\mathbf{x}$ the output vector, and $\overline{\mathbf{p}}\tilde{\mathbf{B}}\mathbf{Q}$ the vertically integrated capital stock. As Brody (1970:126) has shown, the average rate of profit $\bar{r}^0$, computed on the basis of prices and outputs that are not the right- and left-hand eigenvectors of the eigenvalue $\lambda = 1/r$, creates a deviation of the average rates of profit $\bar{r}^0$ and r (the uniform rate of profit). However, as Brody also shows, the distortion is very small, and $\bar{r}^0$ will be close to r. We can now call the difference $\bar{r}_j - \bar{r}^0$ the deviation of any industry rate of profit from the new average rate of profit. Moreover, an actual price p^*_j may be above, equal to, or below the modified production price $\overline{p}_j$. Actual prices may fluctuate, but they are not an arbitrary phenomenon. The modified production prices $\overline{\mathbf{p}}$ can be considered the centers of gravity for actual prices, at least for the period of time for which differential profit rates prevail. Because competition and mobility barriers to capital produce deviations from the average rate of profit—and uniform profit rates never exist—it would be more realistic to assume those modified production prices as centers of gravity for market prices for a certain period of time (see also Semmler 1984b).

At this point, I can make another remark on the measurement of monopoly profit rate, price-cost margin, or profit margin. I already have shown that when $\bar{r}_j > \bar{r}^0$ this difference does not always indicate market power in industries. As we have seen before, the deviation of $\bar{r}_j$ from $\bar{r}^0$ may be caused by the specific supply and demand conditions, by other restrictions on the mobility of capital, or by productivity and cost differentials of firms in industries. Only in the second case may the difference $\bar{r}_j - \bar{r}^0$ express market power and a monopoly profit rate. On the assumption, however, that differential profit rates exist because of the reasons discussed above, a monopoly profit rate cannot be measured as easily as usual. A profit rate above the average need not indicate a monopoly profit rate. It might be that firms have lower input costs because the commodities entering industry j include profit rates below the average (see Steedman 1979b). In this case, we have a higher profit rate in industry j without its being a monopoly profit rate. By referring to the existence of differential profit rates, the cost of production can be redefined too. The cost of production vector is:

$$\bar{\mathbf{c}}' = \mathbf{w}' + \sum_{n=1}^{\infty} \bar{\mathbf{p}}\tilde{\mathbf{B}}\langle \mathbf{r}\rangle\, \tilde{\mathbf{A}}^n, \tag{5.4}$$

since $\mathbf{Q} = (\mathbf{I} - \tilde{\mathbf{A}})^{-1}$ can be expanded as a power series. The cost of production $\bar{\mathbf{c}}'$ is thus the vertically integrated cost of production. Since the vertically integrated cost of production under the condition of a uniform profit rate is

$$\mathbf{c}' = \mathbf{w}' + \sum_{n=1}^{\infty} r\mathbf{p}\tilde{\mathbf{B}}\tilde{\mathbf{A}}^n,$$

the difference $\bar{c}'_j - c'_j$ may cause a differential profit rate for an industry. A higher profit rate is a measure of monopoly power and monopoly profit rate only if the profit is measured as the difference between the average price $\bar{p}_j$ and the vertically integrated cost c'_j, i.e., $\bar{p}_j - c'_j$. Empirically measured profit rates do not account for this possibility of a profit rate above the average; thus, empirically measured profit rates must not indicate monopoly profit rates or profit margins.

Another problem that arises with the existence of differential profit rates and a price vector $\bar{\mathbf{p}}$ is the problem of aggregation. However, as Brody (1970:125) has shown, if we assume prices of production $\mathbf{p}$ with a uniform profit rate r and, on the other hand, production prices $\bar{\mathbf{p}}$ with differential profit rates $\langle \mathbf{r}\rangle$, then the aggregation of industries on the basis of the prices $\bar{\mathbf{p}}$ and a corresponding output vector $\mathbf{x}$ will never increase the deviations of the aggregates. Thus, for individual prices there will be deviations of $\bar{\mathbf{p}}$ from $\mathbf{p}$, but for aggregates the deviations may be much smaller (see also Shaikh 1982). However, the existence of differential profits and a delay of the formation of a uniform profit rate due to the causes discussed above do not mean that the regulating price will not be a production or reproduction price anymore. Against the assumption of the existence of differential profit rates and markups, the objection could be made that prices are not determined any more by their reproduction cost and that in case of structural or other barriers to mobility of capital, differential profit rates would not be used anymore as guideposts for capital mobility. The empirical evidence, however, shows that we can have differential profit rates for a considerably long time while commodities are produced and reproduced. Yet, as also shown, barriers to the mobility of capital are subject to many changes and can be overcome in the course of time.

5.3. Production Prices, Industrial Pricing, and Markups

After having discussed the problem of how the empirical facts of differential profit rates can be integrated into an elaborate concept of production prices, I want to analyze in this section, how theories of industrial pricing that are based on markup or target rate of return pricing can be made consistent with the classical and Marxian theories of competition and prices of production. In section 3.1.2 the problem of markup and target rate of return pricing was discussed with regard to empirical studies on industrial pricing. In section 3.1.3 I made preliminary remarks on the relation of production prices to markup and target rate of return pricing. Here, I want to return to this topic and show how industrial pricing based on markups and target rates of return can be derived from the production price concept. In this section, I assume single-product firms that are able to calculate their standard volume of output and their standard cost. As mentioned in section 3.2., short-run changes in the volume of output do not change the standard cost and standard price (see also Coutts et al. 1978:21). Short-run profit may be affected by fluctuations of output around the standard output, due to short-run cost changes; this, however, does not lead to substitution (see Asimakopulos 1978:281). Substitution and choice of technique is thus, within a certain range of output variation, excluded. (Further reasons why it is possible to make the assumption of no substitution for small variations in output for the case of joint production and corporate pricing as well are discussed in appendix 3 and chapter 6). Moreover, in the first step I leave out the problem of differential profit rates, which will be dealt with later. As already shown in chapter 2, the assumptions mentioned here come close to the assumptions that can be found in the classical and Marxian theories of a production price as the center of gravity for the market price. Here too, normal costs and normal prices do not change because of small fluctuations in output and demand.

As discussed in chapter 3, by referring to the increasing oligopolization of industries, post-Marxian and post-Keynesian writers such as Kalecki, Steindl, Sylos-Labini, Eichner, and Asimakopulos have developed a theory of pricing that seems to contradict the notion of production prices as long-run prices discussed above. In their theories the markup or target rate of return on investment seems to be quite arbitrarily determined and is no longer related to the notion of a general profit rate as determined by the structure of production and the level of reproduction of labor power. Contrary to those writers, I maintain that it is possible to develop a theory for the size of the target rate of return and the markup in which they do not lose their relation to the general profit rate and production prices as centers of gravity for industry profit rates and market prices. As developed in section 3.1.3 (formula 3.10a), production prices can be written as the following formula:

$$\mathbf{p} = \mathbf{pA} + \mathbf{pdl} + \mathbf{pB'} + r\mathbf{p\tilde{B}}, \tag{5.5}$$

where it is assumed that each firm produces only one product, that the volume of output is the standard volume of output, and that $\mathbf{A}$ is the matrix for material inputs, and thus $\mathbf{pA}$ is the vector of material cost; $\mathbf{pdl}$ is equal to w, the unit wage cost; $\mathbf{\tilde{B}}$ is the capital stock matrix; r is the rate of return on the capital stock; and $r\mathbf{p\tilde{B}}$ is the profit per unit of output. The coefficients of the matrix $\mathbf{B'}$ represent the capital stock that is used up during the period of production; thus, $\mathbf{pB'}$ represents the vector of depreciation, where $b'_{ij} = \tilde{b}_{ij}/t_{ij}$; $\tilde{b}_{ij}$ is the capital stock from industry i used up in the production process j; and t_{ij} is the turnover time of the fixed capital represented by $\tilde{b}_{ij} = b'_{ij}t_{ij}$ (see Brody 1970, sec. 1.2). The variable r, the profit rate on the capital stock, can also be considered the target rate of return on invested capital (see sec. 3.1.3).

The markup over variable cost $\mu(MC + WC) = \mu VC$, as it is fundamental for Kalecki's theory and the post-Keynesian oligopoly theory, can be easily derived from this approach. Brody has developed types of price equations for socialist planning which are equivalent to those for markup pricing. But he still maintains that "the mark-up cannot be chosen arbitrarily" (1970:81). Referring to the target rate of return approach, equation (5.5) can be written as follows:

$$r\mathbf{p}\tilde{\mathbf{B}} = \mathbf{p} \ (\mathbf{I} - \overline{\mathbf{A}} - \mathbf{B}'), \qquad (5.6)$$

where $\overline{\mathbf{A}}$ is $\mathbf{A} + \mathbf{dl}$. By multiplying both sides by $(\mathbf{I} - \overline{\mathbf{A}} - \mathbf{B}')^{-1}$, we get the following expression:

$$\mathbf{p} = r\mathbf{p}\tilde{\mathbf{B}}(\mathbf{I} - \mathbf{A} - \mathbf{B}')^{-1} \qquad (5.6a)$$

or

$$\mathbf{p}\tilde{\mathbf{B}}(\mathbf{I} - \overline{\mathbf{A}} - \mathbf{B}')^{-1} = \lambda\mathbf{p}, \qquad (5.7)$$

where $\lambda = 1/r$. If the matrix $\tilde{\mathbf{B}}(\mathbf{I} - \overline{\mathbf{A}} - \mathbf{B}')^{-1}$ is nonnegative and indecomposable, λ is the maximal eigenvalue of the matrix $\tilde{\mathbf{B}}(\mathbf{I} - \overline{\mathbf{A}} - \mathbf{B}')^{-1}$. The size of λ, and thus the target rate of return on capital stock r, is a result of the structure of production and the level of the reproduction of labor power (which determines $\mathbf{dl}$ in the matrix $\overline{\mathbf{A}}$). For a uniform profit rate in all industries, this approach tells us how big the maximum rate of profit, the target rate of return, and the markup on prime cost can be.

Before deriving the different markups for the different industries, I want to show briefly that the target rate of return investment can be positive only if the rate of exploitation is positive. If we start from the value system $\Lambda\tilde{\mathbf{A}} + \mathbf{l} = \Lambda$, where Λ is the vertical integrated labor, the value vector of the commodities, we can write $\Lambda = \mathbf{l}(\mathbf{I} - \tilde{\mathbf{A}})^{-1}$, where $\mathbf{l}$ is again the vector of direct labor requirements and $\tilde{\mathbf{A}}$ the matrix of inputs and depreciation, and $\mathbf{dl}$ is the matrix of consumption goods for the reproduction of labor power. The sufficient condition for a positive rate of exploitation is $\mathbf{dlx} < (\mathbf{I} - \tilde{\mathbf{A}})\mathbf{x}$, where $\mathbf{x}$ is the output vector.[2] In terms of value, the necessary condition for a positive rate of exploitation is $\Lambda\mathbf{dlx} <$

$l(I - \tilde{A})^{-1} (I - \tilde{A})x$ or $\Lambda dlx < \Lambda(I - \tilde{A})x$. If this condition is fulfilled the rate of exploitation is

$$e = \frac{\Lambda(I - \tilde{A})x - \Lambda dlx}{\Lambda dlx}.$$

This positive rate of exploitation is the necessary and sufficient condition for a positive rate of return on capital invested. We know that $\Lambda(A^+ + edl) = \Lambda$. The maximum eigenvalue $\lambda(A^+ + edl)$ is 1, where $A^+ = \overline{A} + B'$. We also know that $p(A^+ + r\tilde{B}) = \lambda p$, with $\lambda(A^+ + r\tilde{B}) = 1$. Since we assume that $\Lambda x = px$, r will be positive only if e is positive (see Abraham-Frois and Berrebi 1976:30). But not only the target rate of return on investment is determined by equations (5.6a) and (5.7); so are the different markups in the different industries.

By referring to the markup pricing discussed above, we can write the following system of industrial prices:

$$p = p\overline{A}\langle\delta\rangle \tag{5.8}$$

or

$$p = p\overline{A} (I + \langle\mu\rangle), \tag{5.8a}$$

where $\langle\delta\rangle$ is diagonal matrix of $(1 + \mu_i)$. Assuming that the prices of production from equation (5.5) and the markup prices that we get from equation (5.8a) are the same, we can write

$$p = p\overline{A} + pB' + rp\tilde{B} = p\overline{A} (I + \langle\mu\rangle) \tag{5.8b}$$

or

$$p\overline{A}\langle\mu\rangle + p\overline{A} = p\overline{A} + pB' + rp\tilde{B}$$

or

$$p\overline{A}\langle\mu\rangle = pB' + rp\tilde{B} \tag{5.9}$$

or

$$\langle C\rangle\langle\mu\rangle = \langle\Pi\rangle, \tag{5.9a}$$

where $\langle C\rangle$ is the diagonal matrix of the unit cost of production in the industries and $\langle\Pi\rangle$ is the diagonal matrix of the unit gross profit Π_i

of the industries. Equation (5.9a) can be rewritten by multiplying both sides by $\langle \mathbf{C} \rangle^{-1}$; thus we get

$$\langle \mu \rangle = \langle \mathbf{C} \rangle^{-1} \langle \Pi \rangle. \tag{5.9b}$$

Since r and $\mathbf{p}$ are given from equation (5.7), we can see that the mark-ups are completely determined by the matrices $\overline{\mathbf{A}}$, $\mathbf{B}'$, and $\tilde{\mathbf{B}}$. The matrix $\langle \mu \rangle$ cannot be determined arbitrarily but is given by the structure of production and the level of reproduction of labor power.

By referring to the example introduced in section 3.1.3, I want to demonstrate the relation of the rate of return on fixed capital advanced (target rate of return) to the markup over prime cost. Here it can be shown that the markup cannot be arbitrary. Using the example in section 3.1.3, and referring to the equation (5.9), which is derived from (5.8b) by leaving out $\mathbf{p}\overline{\mathbf{A}}$ on both sides, we can write

$$(0.072 \quad 0.682 \quad 0.246) \begin{bmatrix} 0.493 & 3.714 & 1.5 \\ 0 & 0 & 0 \\ 0.027 & 0.381 & 0.333 \end{bmatrix} \begin{bmatrix} \mu_1 & 0 & 0 \\ 0 & \mu_2 & 0 \\ 0 & 0 & \mu_3 \end{bmatrix}$$

$$= (0.072 \quad 0.682 \quad 0.246) \begin{bmatrix} 0 & 0 & 0 \\ 0.044 & 0.469 & 0.082 \\ 0 & 0 & 0 \end{bmatrix}$$

or, using the diagonal matrices,

$$\begin{bmatrix} 0.0416 & 0 & 0 \\ 0 & 0.359 & 0 \\ 0 & 0 & 0.189 \end{bmatrix} \begin{bmatrix} \mu_1 & 0 & 0 \\ 0 & \mu_2 & 0 \\ 0 & 0 & \mu_3 \end{bmatrix}$$

$$= \begin{bmatrix} 0.03 & 0 & 0 \\ 0 & 0.319 & 0 \\ 0 & 0 & 0.056 \end{bmatrix},$$

which gives

$$\begin{bmatrix} \mu_1 & 0 & 0 \\ 0 & \mu_2 & 0 \\ 0 & 0 & \mu_3 \end{bmatrix} = \begin{bmatrix} 0.721 & 0 & 0 \\ 0 & 0.888 & 0 \\ 0 & 0 & 0.295 \end{bmatrix}.$$

The markups over prime cost for the three different production processes are $\mu_1 = 0.721$, $\mu_2 = 0.888$, and $\mu_3 = 0.295$. Thus, the classical and Marxian concepts of production prices also provide us with a theory of the determination of markups. Even if the rate of return on fixed capital is uniform, the markups will all be different.

We have to modify this derivation of the markups slightly if we assume a rate of return on the *total* capital *advanced*, not just on the fixed capital. If we refer to the Marxian prices of production, which are determined by the cost of production plus the profit rate on the total capital advanced (fixed plus circulating capital), we can write the following system of prices of production:

$$\mathbf{p} = \mathbf{p}(\mathbf{\bar{A}} + \mathbf{B'} + r\mathbf{B^+}), \tag{5.10}$$

where $\mathbf{\bar{A}}$ again is the matrix of material inputs and necessary consumption; $\mathbf{B'}$ the depreciation matrix, where $b'_{ij} = \tilde{b}_{ij}/t_{ij}$; $\mathbf{B^+}$ the matrix of total capital advanced, where $b^+_{ij} = a^+_{ij}t_{ij}$, since the matrix $\mathbf{A^+} = \mathbf{A} + \mathbf{B'} + \mathbf{dl}$ includes the flow of materials, replacement goods for fixed capital, and consumption goods for the reproduction of labor power (see Brody 1970, sec. 1.2); and t_{ij} the turnover time in years. Here again, since r and $\mathbf{p}$ are determined by the eigenvalue and associated eigenvector of

$$\mathbf{pB^+}(\mathbf{I} - \mathbf{\bar{A}} - \mathbf{B'})^{-1} = \lambda\mathbf{p}, \tag{5.11}$$

where $\lambda = 1/r$, we get the following markups:

$$\mathbf{p\bar{A}}\langle\delta\rangle = \mathbf{p}(\mathbf{\bar{A}} + \mathbf{B'} + r\mathbf{B^+}) \tag{5.12}$$

or

$$\mathbf{p\bar{A}}\langle\mu\rangle = \mathbf{p}(\mathbf{B'} + r\mathbf{B^+}). \tag{5.12a}$$

Using the diagonal matrices for unit costs and unit gross profits, we get

$$\langle C \rangle \langle \mu \rangle = \langle \Pi \rangle$$

or

$$\langle \mu \rangle = \langle C \rangle^{-1} \langle \Pi \rangle. \qquad (5.12b)$$

Here again we can see that the markups or profit margins for each industry are completely determined by the matrices $\overline{A}$, B', and B^+, and that markups or profit margins do not seem to be arbitrary.

This approach can also be extended to the problem of differential profit rates of industries, as formalized in equations (5.1) and (5.1a). In this case we cannot get prices and average rate of return on capital advanced from the eigenvalue equation (5.7 or 5.11), but $\overline{p}$ and $\overline{r}^0$ have to be determined in a different way ($\overline{r}^0$ is the social average profit rate when differential profit rates exist). Under the condition of differential profit rates, a price system that includes a return on total capital invested, i.e., the system of equation (5.5), can be written in the following way:

$$\overline{p} = \overline{p}\overline{A} + \overline{p}B' + \overline{p}B^+\langle \overline{r} \rangle, \qquad (5.13)$$

where $\langle \overline{r} \rangle$ is the diagonal matrix of differential profit rates $\overline{r}_i$. From equation (5.13) we can also get the average profit rate in the economy $\overline{r}^0$, because

$$\overline{r}^0 = \frac{\overline{p}B^+\langle \overline{r} \rangle \, x}{\overline{p}B^+ x}.$$

We can also derive $\overline{r}^0$ by using the concept of vertical integration, as in equation (5.2). The system that allows us to derive the different markups in the industries under the conditions of differential profit rate is as follows:

$$\overline{p}\overline{A} \, (1 + \langle \overline{\mu} \rangle) = \overline{p}\overline{A} + \overline{p}B^+\langle \overline{r} \rangle. \qquad (5.14)$$

Thus we get

$$\overline{p}\overline{A}\langle \mu \rangle = \overline{p}B' + \overline{p}B^+\langle \overline{r} \rangle \qquad (5.15)$$

or, in terms of the diagonal matrices,

$$\langle \mu \rangle = \langle C \rangle^{-1} \langle \Pi \rangle.$$

But I have to remark here that it is possible that equation (5.13), which can also be written

$$\bar{p}\{I - (\bar{A} + B' + B^{+}\langle\bar{r}\rangle))\} = 0, \qquad (5.16)$$

does not necessarily have a positive solution for all elements of $\bar{p}$. We get a positive price vector $\bar{p}$ only if $\langle\bar{r}\rangle$ remains within a certain bounded space (see appendix 4). Yet we can see that modern industrial pricing based on markup or target rate of return pricing can be made consistent with the aforementioned production price concept, assuming either a uniform profit rate or differential profit rates for all industries.

To sum up this discussion, the causes and the empirical evidence for differential profit rates have been shown to be not in contradiction with the dynamic theory of competition developed in chapter 2, but rather in accord with it. As demonstrated in actual economic systems, we can expect differential profit rates between industries and firms for a certain period of time and we also can experience a widespread practice of markup pricing, not only in highly concentrated industries. By referring to a model of industrial pricing containing single-product firms, it has been shown that there is no contradiction between markup, target rate of return pricing, or the existence of differential profit rates and the concept of production prices presented. The first approach can be made consistent with the latter. Markup and target rate of return pricing with differential profit rates have been considered, since Kalecki, a new form of pricing of active oligopoly firms, and the markup was considered the measure of oligopoly power. Yet Kalecki referred only to single-product firms and industrial pricing. As I will show, markup and target rate of return pricing have been developed, not by single-product firms, but by multiplant and multiproduct corporations since the twenties. Markup and target rate of return pricing are closely related to the generation of large, vertically integrated and diversified corporations. Their activities are not activities of single-product firms any more; corporate activities and pricing can best be modeled by theories of joint production. In the next chapter, therefore, I will pursue further the question of whether the activities of large corporations which have many production processes at their disposal and produce many outputs are compatible with the dynamic concept of competition and production price, developed before.

Notes

1. It should be kept in mind that—as shown in sec. 2.3.4—profits of large firms can contain elements of economic rent. If large corporations have extensive ownership of natural resources (land, minerals, mining, etc.), profits can be higher because of a "natural" or "artificial" monopoly on input factors in production processes.

2. With regard to the relation of the rate of profit r and the rate of exploitation e, discussed below in the text, it must be mentioned here that it is possible for a system to be reproductive with a surplus value in terms of labor values, but not in physical terms (see Krause 1981:176). This problem becomes especially important in the discussion on heterogeneous labor and the theory of value (see Bowles and Gintis 1978; Morishima 1978; Krause 1981).

6. PRODUCTION PRICES, JOINT PRODUCTION, AND CORPORATE PRICING

In the previous chapter it was assumed that firms are producing a single product and that the prices for the entire industry are determined by prime cost and a markup (or a target rate of return). I want to extend my approach now to the case of joint production and corporate pricing. Recently more and more attention has been given to a theory of value and price for joint production models. Indeed, it can be said that single production—the activity of one single-product firm in one industry—is not necessarily the common case in industrial production. Joint production, where several products are produced by the same process (or by-products are produced that are salable or not salable), has been known in economic literature since the classics (see Smith 1976:181, 246; Marx 1967b, ch. 5, especially sec. 5.4; Mill 1900, book 3, ch. 16, sec. 1; Marshall 1947:386; Jevons 1965; Hicks 1939, sec. 6.5; Stackelberg 1948:31). Cases of joint production can be found in agricultural production, manufacturing production, the energy sector, and the production of public goods and services.[1] However, as can be seen from the literature on the rise of large corporations since the end of the nineteenth century, joint production became a very common practice for vertically integrated and diversified large corporations.[2] As Chandler (1977) has shown, the rise of large corporations is closely related to joint production cases. As documented by the literature on the history of industrial concentration, at the end of the nineteenth century, large companies already pursued vertical integration and diversification. They first moved into areas where primary products were produced. In this area the most common cases of joint production could be found, i.e., in the production of minerals, agricultural products, coal, gas, and oil and in certain manufacturing sectors (chemical production, coke, refineries, steel mills, meat packing). The vertical integration and diversification of corporations was closely related to this area where joint production was very common. Moreover, with the increase in diversification and the rise of large conglomerates, starting in the twenties, multiplant and multiproduct activities of large firms became a common phenomenon. As can also be seen from the literature of the history of large corporations (see Chandler 1977:445), it was mainly the large multiproduct and multiplant corporations that developed special cost accounting and budget accounting procedures to deal with the problem of multiplant and multiproduct activities. The main goal of the pricing procedure, developed by the large vertically integrated, diversified, and decentralized corporations since the twenties, was control of the reproduction and expansion of their capital. As we will see, markup and target rate of return pricing were developed for this purpose. However, interpreting the activities of such large corporations in terms of a joint production model may—as is well known—lead to some difficulties for the classical and Marxian theories. Therefore, after introducing a simple joint production model for interpreting corporate activities in section 6.2, I will discuss the conditions under which the treatment of corporate activities as joint production activities will lead to reasonable results with regard to the classical and Marxian theories. The last part of the chapter will return to the relation between production prices, corporate pricing, and markups.

6.1. A Simple Model of Joint Production and Corporate Activities

As mentioned before, we assume for this analysis that corporations produce many products and have many production processes available to them. They are decentralized into divisions and subdivisions producing different outputs (multiplant and multi-product corporations), but for each vector of outputs there is—in the short run—only one input vector available. Thus, choice of technique and substitution are excluded in the short run. The rationale for this assumption, as mentioned above, is that there is sufficient empirical evidence that modern corporations calculate production costs and normal rates of return on capital invested under the condition of a standard volume of output, which implies the calculation of the normal cost (see Chandler 1977:446). This procedure of cost calculation was introduced into corporate financial control policies in the twenties and has been widely exercised by corporations since the fifties (see Kaplan et al. 1958). Many econometric price tests, like those presented in chapter 3, lead us to the same conclusion. This allows us to make the assumption that for short-run fluctuations in output returns to scale, choice of technique, and substitution do not play an important role. Moreover, a result reached in a theoretical study by Hinrichsen and Krause (1981) can be taken as a motivation for making the assumption introduced above (see appendix 3).

The following example, which refers to the assumption mentioned above, may illustrate the production of a multiplant and multiproduct corporation. The output program of a corporation as a large unit of capital that produces many outputs may be represented the following vector $\mathbf{x}^h$, where h is the hth corporation and x_1^h, x_2^h, and x_3^h refer to the types of outputs produced by it. The number of corporations, for example, may be three, $h = 1, 2, 3$. We may assume the following activated processes for each of the three

$$
\begin{array}{ccc}
P_1^h & P_2^h & P_3^h
\end{array}
$$

$$
\begin{bmatrix}
\bar{a}_{11} & \bar{a}_{12} & \bar{a}_{13} \\
\bar{a}_{21} & \bar{a}_{22} & \bar{a}_{23} \\
\bar{a}_{31} & \bar{a}_{32} & \bar{a}_{33}
\end{bmatrix}
$$

$$
\downarrow \quad \downarrow \quad \downarrow
$$

$$
\begin{bmatrix}
b_{11} & b_{12} & 0 \\
0 & b_{22} & b_{23} \\
b_{31} & 0 & 0
\end{bmatrix}
$$

corporations P_1, P_2, and P_3. Two processes produce two outputs each, the third one only one output. We can write these production processes in terms of their coefficients, normalized to the unit output level. (For a simple numerical example, see note 11.)

All three corporations ($h = 1, 2, 3$) can activate the three processes; however, only the first two processes produce joint products. The total input requirements for all of the corporations are $\overline{\mathbf{A}}\mathbf{x}$, and the vector of total output is $\mathbf{B}\mathbf{x}$, where $\mathbf{x} = (\mathbf{x}^1 + \mathbf{x}^2 + \mathbf{x}^3)$ and $\mathbf{x}^1$, $\mathbf{x}^2$, and $\mathbf{x}^3$ are the vectors of the outputs of the respective corporations. Moreover, $\overline{a}_{ij}$ of $\overline{\mathbf{A}}$ represents the ith input per unit of output j, and $\mathbf{B}$ is the matrix of output coefficients, with b_{ij} representing the ith output per unit of output of commodity j. Here $\overline{\mathbf{A}} = \mathbf{A} + \mathbf{dI}$, as in section 5.3. The necessary inputs for the production process of any one corporation ($h = 1, 2, 3$) and the outputs produced can be represented by the following relation:

$$\overline{\mathbf{A}}\mathbf{x}^h \leqslant \mathbf{B}\mathbf{x}^h,$$

where $\mathbf{x}^h \geqslant \mathbf{0}$. However, as developed in section 6.2, the production processes for joint products can be separated with regard to the input costs for each product, or they can be left nonseparated.

These characteristics may also be true for any division or subdivision (multiplant corporation) of a company. In this case the vector $\mathbf{x}^h$ becomes $\mathbf{x}^{hg}$, where h is the corporation and g its subdivision. Adding up the production of all g's gives us the output vector $\mathbf{x}^h$. In what follows I want to refer only to this vector $\mathbf{x}^h$. Moreover, it is assumed here that $\mathbf{x}^h$ is the vector of the standard volume of output. Thus, we can exclude the problems of the role of demand, returns to scale, choice of technique, and substitution, as discussed before. As can be seen from the financial control policy of multiplant and multiproduct corporations since the twenties, corporations do in fact calculate such a standard volume of output (see Bradley 1927; Brown 1924, art. 2–5; Chandler 1977:445). Now we can represent the total necessary input and total output produced by all corporations by the following formula

$$\overline{\mathbf{A}}\mathbf{x} \leqslant \mathbf{B}\mathbf{x}. \tag{6.1}$$

Since we assume that the corporations produce a surplus (as a source of profits), we must have the following conditions:

$$(\mathbf{B} - \overline{\mathbf{A}})\mathbf{x} \geqslant \mathbf{0}. \tag{6.1a}$$

When a surplus is produced, a positive growth rate of the corporations and the economic system is possible. If the growth rate is $g > 0$, we get for a model with only circulating capital:

$$(1 + g)\overline{A}x = Bx. \tag{6.2}$$

On the assumption that the corporations will employ not only circulating capital but also fixed capital, the inequality (6.1) looks slightly different. If B' is part of the initial capital stock that is used up by the production processes and has to be replaced (see section 3.1.3), we get the following input-output relation for corporation h:

$$(\overline{A} + B')x^h \leqslant Bx^h.$$

The surplus product for the economic system is

$$(B - \overline{A} - B')x \geqslant 0, \tag{6.1b}$$

and the expanding economic system can be written as

$$(1 + g)(\overline{A} + B')x = Bx \tag{6.2a}$$

or

$$(1 + g) A^{+}x = Bx, \tag{6.2b}$$

where $A^{+} = \overline{A} + B'$.

It has to be mentioned that fixed capital is treated here as it is in Marx and not as it is in the Sraffa/von Neumann system. In the latter fixed capital is treated as a joint product and appears as part of the output Bx. In Marx fixed capital is treated on the input side. I will use this concept of fixed capital, which was developed by Lange (1952), Brody (1970), and Pasinetti (1973), in the following discussion on pricing. As we can see from the corporate pricing and the financial policy that has developed since the twenties, fixed capital is treated in the classical fashion (see Brown 1924, art. 2; Chandler 1977:446). By referring to this treatment of fixed capital in the case of multiplant and multiproduct corporations, we can extend our pricing model for single production and industrial pricing to joint production and corporate pricing.

As mentioned before, multiplant and multiproduct corporations have developed, since the twenties, a pricing mechanism that does not necessarily contradict the classical and Marxian theories of competition, average profit rate, and prices of production as centers of gravity for market prices. As can be seen from the aforementioned documents on the pricing policy of large corporations that tried to decentralize their large units into divisions and subdivisions (see also Chandler 1962), the corporations developed a cost-plus or markup price for each product or product group that was consistent with a normal or averge rate of return on their total capital advanced.[3] The main reasons that were given by corporations that introduce this type of pricing were increased fixed investment, development of multiproduct production, and decentralization. These made it necessary to introduce pricing with fixed profit margins, which made control of the entire corporation's employed capital possible.

Markup pricing does not seem to have much to do with the degree of concentration in industries (as Kalecki interpreted it) but was introduced for the purpose of financial control of the large amounts of fixed capital used by decentralized multiplant and multiproduct corporations. This can be seen from the following quotation:

> The development of industry usually is accompanied by an increase in fixed investment, which results from a further adoption of labor saving machinery, and from the tendency of the industrial unit to become a more complete manufacturer. Total cost may decrease, but the proportion of selling price necessary to cover indirect expense and return on investment tends to increase. The problem of equitably distributing over different products both indirect costs and the profit margin necessary to provide return on the capital employed is, therefore, one of increasing importance, and its solution is facilitated by the periodic development of standard prices, based upon standards of capital requirement and of manufacturing and commercial expenses. (Bradley 1927:433)

How this model of pricing for a decentralized multiplant and multiproduct corporation can sufficiently be described even within the classical and Marxian framework of competition, average profit rate, and prices of production is the subject of the following discussion. The main approach is that each product, product group, or production of a plant should be priced in such a way that it provides a normal or average rate of return on the total capital advanced. This normal rate of return allows for the growth and expansion of the corporation.

We start with the markup pricing of each product or product group of a corporation.[4] This markup or cost-plus pricing by a corporation with joint production can be represented in the following way, considering only prime cost for the markup prices:

$$\mathbf{p}\overline{\mathbf{A}}\langle\boldsymbol{\delta}\rangle = \mathbf{pB}, \qquad\qquad (6.3)$$

where the diagonal matrix $\langle\boldsymbol{\delta}\rangle$ is $\mathbf{I} + \langle\boldsymbol{\mu}\rangle$ and $\langle\boldsymbol{\mu}\rangle$ is the diagonal matrix of markups. The total value of the inputs of corporation h is

$$\mathbf{p}\mathbf{A}^{h}\mathbf{x}^{h},$$

and the total value of the produced output from the different plants and products is

$$\mathbf{pBx}^{h}.$$

This gives us the produced sum of gross profits (including depreciation)

$$\mathbf{pBx}^{h} - \mathbf{p}\overline{\mathbf{A}}\mathbf{x}^{h} = \mathbf{p}\overline{\mathbf{A}}\langle\boldsymbol{\mu}\rangle\mathbf{x}^{h}.$$

As mentioned above, markup pricing or cost-plus pricing was developed by large corporations beginning in the twenties for the purpose of financial control.

The markup on standard cost should provide the company with a normal rate of return on the total capital advanced. We have to show the relation of the markup pricing for each product or product group to prices that include an average rate of return on total capital advanced. The pricing formula for a large corporation with joint production that wants to receive an average rate of return on the total capital advanced can be written in the following way:

$$\mathbf{p}\overline{\mathbf{A}} + \mathbf{pB'} + r\mathbf{pB}^{+} = \mathbf{pB}, \qquad\qquad (6.4)$$

where again, $\overline{\mathbf{A}}$ is a square matrix representing the material inputs and necessary consumption; $\mathbf{B'}$ the depreciation matrix discussed in section 5.3; and $\mathbf{B}^{+}$ the matrix of total capital advanced per unit of output, with $b_{ij}^{+} = a_{ij}^{+}t_{ij}$, as defined in section 5.3. All coefficients refer to a standard or average output. Equation (6.4) can be reformulated as

$$r\mathbf{p}\mathbf{B}^{+} = \mathbf{p}(\mathbf{B} - \overline{\mathbf{A}} - \mathbf{B}').$$ (6.4a)

Weighting the left and the right sides by the vector of the output of corporation h gives us

$$r\mathbf{p}\mathbf{B}^{+}\mathbf{x}^{h} = \mathbf{p}(\mathbf{B} - \overline{\mathbf{A}} - \mathbf{B}')\mathbf{x}^{h},$$

the total net profit of corporation h. Equation (6.4a) can be reformulated as a general eigenvalue problem that takes into account joint production by corporations.

From equation (6.4) we get

$$\mathbf{p}\mathbf{B}^{+} = \lambda\mathbf{p}(\mathbf{B} - \overline{\mathbf{A}} - \mathbf{B}').$$ (6.5)

If we set $(\mathbf{B} - \overline{\mathbf{A}} - \mathbf{B}') = \mathbf{S}$, the surplus product matrix for the joint production case, we get

$$\mathbf{p}\mathbf{B}^{+} = \lambda\mathbf{p}\mathbf{S},$$ (6.5a)

which is equivalent to the formulation of a general eigenvalue problem (see appendix 3). Under certain conditions, equation (6.5a) does have a positive real root λ and a simple nonnegative eigenvector, associated with λ as its solution. The more general characteristics of this solution are discussed in appendix 3, where it is also shown that the number of products does not have to be the same as the number of processes.

Before discussing the formula for markup pricing by corporations and equation (6.5a) further, in the following section I want to differentiate between separated and nonseparated joint production activities.

6.2. Joint Production with Separated and Nonseparated Activities

I will now present a short survey of recent discussion of joint production and the theory of value.[5] I want to explore the conditions under which the treatment of corporate activities in terms of a joint production model will lead to reasonable results in the context of

Marxian theory.[6] Since the case of joint production can lead to negative values and a negative rate of surplus value when treated in a linear production model, the Marxian labor theory of value has been considered anamalous and redundant (Steedman 1977, ch. 2). On these grounds the labor theory of value has been attacked and abandoned, because in joint production systems negative values and rate of surplus value can coexist with positive prices and a positive rate of profit. In this chapter I mainly want to refer to recent Marxist and neo-Ricardian discussion and to work out two main cases that give reasonable results with regard to a theory of price even if corporate activities include joint production. Using a joint production model for interpreting corporate activities means assuming that corporations can activate many processes and produce many products (multiplant and multiproduct corporations). The multiple activities of large corporations can be considered as separated or nonseparated activities.[7] The activities shown in figure 6.1 may be differentiated for joint production processes.

In the case of separated activities (case 1), the joint costs (or common costs) of production processes are divisible (as in the case of common costs for different products) or can be made divisible according to certain accounting principles. The accounting principles that are usually used to separate the joint costs of different products can be either monetary expressions (like sales value or unit costs) or physical units (based on some physical measurement). These principles are widely used in business practice (see Matz and Curry 1972, ch. 24) and in input-output analysis.[8] According to them, joint costs are separated and allocated to each product in each

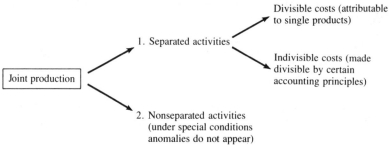

Figure 6.1. Joint Production with Separated and Nonseparated Activities

production process. The production processes are duplicated by this procedure, so that we get multiple processes. The system of joint production processes can then be transformed into a single-product system with multiple activities. (The general idea is very well developed in Flaschel 1979, 1980, 1983). The separation of joint production activities may be illustrated by the simple joint production system $(\mathbf{A}, \mathbf{l}, \mathbf{B})$:

$$\mathbf{A} = \begin{bmatrix} a_{11} & 0 \\ 0 & a_{22} \end{bmatrix}$$

$$\mathbf{l} = (\, l_1 \quad l_2 \,)$$

$$\mathbf{B} = \begin{bmatrix} b_{11} & b_{12} \\ b_{21} & b_{22} \end{bmatrix}.$$

The duplication of the joint production processes leads to

$$\bar{\mathbf{A}} = \begin{bmatrix} a_{11}\beta_{11} & 0 & a_{11}\beta_{21} & 0 \\ 0 & a_{22}\beta_{12} & 0 & a_{22}\beta_{22} \end{bmatrix}$$

$$\bar{\mathbf{l}} = (l_1\beta_{11} \quad l_2\beta_{12} \quad l_1\beta_{21} \quad l_2\beta_{22})$$

$$\bar{\mathbf{B}} = \begin{bmatrix} b_{11} & 0 & b_{21} & 0 \\ 0 & b_{12} & 0 & b_{22} \end{bmatrix}.$$

With this idea of separating joint costs, the matrix $\mathbf{A}$ can be transformed into a multiple-activity matrix, where each column represents the input costs for one type of output produced in different production processes. The β_{ij} assigns a proportion of the inputs of the production process j to the commodity i, produced in the jth production process. The matrix $\mathbf{B}$ is transformed into matrix $\bar{\mathbf{B}}$, where each element $\bar{b}_{ij}$ represents the ith commodity produced by the jth production process. When the joint production processes are separated in such a way, they can be reduced to a single-product system with multiple activities. As we will see, the input matrix $\mathbf{A}$ and the output matrix $\mathbf{B}$ will finally be transformed into matrices $\hat{\mathbf{A}}$ and $\hat{\mathbf{B}}$, where the property of single-product systems $(\hat{\mathbf{B}} - \hat{\mathbf{A}})^{-1} \geqslant \mathbf{0}$, holds. The anomalies of the joint production system will disappear, and negative values and a negative rate of surplus value will not appear. This effect will be discussed below.

In the second procedure, in which joint production activities are not divisible or are not made divisible by assigning to each output a proportion of common costs, there can be pitfalls for the theory of value. An example was introduced by Steedman (1977) in order to show how the labor theory of value runs into difficulties when joint production processes are allowed for. In a circulating capital model, we may assume the following nonseparated joint production activities:

$$\mathbf{A} = \begin{bmatrix} 25 & 0 \\ 0 & 10 \end{bmatrix}$$

$$\mathbf{l} = (5 \quad 1)$$

$$\mathbf{B} = \begin{bmatrix} 30 & 3 \\ 5 & 12 \end{bmatrix}.$$

Although the matrix $(\mathbf{B} - \mathbf{A})\mathbf{x} \geqslant \mathbf{0}$ can be considered productive, generating a semipositive surplus product vector for at least one activity level $\mathbf{x}$, the solution of the value system (after normalizing to the unit output level) is:

$$\Lambda = \mathbf{l}(\mathbf{B} - \mathbf{A})^{-1},$$

showing that $\lambda_1 = -1$ and $\lambda_2 = 2$. This means that the system implies negative values and a negative rate of surplus value even though prices and the profit rate can be shown to be positive. As we can see from the example, the matrix $(\mathbf{B} - \mathbf{A})$ is not nonnegative invertible. The negative values appear because $(\mathbf{B} - \mathbf{A})^{-1} \geqslant \mathbf{0}$ does not hold. Even if joint production processes are not separated with regard to the different outputs they produce, there are several approaches that avoid the result of negative values. I want to discuss mainly two contributions that allow for a nonnegative solution of the value vector Λ. Whereas Flaschel's idea (1979, 1980, 1983) allows for the transformation of the matrices $\mathbf{A}$, $\mathbf{B}$ into matrices $\hat{\mathbf{A}}$, $\hat{\mathbf{B}}$, where $(\hat{\mathbf{B}} - \hat{\mathbf{A}})^{-1} \geqslant \mathbf{0}$ will always be guaranteed under the condition of separated production processes (case 1), the case of nonseparated production processes (case 2) sometimes requires a special joint production system $(\mathbf{A}, \mathbf{l}, \mathbf{B})$, in order to avoid negative values. The first possibility is that we discuss only joint production systems where $(\mathbf{B} - \mathbf{A})^{-1} \geqslant \mathbf{0}$. Thus, we allow only for such joint production systems, where $(\mathbf{B} - \mathbf{A})$ is always nonnegative invertible. Schefold (1978, 1980a, 1980b) considers such systems, which he calls all-engaging systems. The second possibility is that we do allow for joint production systems where $(\mathbf{B} - \mathbf{A})^{-1} \geqslant \mathbf{0}$ does not necessarily hold, and, by introducing weights $\langle \alpha \rangle$ for the vector of direct labor inputs $\mathbf{l}$ in the equation

$$\tilde{\Lambda} = \mathbf{l} \langle \alpha \rangle (\mathbf{B} - \mathbf{A})^{-1},$$

we always will get nonnegative solutions for $\tilde{\Lambda}$, even if the inverse may contain negative elements. This is the approach developed by Krause (1977, 1980), which also allows for the solution of the problem of reducing heterogeneous labor to homogeneous labor for single production as well as for joint production. Moreover, in both the case of separated joint production and that of nonseparated joint production, it is not only possible to show that the values are nonnegative and the rate of surplus value positive, but it is also possible to prove the so-called fundamental Marxian theorem for joint production.

6.2.1. JOINT PRODUCTION AND SEPARATED ACTIVITIES

In many joint production activities joint costs are common costs "allocable among products and services performed because each of the products or services could have been obtained separately" (Matz and Curry 1972:697). However, when there are indivisible joint costs for joint products (or by-products), the joint costs can be divided and separated in accordance with certain cost-causing (monetary or physical) characteristics to determine the unit cost of each product. It must be mentioned, though, that because of the indivisibility of joint costs "cost allocation and apportionment procedures used for establishing the unit cost of a product are far from perfect" (p. 697).

By referring to the sales value method, one of the widely used methods for splitting joint costs, Flaschel (1979, 1980, 1983) has developed an approach for a joint production model which avoids the possible anomalies of such a system and leads to a nonnegative definition of labor values which is very close to the Marxian distinction between individual and social value of a commodity. Following the procedure of Flaschel, we can transform any joint production system into a formal system of multiple activities, represented by a single-product system. However, prices must be taken as given historically for a period of observation (or may be considered as given by a solution of the joint production system developed in section 6.1). This procedure allows us to consider the coexistence of different processes producing the same commodity and assign individual values for the same types of commodities produced by different processes. The weighted averages of the individual values represent—as already worked out by Marx for his notion of a market value of a commodity—social values, which are nonnegative.

Leaving out the problem of fixed capital, which could be included according to the method of Lange, Brody, and Leontief on the input side of the production system, and by referring to a circulating capital model, the joint production system $A \geqslant 0, B \geqslant 0$ (n $\times$ m matrices), and l (the 1 $\times$ m vector of direct labor coefficients) can be written in the following form:

$$\hat{\Lambda}\,\hat{\alpha}\,A\,\hat{\beta} + 1\hat{\beta} = \hat{\Lambda}\,\hat{B}, \tag{6.6}$$

where $\hat{\beta}$ is the following m $\times$ (n · m) matrix:

$$
\begin{bmatrix}
\beta_{11} & 0 & \cdots & 0 & & \beta_{21} & 0 & \cdots & 0 & & \cdots & & & \beta_{n1} & 0 & \cdots & 0 \\
0 & \ddots & & & & 0 & \ddots & & & & & & & 0 & \ddots & & \\
& & \ddots & 0 & & & & \ddots & 0 & & & & & & & \ddots & 0 \\
0 & \cdots & 0 & \beta_{1m} & & 0 & \cdots & 0 & \beta_{2m} & & \cdots & & & 0 & \cdots & 0 & \beta_{nm}
\end{bmatrix}
$$

The coefficients represent the relative share of commodity i in the value of the output of sector j. Therefore

$$\beta_{ij} = p_i b_{ij}/\mathbf{pB}^j$$

and

$$\sum_{i=1}^{n} \beta_{ij} = 1.$$

By using given prices and by referring to the sales value method of joint cost allocation, β_{ij} allows the allocation of the joint costs to each commodity i of each production process j by duplicating the columns of $\mathbf{A}$.[9]

Moreover, $\hat{\alpha}$ may represent the transpose of the n $\times$ (n $\cdot$ m) matrix

$$
\begin{bmatrix}
\alpha_{11} 0 \cdots \cdot \alpha_{1m} & 0 \cdots \cdots 0 & \cdots \cdots \cdots & 0 \cdots \cdots 0 \\
\vdots & \alpha_{21} 0 \cdots \cdots \alpha_{2m} & \vdots & \vdots \\
\vdots & \vdots & \vdots & \vdots \\
0 \cdots \cdots 0 & 0 \cdots \cdots 0 & \cdots \cdots \cdots & \alpha_{n1} \cdots \cdot 0 \, \alpha_{nm}
\end{bmatrix}
$$

The coefficients α_{ij} represent the market share that the process j has with respect to the product i. Therefore,

$$\alpha_{ij} = b_{ij} x_j / \mathbf{B}_i \mathbf{x}$$

and

$$\sum_{j=1}^{m} \alpha_{ij} = 1.$$

Thus, α_{ij}, which duplicates the rows of $\mathbf{A}$, represents the weights of the individual values of the commodities added in order to find the social value of a commodity. Thus, $\hat{\Lambda} \hat{\alpha} = \Lambda$, which represents the vector of social value of the commodities. Also, $\hat{\alpha}$ can be multiplied by $\mathbf{A}\hat{\beta}$, which duplicates the rows of $\mathbf{A}$ and assigns weights to the different input costs entering the production cost of commodity i produced by the production process j, to give a system of $\hat{\Lambda}$ alone.

Furthermore, $l\hat{\beta} = (\beta_{11} l_1, \ldots, \beta_{1m} l_m; \beta_{21} l_1, \ldots, \beta_{2m} l_m; \ldots; \beta_{n1} l_1, \ldots, \beta_{nm} l_m)$ duplicates the labor vector, and $\hat{\mathbf{B}}$ represents a diagonal matrix, whose diagonal is given by $(b_{11}, \ldots, b_{1m}; b_{21}, \ldots, b_{2m}; \ldots, b_{n1}, \ldots, b_{nm})$. Equation (6.6) for individual values can be written as follows:

$$\hat{\Lambda}\hat{A} + \hat{l} = \hat{\Lambda}\hat{B}, \tag{6.7}$$

where $\hat{A} = \hat{\alpha} A \hat{\beta}$ and $\hat{l} = l\hat{\beta}$, or

$$\hat{\Lambda} = \hat{\Lambda} \, \hat{A}\hat{B}^{-1} + \hat{l}\hat{B}^{-1},$$

where the inverse $\hat{B}^{-1} \geq 0$ always holds.

For the vector of the individual values we get

$$\hat{\Lambda} = \hat{l}\hat{B}^{-1}(I - \hat{A}\hat{B}^{-1})^{-1} \tag{6.7a}$$

or

$$\hat{\Lambda} = \hat{l}(\hat{B} - \hat{A})^{-1}. \tag{6.7b}$$

Theorems of Nikaido (1968, theorems, 6.3, 7.1, 7.4) show that $I - \hat{A}\hat{B}^{-1}$ is always nonnegative invertible and that the individual values as well as the social values $\Lambda = \hat{\Lambda}\hat{\alpha}$ will be nonnegative.

A system of individual prices can also be derived from this approach. The price system may be defined by

$$(1 + r)\hat{p}(\hat{A} + \hat{d}\hat{l}) = \hat{p}\hat{B}, \tag{6.8}$$

where the individual values are replaced by a vector of individual prices, including, here, a uniform profit rate, however, generating differential profit rates for each technique at average prices (see Semmler 1984b). $\hat{d} = \hat{\alpha}d$ represents the consumption good vector for the reproduction of labor power. Such a vector of nonnegative individual prices exists (see appendix 3); under certain conditions, discussed in appendix 4, a vector $\hat{p}$ also exists when the profit rate is not uniform but there are differential profit rates for the different joint production processes.

The fundamental Marxian theorem, according to which the rate of surplus value is the necessary and sufficient condition for the money rate of profit, can be proven to hold also for joint production, when the above differentiation between individual and social values is made (see Flaschel 1979). In the case of equal organic composition in all industries, it also can be proven that prices are proportional to labor values (see Flaschel 1980).

Using Steedman's example (1977:153), we can illustrate the existence of nonnegative individual and social values. The anomalies in Steedman's example of a joint production system will disappear.

The matrices **A** and **B** are

$$\mathbf{A} = \begin{bmatrix} a_{11} & 0 \\ 0 & a_{22} \end{bmatrix}$$

and

$$\mathbf{B} = \begin{bmatrix} b_{11} & b_{12} \\ b_{21} & b_{22} \end{bmatrix}.$$

Using the linear system of equations (6.7) for individual values, we can write

$$\hat{\alpha}\mathbf{A}\hat{\beta} = \begin{bmatrix} \alpha_{11} & 0 \\ \alpha_{21} & 0 \\ 0 & \alpha_{12} \\ 0 & \alpha_{22} \end{bmatrix} \begin{bmatrix} a_{11} & 0 \\ 0 & a_{22} \end{bmatrix} \begin{bmatrix} \beta_{11} & 0 & \beta_{21} & 0 \\ 0 & \beta_{12} & 0 & \beta_{22} \end{bmatrix}$$

$$= \hat{\alpha} \begin{bmatrix} a_{11}\beta_{11} & 0 & a_{11}\beta_{21} & 0 \\ 0 & a_{22}\beta_{12} & 0 & a_{22}\beta_{22} \end{bmatrix},$$

where the first and second columns represent the two separated production processes producing the first commodity and the next two columns represent the multiple production processes for the second commodity. The whole production system can be written as

$$\hat{\alpha}\mathbf{A}\hat{\beta} = \begin{bmatrix} \alpha_{11}a_{11}\beta_{11} & 0 & \alpha_{11}a_{11}\beta_{21} & 0 \\ \alpha_{21}a_{11}\beta_{11} & 0 & \alpha_{21}a_{11}\beta_{21} & 0 \\ 0 & \alpha_{12}a_{22}\beta_{12} & 0 & \alpha_{12}a_{22}\beta_{22} \\ 0 & \alpha_{22}a_{22}\beta_{12} & 0 & \alpha_{22}a_{22}\beta_{22} \end{bmatrix}$$

$$\mathbf{1}\hat{\beta} = \begin{bmatrix} l_1\beta_{11} & l_2\beta_{12} & l_1\beta_{21} & l_2\beta_{22} \end{bmatrix}$$

$$\hat{\mathbf{B}} = \begin{bmatrix} b_{11} & 0 & 0 & 0 \\ 0 & b_{12} & 0 & 0 \\ 0 & 0 & b_{21} & 0 \\ 0 & 0 & 0 & b_{22} \end{bmatrix}.$$

In Steedman's numerical example of joint production, the following inputs and outputs are given (before normalization to the unit output level):

$$A = \begin{bmatrix} 25 & 0 \\ 0 & 10 \end{bmatrix}$$

$$l = \begin{bmatrix} 5 & 1 \end{bmatrix}$$

$$B = \begin{bmatrix} 30 & 3 \\ 5 & 12 \end{bmatrix}.$$

In this example the commodity prices are $p_1 = 1/3$ and $p_2 = 1$, and the profit rate is $r = 0.2$ (wages paid ex post). After normalizing to the unit output level and calculating the coefficients for α_{ij} and β_{ij}, we get the following individual values (see Flaschel 1979, 1980a):

$$\hat{\lambda}_1 = 0.24, \qquad \hat{\lambda}_2 = 0.18, \qquad \hat{\lambda}_3 = 0.73, \qquad \hat{\lambda}_4 = 0.53,$$

where $\hat{\lambda}_1 \alpha_{11} + \hat{\lambda}_2 \alpha_{21} = \lambda_1$ (social value of commodity 1) and $\hat{\lambda}_3 \alpha_{12} + \hat{\lambda}_4 \alpha_{22} = \lambda_{11}$ (social value of commodity 2). Since $\Lambda = \hat{\Lambda}\hat{\alpha}$, we can say that social values are the weighted sums of individual values, both of them positive: $\lambda_1 = 0.24$, $\lambda_{11} = 0.59$.[10] As we can see, the anomalies in the example of Steedman disappear, the system has a nonnegative solution for the labor values, and the rate of surplus value will be positive and can be proven to be a necessary and sufficient condition for the money rate of profit ($r = 0.2 > 0$) for the given joint production system (see Flaschel 1979).

In sum, the procedure developed by Flaschel allows us to separate joint production activities of multiplant and multiproduct firms by decomposing the system into a system of multiple activities and treating the latter by means of market shares along the lines suggested by Marx (see sec. 2.3.2). The system of multiple activities—in this case undertaken by different corporations—has the properties of a single-product system. The solutions for the labor vector are always nonnegative, since $(I - \hat{A}\hat{B}^{-1})^{-1}$ or $(\hat{B} - \hat{A})^{-1}$ will always be nonnegative. Thus, positive prices and profit rate will correspond to positive values and rate of surplus value. This procedure for dealing with joint production activities avoids the pitfalls of a joint production system for the theory of value without referring to an optimizing approach or to Morishima's "true labor values." In the latter approach only one technique can prevail and differential profit rates for different techniques producing the same commodity cannot exist.

In the version of a joint production system presented here, there are, as Marx assumed, different techniques and differential profit rates for processes producing the same commodity, and thus differential profit rates for firms. The shortcoming of this approach is that the separation of the joint production processes has to be made according to certain accounting principles that use monetary expressions such as sales values or unit costs. Relative prices enter the definition of labor values, an effect which might be avoided by using physical units based on some physical measurement for allocating proportions of the different inputs to the different outputs. This, however, will be possible only in special cases, since inputs and outputs are usually measured in different units.

6.2.2. JOINT PRODUCTION AND NONSEPARATED ACTIVITIES

The next two approaches avoid the difficulties of using prices (sales value proportions or unit costs) to determine labor values by referring only to a physical system and not separating joint production activities. Special assumptions have to be made in order to get nonnegative solutions. Here the model of Schefold (1978, 1980a) and Krause (1977, 1980) will be discussed.

Schefold examines joint production systems that allow for a nonnegative invertible matrix $\mathbf{B} - \mathbf{A}$. We know that, unlike single-product systems, joint production systems can be productive; however, $\mathbf{B} - \mathbf{A}$ is not necessarily nonnegative invertible. Therefore, setting $\mathbf{B} - \mathbf{A} = \mathbf{C}$, we can say that the system is productive

> if there is one $\mathbf{x} \geqslant \mathbf{0}$ with $\mathbf{C}\mathbf{x} > \mathbf{0}$
> but $\mathbf{C}^{-1} \geqslant \mathbf{0}$ does not hold, then
> $\Lambda = \mathbf{l}\mathbf{C}^{-1} \geqslant \mathbf{0}$ does not hold.

By using this notation, we can show which joint production systems guarantee a nonnegative invertible matrix $\mathbf{C}$ and a nonnegative solution Λ.

Schefold calls a joint production system *all-productive* if in it all goods are separately producible. This means it is possible to increase the net output (**y**) of the system **C** with a nonnegative activity level **x**. Formally:

The system is all-productive if for all $\mathbf{y} \geqslant \mathbf{0}$
there exists an $\mathbf{x} \geqslant \mathbf{0}$ with $\mathbf{Cx} = \mathbf{y}$.

Therefore, separately producible products in a joint production system mean that there exists a nonnegative activity vector **x** such that $\mathbf{y} \geqslant \mathbf{0}$ can be produced. Schefold considers in particular the case when $\mathbf{y} = \mathbf{e}$ (**e** is the unit vector). Under this condition, as shown below, for the system $\mathbf{\Lambda C} = \mathbf{l}$ a nonnegative solution for vector $\mathbf{\Lambda}$ exists.

Schefold calls a system *all-engaging* if the processes are at the same time indispensable.[11] Formally:

The system is all-engaging if for
$\mathbf{Cx} = \mathbf{y}$ with $\mathbf{y} \geqslant \mathbf{0}$
it follows that $\mathbf{x} > \mathbf{0}$.

In other words, if there is some $x_j = 0$, this process would be dispensable to produce the net output vector $\mathbf{y} \geqslant \mathbf{0}$. When the system is all-engaging, a semipositive solution of the joint production system exists.

It remains to be shown why the system with separately producible commodities and indispensable processes generates nonnegative solutions for the value vector $\mathbf{\Lambda}$. Following an idea of Krause (1977), we can prove these statements by making use of Farkas and Minkowski's theorem (see Kemp and Kimura 1978:3). According to this theorem, we have

$\mathbf{C'\Lambda} = \mathbf{l}$ has a solution $\mathbf{\Lambda} \geqq \mathbf{0}$
if and only if for all **x** with $\mathbf{Cx} \geqq \mathbf{0}$
it follows that $\mathbf{lx} \geqslant 0$.

In the first part $\mathbf{C'}$ is the transpose of **C**. The second part means that for all activity vectors that generate a net output $\mathbf{y}$ ($\mathbf{Cx} \geqslant \mathbf{0}$) there are nonnegative labor inputs ($\mathbf{lx} \geqslant 0$). This dual property of the system above can be used to prove the existence of a positive value vector Λ for a system with separately producible products and indispensable processes. Since the second part of the theorem also implies the first part, this proves that all-productive and all-engaging joint production systems $\Lambda C = l$ have nonnegative solutions for Λ. For invertible matrices C this argument is easier, since here it follows that there exists one and only one vector Λ for which $C'\Lambda = l$. For all-productive systems it holds that $C^{-1} \geqslant 0$ and for all-engaging systems that $C^{-1} > 0$.

Some remarks on this special joint production systems that allow for a positive solution of the labor vector are necessary. First, it can be shown that such systems, which are not necessarily single-product systems but have the properties of single-product systems, do exist and have implications for a theory of price and the treatment of technical progress and fixed capital. Second, one of the important characteristics of these joint production systems is that the fundamental Marxian theorem holds for $\Lambda = lC^{-1}$. This follows from the facts that the inverse C^{-1} is semipositive or positive, which leads to a positive solution of the value vector, and that the rate of surplus value will always be positive (see Schefold 1980a). Third, the presence of separately producible products and indispensable processes for joint production systems does not mean that the joint costs for the different outputs of a production process are actually separated and allocated to the commodities i of the process j, as discussed before. In the systems discussed above, the activities are still not separated. Separately producible products and indispensable processes mean only that any composition of the net output vector y (in particular $y = e$, as Schefold assumes) can be produced such that there exists always a gross output vector x, which is semipositive or positive. The dual property is that there is a positive solution of the value vector.

Krause (1977, 1981) has developed a weaker condition for the existence of nonnegative values, which does not allow only for joint production systems where $C^{-1} \geqslant 0$. The weaker condition implies that there can be joint production systems where $C^{-1} \geqslant 0$ does not hold. The example of Steedman, discussed before, actually has the property that $C^{-1} \geqslant 0$ does not hold. An answer to Steedman's critique (1977) of the Marxian theory of value can be given either by separating the joint production activities according to the procedure discussed above or by considering nonseparated joint production systems with the property that the matrix $\mathbf{C}$ is not necessarily nonnegative invertible. Krause discusses joint production systems where the activities are also not separated but where the condition $\mathbf{C}^{-1} \geqslant \mathbf{0}$ does not hold, yet the value vector is positive, provided that weights $(\alpha_1, \ldots, \alpha_n)$ for the labor vector $\mathbf{l}$ are introduced which allow for a positive solution to

$$\tilde{\Lambda} = \mathbf{C}'^{-1} \langle \alpha \rangle \, \mathbf{l}, \tag{6.9}$$

with $\langle \alpha \rangle$ a diagonal matrix.

These systems can be physically characterized as coproductive systems, as Krause calls them. A coproductive joint production system is a system where there is no $\mathbf{x} \geqslant \mathbf{0}$ with $\mathbf{Cx} \leqslant \mathbf{0}$.[12] The reason coproductive systems provide positive solutions for the value vector $\tilde{\Lambda}$ can be derived from a theorem by Gale (see Kemp and Kimura 1978:4). The theorem says

there is no $\mathbf{x} \geqslant \mathbf{0}$ with $\mathbf{Cx} \leqslant \mathbf{0}$
if and only if there is one
$\tilde{\Lambda} \geqslant \mathbf{0}$ with $\mathbf{C}'\tilde{\Lambda} \geqslant \mathbf{0}$

From this follows:

for coproductive systems where $\tilde{\Lambda} \geqslant \mathbf{0}$
with $\mathbf{C}'\tilde{\Lambda} = \mathbf{z}$
there is a $\mathbf{z} = \langle \alpha \rangle \mathbf{l}$
or $\alpha_i = z_i / l_i$.

This theorem may be illustrated by using Steedman's example again. For a labor vector of $\mathbf{l} = (1, 1)$, Steedman's example can be written

$$\mathbf{A} = \begin{bmatrix} 5 & 0 \\ 0 & 10 \end{bmatrix} \qquad \mathbf{B} = \begin{bmatrix} 6 & 3 \\ 1 & 12 \end{bmatrix}$$

$$\mathbf{C} = \begin{bmatrix} 1 & 3 \\ 1 & 2 \end{bmatrix}.$$

The system is coproductive, since from

$$\begin{bmatrix} 1 & 3 \\ 1 & 2 \end{bmatrix}\begin{matrix} x_1 \\ x_2 \end{matrix} \leqslant \mathbf{0}$$

it follows that $x \not\geqslant \mathbf{0}$.

According to the theorem discussed above, there exist (α_1, α_2) such that the value vector becomes nonnegative. For example, assuming $\alpha_1 = 2$ and $\alpha_2 = 5$, we get $\tilde{\lambda}_1 = 1$ and $\tilde{\lambda}_2 = 1$. As we can see, the value vector becomes positive, even if the matrix $\mathbf{C}^{-1}$ is not nonnegative.

We could interpret the multipliers $(\alpha_1, \ldots, \alpha_n)$ by referring to the Marxian discussion on the problem of reducing heterogeneous labor to homogeneous or common labor. The multipliers can be interpreted as reduction coefficients. In our example, the labor input l_2 counts as abstract labor 2.5 times more than the labor input l_1, or, taking l_1 as standard or common labor, l_2 counts 2.5 times more in creating value in production. This idea has been developed further in Krause (1981, 1980), where reduction coefficients are derived that allow for a positive value vector Λ for single-product systems and joint production systems. (In a more complex treatment, however, the vector of direct labor coefficients l must be extended to a matrix of direct labor coefficients **L**.)

We can also explain, from this point of view, the existence of the first process, which produces fewer units of net products for both commodities than the second. We can say that the second production process uses up 2.5 times more labor than the first, measured in terms of common labor, therefore, it can be considered less productive in terms of common labor than in terms of complicated labor. This might be considered the reason the first production process exists and is used, even though it generates fewer net products than the second process.[13] In Steedman's example all labor coefficients already represent homogeneous labor and count as common labor. All reduction coefficients are 1. When the problem of the heterogeneity of labor is taken into account, using reduction coefficients for the different types of labor can eliminate the anomalies of joint production systems and allow for a positive solution of the value vector. Following this approach, it is possible to prove the fundamental Marxian theorem for the case of heterogeneity of labor and joint production (see Krause 1980, 1981).[14]

In sum, treating the activities of large corporations which have many processes at their disposal and produce many outputs in the framework of a joint production process does not necessarily lead to a contradiction with the labor theory of value. Joint production activities of large multiplant and multiproduct corporations either can be considered as separated activities which lead to the same characteristics as single-product activities with multiple processes or can be regarded as nonseparated activities which also do not necessarily lead to an inconsistency in regard to the labor theory of value.

6.3. Production Prices, Corporate Pricing, and Markups

After having shown how corporate activities can be treated in terms of joint production systems without necessarily leading to an inconsistency as regards the Marxian theory, it remains to show how markup pricing by a multiplant and multiproduct corporation, formulated in equation (6.3), can be derived from the corporation's financial goal of receiving an average rate of return on total capital, as expressed in equation (6.4). As in the case of single-product industries, equation (6.3) can be made consistent with equation (6.4). However, I want to deal only with the simple case of nonseparated activities. (For the case of separated activities the results obtained in sec. 6.2.1 can be applied.) Assuming that the markup prices for a standard volume of output are derived from the requirement of normal rate of return on capital invested, we can determine the markups for the outputs of nonseparated activities with the following relation:

$$\mathbf{p\bar{A}} + \mathbf{p\bar{A}}\langle\mu\rangle = \mathbf{p\bar{A}} + \mathbf{pB'} + r\mathbf{pB}^+ = \mathbf{pB}. \qquad (6.10)$$

From this equation we get

$$\mathbf{p\bar{A}}\langle\mu\rangle = \mathbf{pB'} + r\mathbf{pB}^+, \qquad (6.11)$$

where again $\langle \mu \rangle$ is the diagonal matrix of the different markups for products and product groups and $r = 1/\lambda$ from equation (6.5a).

As in the case of single-product industries, the markups or profit margins are completely determined. This can be shown in the following way. We can write the products $\mathbf{p}\bar{\mathbf{A}}$ and $\mathbf{p}(\mathbf{B}' + r\mathbf{B}^+)$ as the diagonal matrices $\langle \mathbf{C} \rangle$ and $\langle \Pi \rangle$, where $\langle \mathbf{C} \rangle$ represents the vector of cost of production (prime cost) and $\langle \Pi \rangle$ the gross profit vector. Thus we get

$$\langle \mathbf{C} \rangle \langle \mu \rangle = \langle \Pi \rangle \tag{6.11a}$$

$$\langle \mu \rangle = \langle \mathbf{C} \rangle^{-1} \langle \Pi \rangle. \tag{6.12}$$

The markups are completely determined by the possible price vector $\mathbf{p}$ of the economic system, the general profit rate r, and the matrices $\bar{\mathbf{A}}$, $\mathbf{B}'$, and $\mathbf{B}^+$. We can see that markup pricing or pricing with profit margins, developed by decentralized multiplant and multiproduct corporations with large fixed capital, is consistent with the classical and Marxian theories of competition, prices of production, and average profit rate, where prices too are determined by cost of production plus an average rate of return on total capital advanced. Thus, we see that modern corporate pricing does not necessarily contradict the classical notion of natural prices or the Marxian notion of prices of production as centers of gravity for market prices; rather, it fits very well into this framework. The modern large corporation can be interpreted as a large pool of capital that has to be reproduced and expanded. Markup pricing and profit margins on standard cost were developed for the purpose of financial control, in order to evaluate the performance of the total capital advanced. This conclusion can be drawn from the original discussion in the twenties: "It becomes apparent, therefore, that the analysis of price in accordance with the method outlined is closely interwoven with the matter of financial control, since the expression of price policy, in terms of rate of return attainable on capital employed, is the most significant factor bearing upon the question of availability of capital for the purpose of operation" (Brown 1924, art. 4, p. 422). The increase in the size of the capital advanced, especially when it was due to an increase in fixed investment, made this price and financial control policy necessary for large corporations. Before drawing some more general conclusions, I have to make two additional remarks. First, returns to scale, choice of technique, and substitution were not taken into consideration in the discussion of the pricing policy of large corporations. Since a standard volume of output of large corporations x^h was assumed for the standard cost and the standard price, slight changes in output do not affect the input-output structure for corporations and the economic system. The input-output structure can remain constant "piecewise" if the output vector varies slightly. Thus, the average rate of return on capital advanced, profit margins, and prices remain the same "piecewise." In the context, returns to scale, choice of technique, and substitution can be neglected (see appendix 3.2). A second remark has to be made about the problem of competition and differential profit rates, discussed in sections 2.3, 4.2, and 4.3. Up to now the assumption has been made that multiplant and multiproduct corporations yield an average rate of return on the total capital advanced. Differential profit rates also exist for multiplant and multiproduct corporations as a result of the causes discussed in section 5.1.

    This problem of differential profit rates was clearly seen when the new form of pricing for multiplant and multiproduct corporations was developed in the twenties.

> Return on investment is the basis of the policy in regard to the pricing on product, but it must be understood that the fundamental consideration is the average return over a protracted period of time, not the specific rate of return over any particular year or short period of time. This long-time rate of return on investment represents the official viewpoint as to the highest average rate of return which can be expected consistent with a healthy growth of business, and may be referred to as the economic return available. The adjudged necessary rate of return on capital will vary as between separated lines of industry, as a result of differences in their economic situation; and within each industry there will be important differences in return on capital resulting primarily from the relatively greater efficiency of certain producers. (Bradley 1927:422)

As can be seen from this quotation, it is not necessary that an average rate of return on capital advanced be received for each product, product group, or plant in certain industries. Differential profit rates for commodities or plants within each industry can be received. But here again differential profit rates for multiplant and multiproduct corporations due to market conditions, limited mobility of capital, or size and efficiency of plants are consistent with the theory of competition and production prices as presented in chapter 2. This, of course, does not exclude the possibility that diversified and vertically integrated corporations with multimarket contacts may exhaust market power—as discussed in section 5.1— and increase profit rates. However, as shown, recent research on the profitability of diversified and integrated corporations that operate in many lines of business has demonstrated that there is no clear-cut evidence for persistence of higher profitability of diversified corporations due only to market power variables (see Ravenscraft 1981; Scott 1981; Gale and Branch 1982). Thus, allowing for differential profit rates according to the reasoning of section 5.1, we have to write a price formula for a joint production system which includes differential profit rates $\langle \bar{r} \rangle$. The prices for nonseparated activities, including differential profit rates, can be derived in the following way, where $\langle \bar{r} \rangle$ has to stay within a certain bounded space:

$$\bar{p}\bar{A} + \bar{p}B' + \bar{p}B^{+}\langle \bar{r} \rangle = \bar{p}B \qquad (6.13)$$

or

$$\bar{p}\left[B - (\bar{A} + B' + B^{+}\langle \bar{r} \rangle) \right] = 0. \qquad (6.13a)$$

The mathematical properties of a positive solution of equation (6.13a) are discussed in appendix 4, where it is also shown that the prices do not necessarily have to be equilibrium prices. Using these prices, which imply differential profitability for the different economic activities, we can derive the markups for each line of business in which a multiplant, multiproduct corporation operates. The formula for the markups, equation (6.11), can be written as follows:

$$\bar{p}\bar{A}\langle \mu \rangle = \bar{p}B' + \bar{p}B^{+}\langle \bar{r} \rangle, \qquad (6.14)$$

from which the markups

$$\langle \mu \rangle = \langle C \rangle^{-1}\langle \Pi \rangle, \qquad (6.15)$$

implying differential profit rates, can be derived again. Yet on the whole we can conclude, as Clifton (1979) does in a recent study, that corporate pricing is not necessarily an expression of the market power of firms in concentrated industries, and that markup pricing, cost-plus pricing, and rigid prices of corporations do not necessarily reflect the degree of monopoly power in industries. Moreover, it seems that the pricing procedure of decentralized, multiplant, and multiproduct corporation with a large amount of fixed investment became very similar to that found in the classical and Marxian theories of competition and production prices. Modern large corporations can be considered large units of capital that attempt to control and to expand their capital and have developed a pricing procedure that fulfills these needs. This analysis of modern corporate pricing is not meant to deny that corporations, as large units of capital, possess economic and financial power. But the corporate power that accompanied the growth of large corporations since the end of the nineteenth century seems to be power not so much over the markets as over production relations. This difference between market power and corporate power will be discussed briefly in the final part of this book.

Notes

1. In an empirically oriented paper, Steedman (1982) gives a long list of cases of joint production for all of these sectors, concluding that single production is only an exceptional case, whereas joint production is a common practice in all sectors. I also maintain that joint production is a very common practice, especially since the rise of large multiproduct and multiplant corporations (see Bailey and Friedlaender 1982). As can be seen in the history of the development of large corporations, vertical integration and diversification was at first closely related to joint production. However, this does not mean that the activities are not or cannot be separated and the joint cost allocated to the different jointly produced commodities by means of some accounting principles. Steedman (1982), in his short paper, does not discuss the possible distinctions of separated and nonseparated activities. If this distinction were made, some problems of joint production could be solved.

2. In a recently published survey article, Bailey and Friedlaender also state that single-product firms have become a rare case and that "most businesses produce many products" (1982:1025). Large multiplant and multiproduct firms operate, as shown, in a wide

range of markets in order to utilize economies of scope, which "arise from the sharing or joint utilization of inputs" (p. 1026).

3. This problem was first discussed by the management of General Motors in the twenties, as can be seen in the following documents, which J. Clifton made available to me: "General Motors is operated as a decentralized organization. Each operating division or subsidiary is in principle entirely self-contained and is responsible for the successful design, manufacture, and sale of its product, subject to general policy of the corporation. . . . The ideal of the corporation is centralization of policy but decentralization of management, which means that the president of each constituent is allowed an altogether free hand in his company. . . ." But this new organizational structure of the multidivisional corporation, together with the increase in fixed capital, necessitated the new pricing policy: it was maintained "that a normal average rate of plant operation is an essential factor in the analysis of price. This determines the so-called standard volume, which is accepted as the basis upon which costs will be measured and upon which the margin of profit is determined as necessary to afford a given average rate of return upon capital employed" (see Brown 1924, art. 3, p. 283). The profit margin was considered a measure for a normal rate of return on the total capital invested. "Thus, the profit margin, translated into its salient characteristic—rate of return on capital employed—is the yardstick by which to gauge the price of a commodity with regard to collateral circumstances affecting supply and demand" (art. 3, p. 286).

4. There is also a huge neoclassical literature on a theory of cost and pricing for a multiplant and multiproduct firm. However, in the main, optimizing techniques or activity analysis is utilized for a theory of joint production, where input and output prices are considered to be given (see Pfouts 1961; Naylor 1965; Maurice and Ferguson 1971).

5. Since this section uses more advanced mathematics, sections 6.2.1 and 6.2.2 may be skipped by nonmathematical readers. A brief summary of the results of the discussion is provided in the section's introduction.

6. In the following discussion, I leave out those debates on joint production and the labor theory of value that use the theory of linear programming to define labor values. This theory defines labor values differently from the approach discussed here, namely, as "true values," which assumes the existence of only optimal techniques for production processes. For such an approach to the problem of joint production, see Morishima 1973; Morishima and Catephores 1978; Wolfstetter 1976.

7. Marshall had already developed the idea in 1890 that common costs of joint products can be separated and allocated to each product of a production process, when the product is salable. Moreover, he holds the opinion that common costs of most of the joint production activities can be separated: "It is only when one of two things produced by the same process is valueless, unsalable, and yet does not involve any expense for its removal, that there is not inducement to attempt to alter its amount, and it is only in these exceptional cases that we have no means of assigning its separate supply price to each of the joint products" (1947:390).

8. In input-output analysis in the United States since 1972, two methods are used to deal with joint products (see Ritz 1980:48) by separating them into primary and secondary products. One method of allocating the input costs to the different products assumes a "constant commodity technology." It uses the input coefficients of the secondary products from those industries where the secondary products are produced as primary products. The second method is the "constant industry technology" method, which uses the input coefficients from those industries where the secondary product is produced. Moreover, the

market share method is used to allocate the input costs to the different products (Ritz 1980:37); see also United Nations 1968; and Stone et al. 1963.

9. The prices used here to allocate the input costs to the different products according to the sales value method could also be thought of as being derived from equation (6.5a).

10. The social values can be calculated in a more direct way. Since $\hat{\Lambda}\hat{\alpha}A\hat{\beta} + I\hat{\beta} = \hat{\Lambda}\hat{B}$, by multiplying both sides by $\hat{B}^{-1}\hat{\alpha}$ and setting $\hat{\Lambda}\hat{\alpha} = \Lambda$, with Λ the vector of social values, we get

$$\hat{\Lambda}A\hat{\beta}\hat{B}^{-1}\hat{\alpha} + I\hat{\beta}\hat{B}^{-1}\hat{\alpha} = \Lambda,$$

the coefficients $\hat{\beta}\hat{B}^{-1}\hat{\alpha}$ can be calculated (after normalizing to unit output levels) and the social values determined (see Flaschel 1980). Using Steedman's matrix (1977:153), the procedure for calculating the social values can be illustrated in a simple way. If the cost of joint production is split according to the proportion of the sales value of the commodity in total output value (evaluated in terms of given prices) of process j, then we get

$$\beta_{11} = 2/3, \beta_{21} = 1/3, \beta_{12} = 1/13, \beta_{22} = 12/13.$$

The input costs of the joint production process can be split and allocated to the different products for the same commodity i. Then we get the following multiple production processes for commodities 1 and 2:

$$\bar{A} = \begin{bmatrix} (2/3) \cdot 25 & 0 & (1/3) \cdot 25 & 0 \\ 0 & (1/13) \cdot 10 & 0 & (12/13) \cdot 10 \end{bmatrix}$$

$$\bar{I} = [(2/3) \cdot 5 \quad 1/13 \quad (1/3) \cdot 5 \quad 12/13 \quad]$$

$$\bar{B} = \begin{bmatrix} 30 & 0 & 5 & 0 \\ 0 & 3 & 0 & 12 \end{bmatrix}.$$

By adding the processes producing the same commodities, we get

$$\lambda_I(2/3) \cdot 25 + \lambda_{II}(1/13) \cdot 10 + (2/3) \cdot 5 + 1/13 = \lambda_I 33$$

$$\lambda_I(1/3) \cdot 25 + \lambda_{II}(12/13) \cdot 10 + (1/3) \cdot 5 + 12/13 = \lambda_{II}17,$$

with the social values $\lambda_I = 0.24$, $\lambda_{II} = 0.59$.

11. An example for such an all-engaging system may be the following:

$$A = \begin{bmatrix} 0 & 0 & 0.8 \\ 0.7 & 0 & 0 \\ 0 & 0.8 & 0 \end{bmatrix} \quad B = \begin{bmatrix} 1 & 0.6 & 0 \\ 0 & 1 & 0.5 \\ 0.4 & 0 & 1 \end{bmatrix}.$$

Calculating the inverse, we get

$$C^{-1} = \begin{bmatrix} 0.77 & 0.02 & 0.60 \\ 0.49 & 0.73 & 0.03 \\ 0.09 & 0.57 & 0.78 \end{bmatrix}.$$

For a given net output vector $y \geqslant 0$, it follows that there exists an $x > 0$ and that $Ix \geqslant 0$ since $x = C^{-1}y$ will be positive, because C^{-1} is positive and y semipositive. Therefore, it is also true that for any given vector of positive direct labor requirements $\Lambda = C^{-1}I$ has a nonnegative solution. Such systems can be used to deal with the problem of fixed capital in linear models without being confronted with anomalies of joint production systems (see Schefold 1980a). However, fixed capital is treated here in the sense of Sraffa, as a special joint product, and not according to the method of Lange (1952), Brody (1970), and Pasinetti (1973), used above.

12. Moreover, as Krause (1977) has shown, coproductive systems have positive prices.

13. If two such techniques are chosen by two corporations, one of which generates a greater net product than the other, the coexistence of the two techniques may be explained by the fact that the superior technique may in the end be as productive as the inferior technique in terms of common labor, once different weights are assigned to the different labor inputs.

14. Although Krause, in his approach, develops solutions of two puzzling problems of the Marxian theory of value and price (the problem of negative values for a joint production system and the problem of heterogeneity of labor), the solutions, especially for the so-called reduction problem, may be considered not very satisfactory. For deriving the reduction coefficients, the real wage for each type of labor input is taken as given and enters the determination of the reduction coefficients. Therefore, the value vector, and thus the exchange values, are influenced by the real wage—a result that seems to be inconsistent with the positions of the classics.

7. MARKET POWER AND CORPORATE POWER—SOME CONCLUSIONS

In this chapter some results of the previous chapters are summarized and the difference between the notions of market or monopoly power and corporate power are discussed, with reference mainly to the post-Marxian and post-Keynesian traditions.

The structural and institutional changes analyzed by post-Marxian or post-Keynesian writers cannot be denied. Indeed, structural and institutional changes in advanced industrial societies, such as increasingly capital-intensive production, an increasing average size of firms, concentration of capital, mergers, and the rise of large multimarket and multinational corporations and banks, have occurred since the end of the nineteenth century. In analyzing these changes, those theorists made a great contribution to the analysis of the impact of large corporations on advanced industrial societies. These changes are quite important and cannot be neglected. Hilferding, with his book "Das Finanzkapital" (1968), made the first important step toward such an analysis. It is also true that the economic and social power of large corporations has increased.[1] Large multiplant and multiproduct corporations take advantage of economies of scope (see Bailey and Friedlaender 1982) and cannot be considered powerless single-product firms located in certain industries or regions and limited in their economic mobility. The large corporations, as multiproduct and multiplant corporations, can operate simultaneously in extractive industry, agriculture, manufacturing, or the service sector. They are large-scale units of capital and have many inputs and production processes across sectors and regions at their disposal. The power over inputs and production processes, however, has another expression: the control of large financial resources, i.e., money capital. Multiplant and multiproduct corporations have large financial resources at their disposal which allow them to allocate capital to different industries and countries and to cross-subsidize operating firms. With their financial power, they can resist the unionization of industries or firms and resist wage and other union demands. Moreover, there are many ways in which they can loosen the constraints of monetary and fiscal policy. Among them are using their independent financial power (house banks or branches abroad) to escape from monetary constraints, using transfer pricing to minimize tax burden, shifting productive capital or money capital from high- to low-wage countries, and varying utilization of capacity in different countries or regions when threatened by labor unrest or government policy (see Clifton 1979). It follows that these large units of capital, which organize production across industries and regions, are more powerful than single-product firms that have large market shares and can take advantage of entry barriers but are located in only one industry. The nature of the economic power of multiplant and multiproduct firms seems to be related more to size and size-related economies than to monopoly position in the market. The corporations, as large units of capital, obviously possess economic power beyond their market power. This power rarely has anything to do with market structure and the degree of concentration; it has rather to do with size, vertical integration, and diversification. This power is, as discussed in chapter 6, power over inputs, production processes, and production relations—not necessarily over all the markets in which these corporations operate.

However, this analysis of the changes in the structure and power of large-scale firms does not lead us necessarily to reject the theory of competition and production prices presented above. The growth of capital—or the growth of the firm—is widely accepted as the aim of large corporations. As shown, the competitive struggles of firms to decrease costs are a result of the effort to grow. Business failures, mergers, and fewer units of capital do not imply decreased competition and decreased rivalry. Industrial concentration of firms does not mean less mobility of capital, as maintained in the post-Marxian theory of monopoly. On the contrary, we can see that historically, as the units of capital have become larger, the mobility of capital—especially of money capital —has increased. Large units of capital, i.e., modern corporations, are independent centers of financial power (see Herman 1981). They can shift money capital quite easily (see Clifton 1977) across regions and industries and cross-subsidize operating units when the competitive struggle of firms makes such actions necessary. The existence of large-scale firms does not imply that the degree of competition and rivalry decreases, and as the studies discussed in chapter 4 have shown, the market shares of multimarket firms do not imply that corporations can exercise market power in all markets where they operate.

We cannot conclude that prices deviate persistently from production prices due to market power and that there is a persistence of differential profit rates due to industrial concentration. As shown, we cannot draw these conclusions from the empirical evidence presented in chapters 3 and 4. Differential profit rates among firms and industries are likely to exist in an actual economic system for a certain length of time, but this is consistent with the aforementioned dynamic theory of competition (see ch. 5). In addition, as shown in chapter 6, the pricing procedure of large corporations does not contradict the theory of production prices. The pricing policy of large corporations is in the main oriented toward long-run normal cost, long-run normal output, and a long-run normal price. Administered prices, markup pricing, and target rate of return pricing can be interpreted as different, but only slightly varying, methods of calculating a long-run production price which guarantees an average rate of return on investment for large multi-product corporations and thus guarantees their survival and their growth at a steady rate.[2] Recent discussion of industrial pricing and the pricing policies of oligopolies or large corporations shows that the pricing procedures and profit rate differentials observed for large corporations can be made consistent with the theory of production prices as presented in chapter 2.

These two concepts—that of market or monopoly power and that of the power of large-scale firms—have different connotations. Therefore, it seems necessary to distinguish monopoly power, which is defined in relation to the market structure, from the power of large firms. The latter implies power beyond market power and competition beyond firm competition in industries.

Notes

1. Their political power is also well known, and is often analyzed (see Epstein 1979). The discretionary power of large corporations is very well analyzed in Hymer 1979; Chandler 1977; Herman 1981.

2. However, as discussed above, it seems to be more realistic to assume not uniform profit rates but differentials of profit rates among firms or industries. In this case too, administered prices and markup pricing are consistent with the concept of production prices (see secs. 5.2 and 5.3 and appendix 4).

Appendixes

Appendix 1. TECHNICAL CHANGE AND CHANGE IN VALUES

For a linear equation system $\Lambda\mathbf{B} = \mathbf{l}$, presented in chapter 2 as $\Lambda\mathbf{B}^* = \mathbf{l}$, the solution Λ is determined by the inverse $\mathbf{B}^{-1}$, since $\Lambda = \mathbf{lB}^{-1}$. The question is how the inverse changes if $\mathbf{B}$ changes to $\mathbf{B} + \delta\mathbf{B}$. We write $\delta\mathbf{B} = \mathbf{E}$, where $\mathbf{E}$ is the disturbance of $\mathbf{B}$. We might examine the maximum error of the new inverse and the effect on the solution of $\tilde{\Lambda}$ by the following method (see Fox 1965: 141).

We can take $(\mathbf{B} + \mathbf{E}) - \mathbf{B} = \mathbf{E}$ and pre- and post-multiply these equations by $(\mathbf{B} + \mathbf{E})^{-1}$ and $\mathbf{B}^{-1}$. We get $\mathbf{B}^{-1} - (\mathbf{B} + \mathbf{E})^{-1} = (\mathbf{B} + \mathbf{E})^{-1}\mathbf{E}\mathbf{B}^{-1}$. To get an estimate of the maximum change in the new inverse, we take norms and use the fact that $(\mathbf{B} + \mathbf{E})^{-1} = (\mathbf{I} + \mathbf{B}^{-1}\mathbf{E})^{-1}\mathbf{B}^{-1}$. We get

$$\|\mathbf{B}^{-1} - (\mathbf{B} + \mathbf{E})^{-1}\| \leqslant \frac{\|\mathbf{B}^{-1}\|^2\|\mathbf{E}\|}{1 - \|\mathbf{B}^{-1}\|\,\|\mathbf{E}\|},$$

assuming that $\|\mathbf{B}^{-1}\|\,\|\mathbf{E}\| < 1$. Multiplying the numerator and denominator on the right side by $\|\mathbf{B}\|/\|\mathbf{B}\|$ and dividing the whole equation by $\|\mathbf{B}^{-1}\|$ gives us the following expression:

$$\frac{\|\mathbf{B}^{-1} - (\mathbf{B} + \mathbf{E})^{-1}\|}{\|\mathbf{B}^{-1}\|} \leqslant \frac{\|\mathbf{B}^{-1}\|\,\|\mathbf{B}\|\,\|\mathbf{E}\|/\|\mathbf{B}\|}{1 - \|\mathbf{B}^{-1}\|\,\|\mathbf{B}\|\,\|\mathbf{E}\|/\|\mathbf{B}\|}$$

We can see that the relative disturbance of the original matrix $\mathbf{B}$ (due to the change in the organic composition of our original matrix **A**) is determined by $\|\mathbf{B}^{-1}\| \, \|\mathbf{B}\|$ and $\|\mathbf{E}\|/\|\mathbf{B}\|$. If $\|\mathbf{B}^{-1}\| \, \|\mathbf{B}\|$ is small, the relative disturbance of the solution will also be small. If $\|\mathbf{B}^{-1}\| \, \|\mathbf{B}\|$ is large, it may no longer be concluded that the disturbance will be small. The literature discusses types of matrices in which the disturbances are very large (see Fox 1965; Ortega 1972; Voievodine 1980). On the other hand, a strong disturbance **E** will also change the solution greatly. But the effect on the new solution is already determined by the original matrix **B**. Of course, as mentioned in the text, the new solution of $\tilde{\Lambda}$ is also influenced if the vector **1** also changes.

Since $\tilde{\Lambda}(\mathbf{B} + \mathbf{E}) = \mathbf{1} + \delta\mathbf{l}$, a possible disturbance of **l** (the direct labor coefficients) also has an influence on the solution $\tilde{\Lambda}$, since $\tilde{\Lambda} = (\mathbf{l} + \delta\mathbf{l})(\mathbf{B} + \mathbf{E})^{-1}$. But the most influential part is always the inverse $(\mathbf{B} + \mathbf{E})^{-1}$, the degree of ill-conditioning of matrix **B**, and therefore of matrix **A**. By using equation (2.6), $\delta\Lambda = (\delta\mathbf{l} - \Lambda\delta\mathbf{B})\mathbf{B}^{-1}(\mathbf{I} + \delta\mathbf{B}\mathbf{B}^{-1})^{-1}$, we can also estimate the relative change in the vector for the values. By taking norms of this equation and using the upper bound for the inverse

$$\|(\mathbf{I} + \delta\mathbf{B}\mathbf{B}^{-1})^{-1}\| \leqslant \frac{1}{1 - \|\delta\mathbf{B}\| \, \|\mathbf{B}^{-1}\|},$$

if $\|\delta\mathbf{B}\| \, \|\mathbf{B}^{-1}\| < 1$, and dividing both sides of the inequality by $\|\Lambda\|$, we get

$$\frac{\|\delta\Lambda\|}{\|\Lambda\|} \leqslant \left(\frac{\|\delta\mathbf{l}\|}{\|\Lambda\|} - \|\delta\mathbf{B}\| \right) \cdot \frac{\|\mathbf{B}^{-1}\|}{1 - \|\delta\mathbf{B}\| \, \|\mathbf{B}^{-1}\|}.$$

Λ is usually a continuous function of **B**, but this does not say anything about the size of the change $\delta\Lambda$, which is determined by the degree of ill-conditioning of matrix **B**. Ill-conditioned matrices will prevail, for example, when two rows (or two columns) are very close to each other (see Fox 1965:139). I want to give two examples of the change in the value Λ due to a small change in **l** or **B** (see Semmler 1984a). One example may be the following:

$$\Lambda\left\{ \begin{bmatrix} 1 & 0 \\ 0 & 1 \end{bmatrix} - \begin{bmatrix} 0.3 & 0.699 \\ 0.7 & 0.3 \end{bmatrix} \right\} = (0.1, 0.1).$$

The matrix for the material inputs, as well as the labor vector, shows positive elements, and the matrix is productive. The solution of the system

$$\Lambda \begin{bmatrix} 0.7 & -0.699 \\ -0.7 & 0.7 \end{bmatrix} = (0.1, \, 0.1)$$

is $\lambda_1 = 200$ and $\lambda_2 = 199.86$. Now we change one element in the matrix for material inputs. We want to solve the following system:

$$\Lambda \begin{bmatrix} 0.7 & -0.6999 \\ -0.7 & 0.7 \end{bmatrix} = (0.1, \, 0.1).$$

We get the solution $\lambda_1 = 2000$ and $\lambda_2 = 1999.29$.

Another example may be this one, in which the matrix of the material inputs and the labor vector show positive elements and the matrix is productive:

$$\Lambda \begin{bmatrix} 0.7700 & -0.5000 & -0.3333 \\ -0.5000 & 0.6667 & -0.2500 \\ -0.3333 & -0.2500 & 0.8000 \end{bmatrix} = (0.8, \, 0.4, \, 0.6).$$

The solution of the system is $\lambda_1 = 150.427$, $\lambda_2 = 155.407$, $\lambda_3 = 111.986$. However, if we change b_{23} from -0.2500 to -0.2400 we get the solution $\lambda_1 = 88.679$, $\lambda_2 = 90.903$, $\lambda_3 = 66.103$.

In this case, as well as in the first case, it may be argued that the relative values change only slightly, whereas the absolute values change very sensitively. However, from an economic point of view, the second property (sensitive change of prices, even if the change is a continuous function of the coefficients) already creates serious problems. If we assume, for example—as Ricardo (1951, ch. 7) did—that gold is produced outside a country and that one unit of labor is embodied in one ounce of gold, the price level in the country, in which the production coefficients have changed slightly, would have to change sensitively. This would also change the absolute or comparative cost advantage of a country and lead to a new international division of labor, depending on what mechanism is assumed to establish the new absolute or relative cost advantage (see also Steedman 1979b). However, there does not seem to be a

conceivable economic mechanism that could lead to an adjustment toward the new price level and toward a new international
division of labor. The same problem of an economic adjustment
will arise if relative values change. In cases where such an economic
adjustment process is not conceivable, we can conclude that the
new equilibrium might not be a very relevant one.

Appendix 2. TECHNICAL CHANGE AND CHANGE IN PRODUCTION PRICES

Equation (2.8),

$$(\overline{A}' + \delta\overline{A}')(p^{(r)} + \delta p^{(r)}) = (\lambda_r + \delta\lambda_r)(p^{(r)} + \delta p^{(r)}),$$

can be written as

$$\tilde{A}'\tilde{p}^{(r)} = \tilde{\lambda}_r\tilde{p}^{(r)}, \qquad (A2.1)$$

where $\tilde{A}'$ is the changed matrix $\overline{A}'$, λ_r the new maximum eigenvalue, and $\tilde{p}^{(r)}$ the corresponding eigenvector, which can be interpreted as the new vector of prices of production. In order to simplify the following derivations, we substitute for $\overline{A}' + \delta\overline{A}'$ the expression $A + \delta A$ and for δA the term ϵB, where ϵ is a small number and B a matrix (see Fox 1965:277). Thus, we can write equation (A2.1) as

$$(A + \epsilon B)p^{(r)}(\epsilon) = \lambda_r(\epsilon)p^{(r)}(\epsilon). \qquad (A2.1a)$$

On the other hand, for the original structure of production— represented by the matrix A—we get the following prices of production and eigenvalue:

$$Ap^{(r)} = \lambda_r p^{(r)} \qquad (A2.2)$$

We know that all eigenvalues of matrix A can be expressed by the similarity transformation of matrix A; i.e., that if A can be transformed into a diagonal matrix, then

$$\mathbf{X'AP} = \Lambda, \tag{A2.2a}$$

where $\mathbf{X'} = \mathbf{P}^{-1}$. $\mathbf{X'}$ is the transposed matrix of the left-hand eigenvectors of $\mathbf{A}$ and $\mathbf{P}$ the matrix of the right-hand eigenvectors of $\mathbf{A}$ corresponding to the eigenvalues of Λ. (Λ is a diagonal matrix of the eigenvalues $\lambda_1, \lambda_2, \ldots, \lambda_n$.) The individual vectors of $\mathbf{X'}$ and $\mathbf{P}$ can be normalized so that $\mathbf{x}^{(r)'}\mathbf{x}^{(r)} = 1$ and $\mathbf{p}^{(r)'}\mathbf{p}^{(r)} = 1$. For a symmetric matrix $\mathbf{A}$ we get $\mathbf{x}^{(r)'}\mathbf{p}^{(r)} = \mathbf{p}^{(r)'}\mathbf{p}^{(r)} = 1$. For a more general matrix (nonsymmetric matrix $\mathbf{A}$), we can write $\mathbf{x}^{(r)'}\mathbf{p}^{(r)} = q_r$ ($q_r = 1$ for a symmetric matrix). For the perturbed matrix $\tilde{\mathbf{A}} = \mathbf{A} + \epsilon\mathbf{B}$ we get the following general similarity transformation:

$$\mathbf{X'}(\mathbf{A} + \epsilon\mathbf{B})\mathbf{P} = \Lambda + \epsilon\mathbf{C}, \tag{A2.3}$$

where the element c_{rs} of $\mathbf{C}$ is given by $\mathbf{x}^{(r)'}\mathbf{Bp}^{(s)}/q_r$. This is true, since $\mathbf{X'AP} = \Lambda$.

From equation (A2.1a) we know that $\mathbf{p}^{(r)}(\epsilon)$ is an eigenvector of $(\mathbf{A} + \epsilon\mathbf{B})$ associated with the eigenvalue $\lambda_r(\epsilon)$. An eigenvector of the matrix in equation (A2.3) can be written as $\mathbf{z}^{(r)}(\epsilon)$, so that we get

$$\mathbf{X'}(\mathbf{A} + \epsilon\mathbf{B})\mathbf{Pz}^{(r)}(\epsilon) = (\Lambda + \epsilon\mathbf{C})\mathbf{z}^{(r)}(\epsilon) = \lambda_r(\epsilon)\mathbf{z}^{(r)}(\epsilon) \tag{A2.4}$$

and $\mathbf{p}^{(r)}(\epsilon) = \mathbf{Pz}^{(r)}(\epsilon)$.

Equation (A2.4) is equal to equation (A2.1a), since we can substitute for $\mathbf{z}^{(r)}(\epsilon)$ in equation (A2.4) the expression $\mathbf{P}^{-1}\mathbf{p}^{(r)}(\epsilon)$. Thus, we can write

$$\mathbf{X'}(\mathbf{A} + \epsilon\mathbf{B})\mathbf{PP}^{-1}\mathbf{p}^{(r)}(\epsilon) = \lambda_r(\epsilon)\mathbf{P}^{-1}\mathbf{p}^{(r)}(\epsilon).$$

Since we know that $\mathbf{X'} = \mathbf{P}^{-1}$ we get equation (A2.1a). If in equation (A2.4) ϵ is equal to zero, the rth component of $\mathbf{z}^{(r)}(0)$ is unity and all the rest zero, since $\mathbf{p}^{(r)}(0) = \mathbf{Pz}^{(r)}(0)$ and $\mathbf{p}^{(r)}(0)$ is the rth column of $\mathbf{P}$. Moreover, we assume the rth component of $\mathbf{z}^{(r)}(\epsilon)$ is the largest, and we normalize so that this component is unity. Then, according to equation (A2.4), for the sth component of $\mathbf{z}^{(r)}(\epsilon)$, with $s \neq r$, we get the result

$$\lambda_r(\epsilon)z_s^{(r)}(\epsilon) = \lambda_s z_s^{(r)}(\epsilon) + \epsilon\sum_{t=1}^{n} c_{st} z_t^{(r)}(\epsilon). \tag{A2.4a}$$

Since the components of $\mathbf{z}^{(r)}$ are equal to or less than unity and $c_{st} = x^{(s)}\mathbf{B}\mathbf{P}^{(t)}/\mathbf{q}_s$ (see equation [A2.3]), we get the following result:

$$|\lambda_r(\epsilon) - \lambda_s| \, |z_s^{(r)}(\epsilon)| \leqslant \epsilon|\mathbf{q}_s^{-1}| \sum_{t=1}^{n} |\mathbf{x}^{(s)}{}'\mathbf{B}\mathbf{p}^{(t)}|. \qquad (A2.4b)$$

From equation (A2.4b) we get

$$|z_s^{(r)}(\epsilon)| \leqslant \frac{\epsilon|\mathbf{q}_s^{-1}| \sum_{t=1}^{n} |\mathbf{x}^{(s)}{}'\mathbf{B}\mathbf{p}^{(t)}|}{|\lambda_r(\epsilon) - \lambda_s|}. \qquad (A2.4c)$$

We can see immediately that the components $z_s^r(\epsilon)$ may not be small any more, in which case a latent root (belonging to the undisturbed system of production $\overline{\mathbf{A}}'$) is near to the $\lambda_r(\epsilon)$ corresponding to $\mathbf{z}^{(r)}$. Moreover, all the components $\mathbf{p}^{(r)}(\epsilon) = \mathbf{P}\mathbf{z}^{(r)}(\epsilon)$ may be disturbed badly. We also see that even if, for example, the new maximum eigenvalue $\lambda_r(\epsilon)$ for the disturbed matrix $\tilde{\mathbf{A}}'$ is near the old maximum eigenvalue of the matrix $\overline{\mathbf{A}}'$ (e.g., near λ_s), the new price vector $\mathbf{p}^{(r)}(\epsilon)$ can be greatly affected.[1]

From Frobenius' theorem we know that the maximum eigenvalue of an indecomposable matrix $\overline{\mathbf{A}}'$ is increasing (decreasing) if its elements increase (decrease), and that the maximum profit rate falls (increases). But we do not know how much the eigenvector is disturbed. Formula (A2.4c) gives us an estimate of such disturbance. In a case where elements of the matrix $\overline{\mathbf{A}}'$ change in different directions, the change of the maximum eigenvalue can also be estimated (see Gantmacher 1970, vol. 2, ch. 13, sec. 2; Fox 1965:276). We can now discuss the three cases mentioned in section 2.3.3 of this book.

1. In the first case, where we assumed an increasing organic composition of capital, due to an increase in the elements of matrix $\mathbf{A}$, $\epsilon\mathbf{B}$ can be regarded as $(\delta\mathbf{A})'$. According to formula (A2.4c), we may get great disturbances of the price vector $\mathbf{p}^{(r)}$ if the differences between the latent roots $|\lambda_r(\epsilon) - \lambda_s|$ are very small and $|\mathbf{q}_s^{-1}|$ differs from 1 greatly.

2. In the second case, in which matrix $\overline{\mathbf{A}}'$ changes as a result of a change in the real wage vector $\mathbf{d}$, $\epsilon\mathbf{B}$ can be regarded as $(\delta\mathbf{d}\mathbf{l})'$. The price change can be great, depending on whether or not $\lambda_r(\epsilon)$

is near λ_s and $|q_s^{-1}|$ differs greatly from 1. But the fact that prices may change greatly depends not so much on the change in **d** (represented by **B** in formula [A2.4c]) as on the original matrix $\overline{\mathbf{A}}'$ (the ill-conditioning of the vector problem).

3. In the third case, if $\epsilon\mathbf{B}$ is $(\delta\mathbf{A} + \mathbf{d}\delta\mathbf{l})'$, the tolerance for the price change can be estimated from formula (A2.4c), but prices may change in different directions and different magnitudes, depending again on the difference $|\lambda_r(\epsilon) - \lambda_s|$ and on $|q_s^{-1}|$ and **B**. But here again, $|q_s^{-1}|$ is already given by matrix $\overline{\mathbf{A}}'$, i.e., by the degree of ill-conditioning of matrix $\overline{\mathbf{A}}'$. The change in matrix $\epsilon\mathbf{B} = (\delta\mathbf{A} + \mathbf{d}\delta\mathbf{l})'$ is of special interest for the discussion on choice of technique and falling rate of profit. Usually, a reference to the neoclassical choice of technique criterion is assumed to mean that the new matrix $\tilde{\mathbf{A}}' = \overline{\mathbf{A}}' + \epsilon\mathbf{B}$ weighted by the old price vector will lead to a decreasing eigenvalue. A higher profit rate (associated with a new price vector) will be the result (see Okishio 1961; Roemer 1979). However, this result is not true if we allow for a more general criterion of structural change, by which some columns of $\tilde{\mathbf{A}}'$ have increased and some decreased in comparison with $\overline{\mathbf{A}}'$. The result is also not true if there is a technical change which increases the requirements for fixed capital more than it decreases the sum of depreciation, intermediate inputs, and direct labor inputs (weighted by the previous price vector). The method of estimating the change in the direction of the eigenvalue presented in Gantmacher (1970, vol. 2, ch. 13, sec. 2) and Fox (1965: 276) can be applied to this problem. In this case, the eigenvalue in formula A2.1 can increase and the profit rate fall, in spite of the fact that cost decreases and the profit margin rises (see Semmler 1984b).

Appendix 3. JOINT PRODUCTION, UNIFORM PROFIT RATE, PRICES, AND NONSUBSTITUTION

A3.1. Generalized Eigenvalue Problem and Prices

As mentioned in chapter 6, the prices and output proportions of joint production activities can be modeled in terms of a general eigenvalue system. To prove the existence of a nonnegative uniform profit rate and positive prices in such a joint production system, I refer to a theorem of Mangasarian (1971).

In a simple eigenvalue system, the maximum eigenvalue in $\mathbf{Ax} = \lambda\mathbf{x}$ or in $\mathbf{A'p} = \lambda\mathbf{p}$ can be interpreted as $1/(1 + r)$ or, as in sections 3.1.3 and 6.1, as $1/r$, where r is the uniform profit rate and $\mathbf{p}$ and $\mathbf{x}$ the vectors of semipositive prices and of outputs respectively. For the simple eigenvalue problem of the form $\mathbf{Ax} = \lambda\mathbf{x}$ or $\mathbf{A'p} = \lambda\mathbf{p}$, the theorem of Frobenius states that for an indecomposable square matrix there exist an eigenvalue λ with the largest absolute value which is real and nonnegative and a corresponding eigenvector $\mathbf{x}$ or $\mathbf{p}$ which is semipositive. This theorem has been used in chapters 2 and 3. A generalized eigenvalue problem, which has been used in equation (6.5a), has the following form:

$$\mathbf{Ax} = \lambda\mathbf{Bx}$$

where $\mathbf{A}$ and $\mathbf{B}$ are $m \times n$ real matrices such that the rank of $\mathbf{A}$ or

B is n. The extended Frobenius' theorem for a general eigenvalue problem states (see Mangasarian 1971:87) that if $\mathbf{B}'\mathbf{y} \geqq \mathbf{0}$ implies that $\mathbf{A}'\mathbf{y} \geqq \mathbf{0}$, then for the generalized eigenvalue problem $\mathbf{Ax} = \lambda\mathbf{Bx}$, the eigenvalue with the largest absolute value is real and nonnegative, and a corresponding eigenvector $\mathbf{x}$ is semipositive. For the dual problem $\mathbf{A}'\mathbf{p} = \lambda\mathbf{B}'\mathbf{p}$ an analogous statement holds.

  1. The basic tool for proving this statement is a theorem of the alternative for linear inequalities. It states:

$$\mathbf{B}'\mathbf{y} \geqq \mathbf{0} \qquad \text{implies that} \qquad \mathbf{A}'\mathbf{y} \geqq \mathbf{0}$$

if and only if there exists an $n \times n$ matrix $\mathbf{X}$ such that

$$\mathbf{A} = \mathbf{BX} \qquad \text{and} \qquad \mathbf{X} \geqq \mathbf{0}$$

From this theorem, for which the proof is given by Mangasarian (1971:90), it follows that for such an $\mathbf{X}$, with $\mathbf{A} = \mathbf{BX}$ and $\mathbf{X} \geqq \mathbf{0}$, the eigenvalue system stated above has a maximum nonnegative eigenvalue which is real, and a corresponding eigenvector is semipositive. In other words, the joint production system with a uniform profit rate $1/(1 + r)$ or $1/r$—depending on how it is formalized—will have a semipositive price vector as its solution.

  2. However, it still has to be shown that for an economic system it is reasonable to assume that $\mathbf{B}'\mathbf{y} \geqslant \mathbf{0}$ implies $\mathbf{A}'\mathbf{y} \geqslant \mathbf{0}$. We can give an economic interpretation of this relation by setting $\mathbf{y} = \mathbf{p}^1 - \mathbf{p}^2$, where the prices $\mathbf{p}^1 \geqslant \mathbf{0}$ and $\mathbf{p}^2 \geqslant \mathbf{0}$. Then we can write $\mathbf{p}^1\mathbf{B} \geqslant \mathbf{p}^2\mathbf{B}$, which implies $\mathbf{p}^1\mathbf{A} \geqslant \mathbf{p}^2\mathbf{A}$; that is, if the value of output is greater for $\mathbf{p}^1$ than for $\mathbf{p}^2$, this fact implies that the evaluation of the inputs (the costs) will also be greater for $\mathbf{p}^1$ than for $\mathbf{p}^2$. In other words, it is not reasonable to assume that $(\mathbf{p}^1\mathbf{A})_i < (\mathbf{p}^2\mathbf{A})_i$ for some i and $\mathbf{p}^1\mathbf{B} \geqslant \mathbf{p}^2\mathbf{B}$. This means that for our price equation (6.5a) it is not reasonable to assume that $(\mathbf{p}^1\mathbf{B}^+)_i < (\mathbf{p}^2\mathbf{B}^+)_i$ for some i and $\mathbf{p}^1\mathbf{S} \geqslant \mathbf{p}^2\mathbf{S}$. For an economic system in which such reasonable relations exist, and which is productive, the system will guarantee a uniform nonnegative profit rate r and the existence of a semipositive price vector.[2] On the basis of those systems it is possible to derive the markups for the different lines of business of large corporations (see sec. 6.3).

A3.2. Joint Production and Nonsubstitution Theorem

For a single-product system $(\mathbf{A}, \mathbf{l}, \mathbf{B})$ where there are m processes and n goods with homogeneous labor as the only primary input, each row of $\mathbf{B}$ has exactly one positive entry. Assuming constant returns to scale, it has been shown that the so-called nonsubstitution theorem holds: no variation in the composition of the final demand vector will lead to substitution (see Samuelson 1951; Koopmans 1951b; Arrow 1951: Dorfman et al. 1958, sec. 9). More precisely, this theorem—for which the second part is true only for prices in terms of direct and indirect labor requirements, not necessarily for production prices (see appendix 2)—states that for a linear production system $(\mathbf{A}, \mathbf{l}, \mathbf{B})$ of this kind which is also productive, there exists a single productive subsystem $(\mathbf{A}_I, \mathbf{l}_I, \mathbf{B}_I)$ having the following property: $(\mathbf{A}_I, \mathbf{l}_I, \mathbf{B}_I)$ is a selection of exactly n processes from $(\mathbf{A}, \mathbf{l}, \mathbf{B})$ such that for any final demand $\mathbf{y} \geqslant \mathbf{0}$ there exists a unique solution $\mathbf{x}(\mathbf{y}) \geqslant \mathbf{0}$ if $\mathbf{x}(\mathbf{y})(\mathbf{B}_I - \mathbf{A}_I) = \mathbf{y}$, and $\mathbf{y}$ can be produced with minimal labor expenditure using the activity vector $\mathbf{x}(\mathbf{y})$.

It has been maintained that the classical political economists (Smith, Ricardo) and Marx assumed constant returns to scale for a linear production system, in which the property of nonsubstitution holds. Whether or not these were the assumptions in the classics and Marx is still an object of controversy in economic literature. Yet the only assumption that Smith, Ricardo, and also Marx made was the assumption—as shown in chapter 2—that short-term fluctuations in output and in relative input prices do not affect the long-run centers of gravity: in Smith the natural prices, in Ricardo the direct and indirect labor requirements, and in Marx the market values (or production prices). Of course, Ricardo and Marx, in particular, knew that the "facility" or "difficulty" of production can change the center of gravity for the market price when the long-run "social" (or "effectual") demand changes (see secs. 2.3.2 and 3.3 and Schefold 1981), but for a given state of the economy they neglect the impact of the variation of output or demand on relative prices and the allocation of resources. This position has been criticized by neoclassical theorists (see Arrow and Hahn 1971, ch. 1; Hollander 1973:3). However, it must not be overlooked that the classics and Marx did not have a concept of a linear production model with constant returns to scale. They only maintained that fluctuations in output and relative input prices—as in modern theories of industrial and corporate pricing —do not play a role in determining the long-run prices. This relation of the classics to modern theories of industrial prices has also been pointed out by Robinson (1962). Because of the similarities of the properties of the classical/Marxian production prices to the properties of prices in linear production models with constant returns to scale, the latter have been used to interpret the classics and Marx. The differences between the two concepts are not so obvious in the case of single-product industries; yet they become very obvious if cases of joint production are allowed for. If on the basis of activity analysis joint production systems with m processes and n goods are discussed, the additional question arises of whether a new technique has to be activated in order to satisfy a changing demand $\mathbf{y}$. According to the nonsubstitution theorem this is not the case for a single-product system. In general, for joint production systems $(\mathbf{A}, \mathbf{l}, \mathbf{B})$ it is no longer possible to find a single subsystem ·which produces every $\mathbf{y}$ using a minimum amount of labor. The techniques chosen and the minimum amount of labor will vary with $\mathbf{y}$. However, by using a linear programming approach which includes processes of disposal (costly or not) and writing

$$\min \mathbf{xl},$$
$$\text{subject to} \quad \mathbf{x(y)(B - A) = y}, \quad \mathbf{x} \geq \mathbf{0},$$

Hinrichsen and Krause (1981) developed a theorem that shows that even for a joint production system, a *small* change in $\mathbf{y}$ can be satisfied by changes in $\mathbf{x(y)}$ without activating a new technique and that therefore the traditional formulation of the direct and indirect labor requirements $\Lambda = (\mathbf{B}_I - \mathbf{A}_I)^{-1}\mathbf{l}_I$ still holds for a subsystem $(\mathbf{A}_I, \mathbf{l}_I, \mathbf{B}_I)$. This is a property of joint production systems that is consistent with the concepts of normal output, normal cost, and normal price mentioned in section 6.1.

Appendix 4. JOINT PRODUCTION, DIFFERENTIAL PROFIT RATES, AND PRICES

Sections 5.2, 5.3, and 6.3 show price models that allow for differential profit rates. Equation (5.16),

$$\overline{p}[I - (\overline{A} + B' + B^+\langle\overline{r}\rangle)] = 0,$$

an extension of equation (5.1a), and equation (6.13a),

$$\overline{p}[B - (\overline{A} + B' + B^+\langle\overline{r}\rangle)] = 0,$$

are introduced to allow us to consider differential profit rates and their influence on classical and Marxian production prices.

1. Referring to the more general case covered in section 6.3, we can write

$$\overline{p}C(\overline{r}) = 0,$$

where $C(\overline{r}) = B - (\overline{A} + B' + B^+\langle\overline{r}\rangle)$. To discuss the properties of the solution of $\overline{p}C(\overline{r}) = 0$, we can use Stiemke's theorem (see Kemp and Kimura (1978:3), which states:

> there exists a $\overline{p} > 0$ such that $\overline{p}C(\overline{r}) = 0$
> if and only if $C(\overline{r})x \geq 0$ has no solution or,
> setting $x = x^1 - x^2$,
> if and only if $C(\overline{r})x^1 \geq C(\overline{r})x^2$ for no vectors
> $x^1, x^2 \geq 0$.

Especially for certain values of $\langle \bar{r} \rangle$ for which $C(\bar{r}) \geqslant 0$, the theorem implies that there is no $\bar{p} > 0$. In other words, $\langle \bar{r} \rangle$ cannot fall below a certain minimum without violating the condition $\bar{p} > 0$. (On the other hand, it is obvious that $\langle \bar{r} \rangle$ cannot increase above a certain maximum without violating the condition $\bar{p} > 0$.) The theorem stated above can be interpreted economically. The first part holds if and only if $C(\bar{r})x \geqslant 0$ has no solution or $C(\bar{r})x^1 \geqslant C(\bar{r})x^2$ is impossible for x^1, $x^2 \geqslant 0$. Setting $x^2 = 0$, it follows that $C(\bar{r})x^2 \geqslant 0$. This cannot be true for any $x^1 \geqslant 0$, since it would imply that

$$(\bar{A} + B' + B^+\langle \bar{r} \rangle)x^1 \leqslant Bx^1.$$

In other words, it assumes that the economic system produces an excess supply which is not used up for production or the reproduction of labor power. Therefore, assuming that all products being produced are used up and that the markets clear at prevailing prices, it follows that any solution of $C(\bar{r})x \geqslant 0$ must be such that $C(\bar{r})x = 0$. This implies that every row of $C(\bar{r})$ must have at least one negative element.

2. However, the question remains, What happens if the price vector generated by the differential profit rates $\langle \bar{r} \rangle$ —or by setting markups for the different lines of businesses—represents "normal" or "average" prices (including differential profit rates) but is not necessarily an equilibrium price vector? In this case, for example, we must allow for a vector $\bar{p} > 0$ for which[3]

$$\bar{p}[B - (\bar{A} + B' + B^+\langle \bar{r} \rangle)] \geqq 0.$$

Prices may include differential profit rates for which the value of outputs exceeds the value of purchased inputs for the production processes and for the reproduction of labor power. This will allow for the case where

$$[B - (\bar{A} + B' + B^+\langle \bar{r} \rangle)]x \geqq 0.$$

Not all outputs are sold. There can be an excess supply.[4] Accumulation of stocks of finished commodities will occur, but the transaction on the market can go on in terms of a price vector which is not necessarily an equilibrium price vector. A conclusion similar to that stated above for production prices can be made when markup pricing with differential profit rates is assumed. This can lead to

$$\overline{p}[B - (\overline{A} + \overline{A}\langle\mu\rangle)] \geqq 0$$

and correspondingly

$$[B - (\overline{A} + \overline{A}\langle\mu\rangle)]x \geqq 0.$$

Appendix 5. THE LAW OF SUPPLY AND DEMAND: THE EXISTENCE AND STABILITY OF A GENERAL EQUILIBRIUM

1. In neoclassical general equilibrium analysis, the most fundamental law for price determination is the *law of supply and demand* (Arrow and Hahn 1971:22, 265). This law, in a modern formulation, states that the excess demand vector $z(p) = D(p) - S(p)$
is a continuous function of actual prices p and that prices change
if excess demand changes. This law is used to prove the existence
of an equilibrium and of convergence toward it if the economic
system is out of equilibrium (see Arrow and Hahn 1971, chs. 2
and 11).

2. The existence of an equilibrium, where the excess demand
vector $z(p^0) = D(p^0) - S(p^0)$ is zero and equilibrium prices p^0
allow for a consistent exchange, can be derived from Brouwer's
fixed point theorem, which can be written as $p^0 = T(p^0)$ (see
Arrow and Hahn 1971:27) and means that, for a continuous map-
ping of a compact and convex set into itself, there exists a fixed
point. The vector p^0 can be interpreted as equilibrium prices with
$\Sigma p^0 = 1$. Setting

$$T(p) = \frac{p + M(p)}{[p + M(p)]e},$$

where $\mathbf{p}$ is any actual price vector, $\mathbf{M}(\mathbf{p})$ the adjustment to an existing price vector, and $\mathbf{e}$ the unit vector. Let us assume that $M_i(\mathbf{p}) > 0$ if and only if $z_i(\mathbf{p}) > 0$; that $M_i(\mathbf{p}) = 0$ if $z_i(\mathbf{p}) = 0$; and that $p_i + M_i(\mathbf{p}) \geqslant 0$. These properties are fulfilled, for example, when $M_i(\mathbf{p}) = \max[0, kz_i(\mathbf{p})]$, $k > 0$. These assumptions about the price adjustment represent the neoclassical assumption that prices respond to the excess demand $z_i(\mathbf{p})$ on markets. The price p_i is thus transformed, because $z_i(\mathbf{p}) > 0$ and $M_i(\mathbf{p}) > 0$, into the price $p_i + M_i(\mathbf{p})$. Brouwer's fixed point theorem provides that there exists a fixed point for which the equations system $\mathbf{p}^0 = \mathbf{T}(\mathbf{p}^0)$ holds. The fixed point for $\mathbf{T}$ is an equilibrium. This can be shown in the following way. Setting $\{[\mathbf{p}^0 + \mathbf{M}(\mathbf{p}^0)]\mathbf{e}\}\mathbf{p}^0 = \mathbf{p}^0 + \mathbf{M}(\mathbf{p}^0)$ or $\mathbf{M}(\mathbf{p}^0) = \lambda\mathbf{p}^0$, where $\lambda = [\mathbf{p}^0 + \mathbf{M}(\mathbf{p}^0)]\mathbf{e} - 1$; multiplying both sides by $\mathbf{z}(\mathbf{p}^0)$; and applying Walras' law, according to which for any price vector $\mathbf{p}$ it is true that $\mathbf{p}\mathbf{z}(\mathbf{p}) = 0$, we get $\mathbf{M}(\mathbf{p}^0)\mathbf{z}(\mathbf{p}^0) = \lambda\mathbf{p}^0\mathbf{z}(\mathbf{p}^0) = 0$. The inequality $z_i(\mathbf{p}^0) > 0$ would imply that $M_i(\mathbf{p}^0) = 0$, which contradicts the first assumption above; thus, $\mathbf{z}(\mathbf{p}^0) = \mathbf{0}$. This proof means that there exists at least one price vector which allows for a consistent exchange.

3. In most of the neoclassical literature it is assumed that the adjustment process is stable and that actual prices and quantities converge, after a disturbance, back toward the equilibrium. Only recently has it been discussed in neoclassical economics that the adjustment process can be unstable. Under what conditions the adjustment process will be stable can be demonstrated as follows. Let $M_i(\mathbf{p})$ represent the price adjustment for the commodity i, so that a price vector $\mathbf{p}$ is transformed, as a result of excess demand, into a new price vector $\mathbf{p} + \mathbf{M}(\mathbf{p})$. As shown above, according to neoclassical assumptions the price vector responds to excess demand. The adjustment mechanism is usually represented by a tatonnement, according to which an "auctioneer" adjusts prices when the excess demand is positive or negative. Thus, it is assumed that for any product $M_i(\mathbf{p}) > 0$, if and only if $z_i(\mathbf{p}) > 0$, and $M_i(\mathbf{p}) = 0$, if $z_i(\mathbf{p}) = 0$. Using the notation for the dynamic stability analysis and the index t for the time sequence, we can say that the excess demand function $\mathbf{z}(\mathbf{p}_t) > 0$ transforms the actual price vector $\mathbf{p}_t$ into a price vector $\mathbf{p}_{t+1}$. Thus we get $\mathbf{p}_{t+1} = \mathbf{p}_t + \mathbf{M}(\mathbf{p}_t)$. Using the

Euclidean vector norm, we can say that the equilibrium is stable if $\| T(p_t) - T(p°) \| \leqq q \| p_t - p° \|$, where $0 < q < 1$. p is the actual price vector and p^0 the equilibrium price vector. This means that any given vector of actual prices p_t will converge to p^0 as $t \to \infty$, which implies that $z(p_t)$ converges to $z(p^0) = 0$. The actual price vector converges to the equilibrium price vector, and the excess demand becomes zero. The most important economic condition that has been discovered to guarantee a convergence of actual prices to equilibrium prices is the gross substitution of the commodities discovered by Hicks in the thirties. If the commodities are gross substitutes, an equilibrium is locally and globally stable. Thus, we can define three kinds of stability: the equilibrium is locally stable if there are small disturbances and for any p belonging to a sufficiently small neighborhood of p^0 it follows that p converges to p^0 as $t \to \infty$; the equilibrium is globally stable if the equilibrium is unique and for large disturbances the vector p converges to p^0 as $t \to \infty$; and the equilibrium possesses system stability if there are some equilibrium positions and any vector p converges to some p^0 as $t \to \infty$ (see Quirk and Saposnik 1968, ch. 5). However, it must be mentioned that cases have been worked out in which excess demand does not respond to price changes in the usual sense and the equilibrium is unstable (see Scarf 1960; D. Gale n.d.). Moreover, as has been shown by Arrow and Hahn (1971, chs. 13, 14), the stability of the equilibrium becomes problematic if there is no tatonnement but trade takes place in a market out of equilibrium or expectation and money are taken into account.

Notes

1. The estimate of the disturbance of the eigenvector (price vector) due to a change in the elements of $\bar{A}'$, given by formula (A2.4c), is very important for the discussion of technical progress and the falling rate of profit, since with that formula the change in the price vector in response to technical progress can be estimated. The estimate discussed above can also be used to analyze possible deviations of value from price of production, if both the value system and the prices of production are formulated in terms of an eigen-

Appendixes

value problem. For example, the value system can be written $(\overline{A} + edl)'\Lambda = \Lambda$. We set $\Lambda = p^0$. The price of production system is written $\overline{A}'p = p$. Writing the deviation in terms of the approach used above, we can write $(B - \delta B)(p^{0(r)} - \delta p^{(r)}) = \lambda_r^0 - \delta \lambda_r)(p^{0(r)} - \delta p^{(r)})$, where $B = (\overline{A} + edl)'$, $\delta B = (edl)$ and e is the rate of exploitation. The maximum eigenvalue of the first equation system is 1. The differences between the solutions of the two systems can be estimated according to formula (A2.4c).

2. For a further discussion on the existence and uniqueness of the solution of a generalized eigenvalue system, see Manara 1980.

3. This statement can be derived from the theorem of Gale (see Kemp and Kimura 1978, p. 4, corollary 1), according to which the following alternative holds:

$A'u \geqq 0$ has a semipositive solution, if and only if
for $xA' < 0$ there is no nonnegative solution.

4. This can be the case, for example, if the differential profit rates $\langle r \rangle < \min \langle r \rangle$. It might be argued on the basis of Walras' law (see appendix 5) that excess supply of commodities may be compensated for by "excess demand for money" (if a money commodity were included in the system of inequality above). In this way, it could be concluded that Walras' law still holds, where $pz(p) = 0$, with $z_i(p) < 0$ for $i = 2, 3, \ldots, n$ and $z_i(p) > 0$ for $i = 1$ (the money commodity). But, as has been shown, Walras' law does not appear to be relevant when exchange at prices which are not equilibrium prices is allowed for and a quantity adjustment process prevails (see Benassy 1975 and Wolfstetter 1977:115).

References

Abraham-Frois, G. and E. Berrebi. 1976. *Théorie de valeur, des prix et de l'accumulation*. Paris: Economica, (Theory of Value, Prices and Accumulation). Cambridge: Cambridge University Press 1979).

Abraham-Frois, G. and E. Berrebi. 1979. *A propos d'une incohérence logique de P. Sraffa*. (On a logical incoherence of P. Sraffa) *Cahiers d'Economie Politique* (Paris), no. 5, pp. 5–11.

Abraham-Frois, G. and E. Berrebi. 1980. *Rentes, rareté, surprofits* (Rent, scarcity, and surplus profit). Paris: Economica.

Abraham-Frois, G. and E. Berrebi. 1982. *Taux de profit minimum dans les modèles de production* (Minimum profit rates in production models). Conference Centre de Recherches Economiques et Sociales, Paris-Nanterre, mimeo.

Altvater, E. 1975. Wertgesetz und Monopolmacht (The law of values and monopoly power). *Das Argument*, Argument-Sonderbaende, AS 6, Berlin, pp. 129–199.

Altvater, E., J. Hoffman, and W. Semmler. 1979. *Vom Wirtschaftswunder zur Wirtschaftskrise—Okonomie und Politik in der Bundesrepublik Deutschland* (From economic prosperity to crisis—Economic growth and economic policy in West Germany). Berlin: Olle and Wolter.

Arrow, K. J. 1951. Alternative Proof of the Substitution Theorem for Leontief Models in the General Case. In Koopmans, ed., *Activity Analysis* (q.v.), pp. 155–164.

Arrow, K. J. 1959. Toward a Theory of Price Adjustment. In M. Abramovitz et al., *The Allocation of Economic Resources*, pp. 41–51. Stanford, Calif.: Stanford University Press.

Arrow, K. J., and F. H. Hahn. 1971. *General Competetive Analysis*. San Francisco: Holden Jay.

Ash, P. and J. J. Seneca. 1976. Is Collusion Profitable? *Review of Economics and Statistics* (February), 58(1):1–12.

Asimakopulos, A. 1975. A Kaleckian Theory of Income Distribution. *Canadian Journal of Economics*, 8(3):313–333.

Asimakopulos, A. 1978. *An Introduction to Economic Theory: Microeconomics.* Oxford: Oxford University Press.

Bailey, E. E. and A. F. Friedlaender. 1982. Market Structure and Multiproduct Industries. *Economic Literature* (September), 20(3):1024–1048.

Bain, J. S. 1951. Relation of Profit Rate to Industry Concentration. American Manufacturing 1936–40. *Quarterly Journal of Economics* (August), 65(3):293–324.

Bain, J. S. 1956. *Barriers to New Competition.* Cambridge: Harvard University Press.

Baran, P. and P. Sweezy. 1976. *Monopoly Capital.* New York: Monthly Review Press.

Baron, D. P. 1973. Limit Pricing, Potential Entry and Barriers to Entry. *American Economic Review* 63(4):666–674.

Baumol, W. J. 1962. On the Theory of Expansion of the Firm. In G. Archibald, ed., *The Theory of the Firm*, pp. 318–328. Harmondsworth, England: Penguin.

Beal, S. R. 1975. Concentrated Industries, Administered Prices and Inflation: A Survey of Recent Empirical Research. Council on Wage and Price Stability, publication CWPS-52. Washington, D.C.

Benassy, J. P. 1975. Neo-Keynesian Disequilibrium Theory in a Monetary Economy. *Review of Economic Studies* 42(132):503–523.

Benetti, C. 1981. La question de la gravitation de prix de marché dans la richesse des nations (On the question of the gravitation of market prices in the wealth of nations). *Cahiers d'Economie Politique* (Paris), no. 6, pp. 9–33.

Blair, J. M. 1972. *Economic Concentration, Structure, Behavior and Policy*, New York: Harcourt Brace Jovanovich.

Blair, J. M. 1974. Market Power and Inflation. *Journal of Economic Issues* (June), 8(2):453–483.

Bodoff, J. 1973. Monopoly and Price Revisited. Ph.D. dissertation, New School for Social Research, New York.

Boehm-Bawerk, E. 1949. *Karl Marx and the Close of His System*, P. M. Sweezy, ed. New York: Kelley.

Bohi, O. R. and G. W. Scully. 1975. Buyer's Prices, Seller's Prices and Price Flexibility: Comment. *American Economic Review* 65(3):517–520.

Bowles, S. and H. Gintis. 1978. Professor Morishima on Heterogeneous Labor and Marxian Value Theory. *Cambridge Journal of Economics* 2(2):311–314.

Bradley, A. 1927. Financial Control Policies of General Motors Corporation and Their Relationship to Cost Accounting. *National Association of Cost Accounting Bulletin* Vol. 8, no. 9, sec. 1, pp. 412–432.

Brody, A., 1970. *Proportions, Prices, and Planning.* Budapest; Akademiai Kiado. Reprint, Amsterdam: North Holland, 1974.

Brown, D. 1924. Pricing Policy in Relation to Financial Control. Articles 2–4. *Management and Administration*, vol. 7, pp. 195–198, 283–286, 417–422.

Brozen, Y. 1971a. Bain's Concentration and Rates of Return Revisited. *Journal of Law and Economics* (October), 14:351–369.

Brozen, Y. 1971b. The Persistence of "High Rates of Return" in High Stable Concentration Industries. *Journal of Law and Economics* (October), 14:501–512.

Brozen, Y. 1973. Concentration and Profits—Does Concentration Matter? in Weston and Ornstein, eds., *The Impact of Large Firms* (q.v.), pp. 59–85.

Bukharin, N. 1973. *Imperialism and the World Economy.* New York: Monthly Review Press.

Bruzzel, R., B. Gale, and G. Sultan. 1975. Market Share—A Key to Profitability. *Harvard Business Review* (January–February), 53:97–106.

Cagan, P. 1974. The Hydra-Head Monster: The Problem of Inflation in the United States. American Enterprise Institute for Public Policy Research publication no. 26. Washington, D.C.

Cagan, P. 1975. Changes in the Recession Behavior of Wholesale Prices in the 1920s and Post–World War II. *Explorations of Economic Research* (Winter), vol. 2, pp. 54–104.

Cartelier, J. 1979. La théorie de la rente dans la logique Ricardienne (The theory of rent in neo-Ricardian logic). *Cahiers d'Economie Politique* (Paris), no. 5, pp. 11–21.

Carter, A. P. 1970. *Structural Change in the American Economy.* Cambridge: Harvard University Press.

Caves, R., B. T. Gale, and M. E. Porter. 1977. Interfirm Profitability Differences: Comment. *Quarterly Journal of Economics* (November), 91(4):667–675.

Caves, R. and M. E. Porter. 1976. Barriers to Exit. In R. T. Masson and P. D. Qualls, eds., *Essays on Industrial Organization*, pp. 39–69. Cambridge: Ballinger.

Caves, R. and M. E. Porter. 1977. From Entry Barriers to Mobility Barriers: Conjectural Decisions and Contrived Deference to New Competition. *Quarterly Journal of Economics* (May), 91(2):241–261.

Chandler, A. D. 1962. *Strategy and Structure: Chapters in the History of American Industrial Enterprise.* Cambridge: MIT Press.

Chandler, A. D. 1977. *The Visible Hand: The Managerial Revolution in American Business.* Cambridge: Harvard University Press.

Clifton, J. A. 1977. Competition and the Evolution of Capitalist Mode of Production. *Cambridge Journal of Economics* 1(2):137–151.

Clifton, J. A. 1979. Administered Prices and Corporate Power. Department of Economics, University of Maryland, College Park. Mimeo.

Collins, N. and L. Preston. 1970. *Concentration and Price-Cost Margin in Manufacturing Industries.* Berkeley: University of California Press.

Comanor, W. and T. Wilson. 1967. Advertising Market Structure and Performance. *Review of Economics and Statistics* (November), 49(4):423–440.

Coutts, K., W. Godley, and W. Nordhaus. 1978. *Industrial Prices in the United Kingdom.* Cambridge: Cambridge University Press.

Cowling, K. and D. Mueller. 1978. The Social Costs of Monopoly Power. *Economic Journal* (December), 88(352):727–749.

Dalton, J. A. 1973. Administered Inflation and Business Pricing: Another Look. Review of Economics and Statistics (November), 55(4):516–519.

Deleplace, G. 1974. Sur la differentiation des taux de profit (On profit rate differentials). Cahiers d'Economie Politique (Paris), no. 1, pp. 18–28.

Deleplace, G. 1981. Marché et concurrence chez Marx (Market and competition in Marx). Cahiers d'Economie Politique (Paris), no. 6, pp. 77–99.

Demsetz, H. 1973a. Industry Structure, Market Rivalry and Public Policy. Journal of Law and Economics (April), 16:1–9.

Demsetz, H. 1973b. The Market Concentration Doctrine. Washington: American Enterprise Institute.

DeRosa, D. A. and M. Goldstein. 1982. The Cross-Sectional Price Equation: Comment. American Economic Review (September), 72(3):876–883.

Dobb, M. 1973. Theories of Value and Distribution Since Adam Smith. Cambridge: Cambridge University Press.

Dorfman, R., P. A. Samuelson, and R. M. Solow. 1958. Linear Programming and Economic Analysis. New York: McGraw-Hill.

Eatwell, J. 1971. Growth, Profitability and Size—The Empirical Evidence. In R. Marris and A. Wood, eds., The Corporate Economy, pp. 379–422. Cambridge: Harvard University Press.

Eatwell, J. 1981. Competition. In I. Bradley and M. Howard, eds., Classical and Marxian Political Economy: Essays in Memory of Ronald Meek, pp. 23–46. London: Macmillan.

Eckstein, O. ed. 1972. The Econometrics of Price Determination. Washington, D.C.: Board of Governors of the Federal Reserve System and Social Science Research Council.

Eckstein, O. and G. Fromm. 1968. The Price Equation. American Economic Review (December), 58(4):1159–1183.

Eichner, A. S. 1973. A Theory of Determination of the Mark-up Under Oligopoly. Economic Journal 83(332):1184–1200.

Eichner, A. S. 1976. The Megacorp and Oligopoly: Microfoundations of Macrodynamics. Cambridge: Cambridge University Press.

Eichner, A. S. 1980. A General Model of Investment and Pricing. In E. D. Nell, ed., Growth, Profits and Property: Essays in the Revival of Political Economy, pp. 118–133. Cambridge: Cambridge University Press.

Engels, F. 1978. Socialism: Utopian and Scientific. In Robert C. Tucker, ed., The Marx-Engels Reader, pp. 683–717. New York: W. W. Norton.

Epstein, E. M. 1979. Firm Size and Structure, Market Power and Business Political Influence: A Review of the Literature. School of Business Administration, University of California, Berkeley. Mimeo.

Fine, B. 1979. On Marx's Theory of Agricultural Rent. Economy and Society (August), 8(3):241–278.

Flaschel, P. 1979. The True Labor Theory of Value and the von Neumann Model —An Alternative. Discussion Papers of the Economics Department, Free University of Berlin, no. 5.

Flaschel, P. 1980. Employment Multipliers and Labor Values in Pure Joint Production Systems. Discussion Papers of the Economics Department, Free University of Berlin, no. 3.

Flaschel, P. 1983. *Marx, Sraffa, und Leontief.* Frankfurt: Peter Lang.

Flaschel, P. and W. Semmler. 1984. The Dynamic Equalization of Profit Rates on Multiproduct Industry Levels. New School for Social Research, New York. Mimeo.

Fox, L. 1965. *An Introduction to Numerical Linear Algebra.* New York: Oxford University Press.

Fraas, A. G. and D. R. Greer. 1977. Market Structure and Price Collusion—An Empirical Analysis. *Journal of Industrial Economics* (September), 26:21–44.

Fuchs, V. R. 1961. Integration, Concentration and Profits in Manufacturing Industries. *Quarterly Journal of Economics* (May), 75(2):278–291.

Fujimori, Y. 1981. *Modern Analysis of Value Theory.* Josai, Japan: University of Josai Press.

Gale, B. 1972. Market Share and Rate of Return. *Review of Economics and Statistics* (November), 54(4):412–423.

Gale, B. and B. S. Branch. 1982. Concentration Versus Market Share: Which Determines Performance and Why Does It Matter? *Anti-trust Bulletin* 27(1):83–105.

Gale, D. (n.d.). A Note on Global Instability of Competitive Equilibrium. Department of Mathematics, Brown University. Mimeo.

Gantmacher, F. R. 1970. *Matrizenrechnung.* (Matrix algebra). 2 vols. Berlin: VEB-Verlag.

Garegnani, P. 1976. On a Change in the Notion of Equilibrium in Recent Work on Value and Distribution: A Comment on Samuelson. In M. Brown et al., eds., *Essays in Modern Capital Theory*, pp. 25–47. Amsterdam: North-Holland.

Garegnani, P. 1977. On the Theory of Distribution and Value in Marx and the Classical Economists. Department of Economics, University of Rome. Mimeo.

Garegnani, P. 1978. Changes and Comparisons—A Reply to Joan Robinson. *Cambridge Journal of Economics* (June), 3(2):181–189.

Garegnani, P. 1981. *Marx e gli Economisti Classici* (Marx and the classical economists). Turin: Einaudi.

German Bundestag. 1964. *Bericht ueber das Ergebnis einer Untersuchung in der Wirtschaft* (Report on the results of the analysis of industrial concentration). Document of the German Bundestag IV/2320. Bonn: Government Printing Office.

Godley, W. A. H. 1959. Cost, Prices, and Demand in the Short Run. In M. J. G. Surrey, ed., *Macroeconomic Themes*, 306–309. Oxford: Oxford University Press.

Gordon, R. L. 1967. A Pure Theory of Exhaustion. *Journal of Political Economy* (June), 31(2):274–286.

Gray, L. C. 1914. Rent Under the Assumption of Exhaustibility. *Quarterly Journal of Economics* 28(3):466–489.

Hall, M. and L. Weiss. 1967. Firm Size and Profitability. *Review of Economics and Statistics* (August), 49(13):319–331.

Harcourt, G. G. and P. Kenyon. 1976. Pricing and the Investment Decision. *Kyklos* 29:449–477.

Hazledine, T. 1974. Determination of the Mark-Up Under Oligopoly: A Comment. *Economic Journal* (December), 84(336):967–970.

Herman, E. S. 1981. *Corporate Control,Corporate Power*. Cambridge: Cambridge University Press.

Hicks, J. R. 1939. *Value and Capital: An Inquiry into Some Fundamental Principles of Economic Theory*. Oxford: Clarendon Press.

Hilferding, R. 1968. *Das Finanzkapital* (Finance Capital). Frankfurt: Europaeische Verlagsanstalt.

Hinrichsen, D. and U. Krause. 1981. A Substitution Theorem for Joint Production Models with Disposal Processes. University of Bremen. Mimeo.

Hollander, S. 1973. *The Economics of Adam Smith*. Toronto: University of Toronto Press.

Hotelling, H. 1931. The Economics of Exhaustible Resources. *Journal of Political Economy* (April), 39(2):137–175.

Houthakker, H. 1979. Growth and Inflation: Analysis by Industry. Brooking Papers on Economic Activity, No. 1, pp. 241–257.

Hymer, S. H. 1979. *The Multinational Corporation: A Radical Approach*. Cambridge: Cambridge University Press.

Itoh, M. 1980. Marx's Theory of Market Value. In M. Itoh, *Value and Crisis: Essays in Marxian Economics in Japan*, pp. 80–93. New York: Monthly Review Press.

Jevons, W. S. 1965. *The Theory of Political Economy*. New York: Angus Kelley.

Kalecki, M. 1971. Costs and Prices. In M. Kalecki, *Selected Essays on the Dynamics of the Capitalist Economy, 1933–1970*, pp. 43–62. Cambridge: Cambridge University Press.

Kaplan, A. D., J. B. Dirlam, and R. Y. Lanzilotti. 1958. *Pricing in Big Business: A Case Approach*. Washington, D.C.: The Brookings Institution.

Kemp, M. C. and Y. Kimura. 1978. *Introduction to Mathematical Economics*. New York, Berlin: Springer-Verlag.

Kirzner, I. M. 1973. *Competition and Entrepreneurship*. Chicago: University of Chicago Press.

Koopmans, T. C., ed. 1951a. *Activity Analysis of Production and Allocation: Proceedings of a Conference*. New York: Wiley.

Koopmans, T. C. 1951b. Alternative Proof of the Substitution Theorem for Leontief Model in the Case of Three Industries. In Koopmans, ed., *Activity Analysis* (q.v.), pp. 147–154.

Koshimura, S. 1975. *Theory of Capital Reproduction and Accumulation*. Ontario: DPG.

Koshimura, S. 1977. *Schemes of Reproduction Under a System of Monopoly Price*. Yokohama National University. Mimeo.

Krause, U. 1977. *Ueber Negative Werte* (On negative values). University of Bremen. Mimeo.

Krause, U. 1980. Abstract Labor in General Joint Systems. *Metroeconomica* 32: 115–135.

Krause, U. 1981. Heterogeneous Labor and the Fundamental Marxian Theorem. *Review of Economic Studies* 48(2):173–178.

Kregel, J. A. 1973. *The Reconstruction of Political Economy.* London: Macmillan.

Krengel, R., E. Baumgart, A. Boness, K. Droege, R. Pischner, and J. Schintke. 1977. *Produktionsvolumen und -potential: Produktionsfaktoren der Industrie im Bebiet der Bundesrepublik Deutschland* (Production and production capacity: Factors of production for manufacturing production in West Germany). Series 19. Berlin: Institute for Economic Research.

Kuruma, S. 1973. *Marx-Lexikon zur Politischen Okonomie.* vol. 1, *Konkurrenz* (Marx-Dictionary on Political Economy. vol. 1, Competition). Berlin: Oberbaum.

Lange, O. 1952. *Some Observations on Input-Output Analysis.* Warsaw, Poland: Sankhya 17, Part 4.

Lange, O. 1963. *Political Economy.* Warsaw, Poland: Pergamon Press.

Lanzilotti, R. F. 1958. Pricing Objectives in Larger Companies. *American Economic Review* (December), 48(4):921–940.

Lenin, V. I. 1965. *Imperialism, the Highest Stage of Capitalism.* Peking: Language Press.

Lerner, A. P. 1933. The Concept of Monopoly Power and the Measurement of Monopoly Power. *Review of Economic Studies* 1(1):157–175.

Levine, D. P. 1980. Aspects of the Classical Theory of Markets. *Australian Economic Papers,* June, pp. 1–15.

Levinson, H. 1960. Post War Movements of Prices and Wages in Manufacturing Industries. Joint Economic Committee, Studies in Employment, Growth and Price Levels, Study Paper no. 21.

Lipietz, A. 1979. Les Mystères de la rente absolue: Commentaire sur les coherences d'un texte de Sraffa (The Mysteries of Absolute Rent: A Comment on the Coherence of a Text of Sraffa). *Cahiers d'Economie Politique* (Paris), no. 5, pp. 21–37.

Lustgarden, S. 1975a. *Industrial Concentration and Inflation.* Washington, D.C.: American Enterprise Institute for Public Policy Research, Domestic Affairs Study 31.

Lustgarden, S. 1975b. Administered Inflation: A Reappraisal. *Economic Inquiry* (June), 13:191–206.

MacAvoy, P. W., J. W. McKie, and L. R. Preston. 1971. High and Stable Concentration Levels: Profitability and Public Policy: A Response. *Journal of Law and Economics* (October), 14:493–499.

McEnally, R. W. 1976. Competition and Dispersion in Rates of Return–A Note. *Journal of Industrial Economics* 25:69–75.

Manara, C. F. 1980. Sraffa's Model for Joint Production of Commodities by Means of Commodities. In Pasinetti, ed., *Essays* (q.v.), pp. 1–11.

Mancke, R. B. 1974. Causes of Interfirm Profitability Differences: A New Interpretation of the Evidence. *Quarterly Journal of Economics* (May), 88(2):181–193.

Mangasarian, O. L. 1971. Perron—Frobenius properties of **Ax** − λ**Bx**. *Journal of Mathematical Analysis and Applications.* 36:86–102.

Mann, M. 1966. Seller Concentration, Barriers to Entry and Rates of Return in Thirty Industries, 1950–60. *Review of Economics and Statistics* (August), 48(2): 296–307.

Marcus, M. 1969. Profitability and Size of Firm: Some Further Evidence. *Review of Economics and Statistics* 51(1):104–107.

Marris, R. 1964. *The Economic Theory of Managerial Capitalism.* New York: Macmillan.

Marshall, A. 1947. *Principles of Economics: An Introductory Volume.* London: Macmillan.

Marx, K. 1967a. *Capital: A Critique of Political Economy.* Vol. 1, *The Process of Capitalist Production.* New York: International Publishers.

Marx, K. 1967b. *Capital: A Critique of Political Economy.* Vol. 3, *The Process of Capitalist Production as a Whole.* New York: International Publishers.

Marx, K. 1970. Wages, Price, and Profit. In *Karl Marx and Frederick Engles: Selected Works in One Volume*, pp. 186–224. New York: International Publishers.

Marx, K. 1977. *Marx-Engles Werke.* Vol. 26.2, *Theorien ueber den Mehrwert* (Theories of Surplus Value). Berlin: Dietz.

Marzi, G. and P. Varri. 1977. *Variazioni de produttività nell'economia italiana 1959–1967* (Changes of productivity in the Italian economy 1959–1967). Bologna: Mulino.

Matz, A. and O. J. Curry. 1972. *Cost Accounting: Planning and Control.* Chicago: South-Western.

Maurice, C. and C. E. Ferguson. 1971. The General Theory of Factor Usage with Variable Factor Supply. *Southern Economic Journal* (October), 38(2):133–140.

Means, G. C. 1935. *Industrial Prices and Their Relative Inflexibility.* 74th Cong., 1st sess. S. Doc. 13.

Means, G. C. 1959. *Hearings on Administered Prices.* Part 9. Senate Subcommittee on Antitrust and Monopoly. 86th Cong. 2d sess., pp. 4745–4760.

Means, G. C. 1972. The Administered Price Thesis Reconfirmed. *American Economic Review* (June), 61(2):292–306.

Mill, J. S. 1900. *Principles of Political Economy.* New York: Colonial Press.

Modigliani, F. 1958. New Developments on the Oligopoly Front. *Journal of Political Economy* 64(3):215–233.

Monopolkommission. 1976. Mehr Wettbewerb ist moeglich (More competition is possible). Baden-Baden: Nomos.

Morishima, M. 1973. *Marx's Economics–A Dual Theory of Value and Growth.* Cambridge: Cambridge University Press.

Morishima, M. 1978. S. Bowles and H. Gintis on the Marxian Theory of Value and Heterogeneous Labor. *Cambridge Journal of Economics*, no. 2, pp. 305–309.

Morishima, M. and G. Catephores. 1978. *Value, Exploitation and Growth: Marx in the Light of Modern Economic Theories.* London: McGraw-Hill.

Mott, C. S. 1924. Organizing a Great Industry. Article 5. *Management and Administration* 7:523–527.

Mueller, D. C. 1977. The Persistence of Profits Above the Norm. *Economica* 44(176):371–380.

Mueller, D. C. 1981. Economies of Scale and Concentration. Bureau of Economics, Federal Trade Commission, Washington, D.C. Mimeo.

Mueller, W. F. 1974. Industrial Concentration, an Important Inflationary Force. In H. J. Goldschmid, H. M. Mann, and J. F. Weston, eds., *Industrial Concentration: The New Learning*, pp. 280–306. Boston: Little, Brown.

Murray, R. 1977. Value and Theory of Rent. Part I. *Capital and Class*, no. 3, pp. 100–122.

Naylor, T. H. 1965. A Kuhn-Tucker Model of the Multi-Product, Multi-Factor Firm. *Southern Economic Journal*, April, pp. 324–330.

Neal, A. C. 1942. *Industrial Concentration and Price Inflexibility*. Washington, D.C.: American Council of Public Affairs.

Negishi, T. 1961. Monopolistic Competition and General Equilibrium. *Review of Economic Studies* 28(2):196–201

Nikaido, H. 1968. *Convex Structures and Economic Theory*. New York: Academic Press.

Nikaido, H. 1983. Marx on Competition. *Zeitscheift für Nationalökonomie*, 43(4):337–362.

Nordhaus, W. D. and W. Godley. 1972. Pricing in the Trade Cycle. *Economic Journal* (September), 82(327):853–882.

Okishio, N. 1956. Monopoly and the Rates of Profit. *Kobe University Economic Review* 5:71–88.

Okishio, N. 1961. Technical Change and the Rate of Profit. *Kobe University Economic Review* 7:85–90.

Ornstein, S. I. 1973. Concentration and Profits. In Weston and Ornstein, eds., *The Impact of Large Firms* (q.v.), pp. 87–102.

Ornstein, S. I., J. F. Weston, M. O. Intriligator, and R. E. Shrieves. 1973. Determinants of Market Structure. *Southern Economic Journal* (April), 39: 612–625.

Ortega, J. M. 1972. *Numerical Analysis*. New York: Academic Press.

Pasinetti, L. L. 1973. The Notion of Vertical Integration in Economic Analysis. *Metroeconomica* 25:1–29.

Pasinetti, L. L. 1977. *Lectures on the Theory of Production*. New York: Columbia University Press.

Pasinetti, L. L., ed. 1980. *Essays on the Theory of Joint Production*. New York: Columbia University Press.

Pfouts, R. W. 1961. The Theory of Cost and Production in the Multi-Product Firm. *Econometrica* 29(4):650–658.

Phelps, E., ed., 1970. *The Microeconomics of Inflation and Unemployment*. New York: Norton.

Phlips, L. 1969. Business Pricing Policies and Inflation: Some Evidence from EEC. *Journal of Industrial Economics* (November), 18(1):1–14.

226   References

Pugil, T. 1976. The Effects of International Market Linkage on Price, Profits and Wages in U.S. Manufacturing Industries. Ph.D. diss., Department of Economics, Harvard University.

Qualls, D. 1972. Concentration, Barriers to Entry, and Long Run Economic Profit Margins. *Journal of Industrial Economics* 20(2):231–242.

Qualls, D. 1974. Stability and Persistence of Economic Profit Margins in Highly Concentrated Industries. *Economic Journal* 40(4):604–612.

Quirk, J. and R. Saposnik. 1968. *Introduction to General Equilibrium Theory and Welfare Economics*. New York: McGraw-Hill.

Ravenscraft, D. 1981. *Structure-Profit Relations at the Line of Business and Industry Level*. Bureau of Economics, Federal Trade Commission, Washington, D.C.

Ricardo, D. 1951. *Principles of Political Economy and Taxation*. In *Works and Correspondence*, P. Sraffa, ed., with M. Dobb. vol. 1. Cambridge: Cambridge University Press.

Ripley, F. and L. Segal. 1973. Price Determination in 395 Manufacturing Industries. *Review of Economics and Statistics* (August), 55(2):263–271.

Ritz, P. M. 1980. *Definitions and Conventions of the Input-Output Study*. Bureau of Economic Analysis Staff Paper, Department of Commerce, Bureau of Economic Analysis. Washington, D.C.: Government Printing Office.

Roberts, J. and H. Sonnenschein. 1977. On the Foundations of the Theory of Monopolistic Competition. *Econometrica* 45(1):101–113.

Robinson, J. 1962. The Basic Theory of Normal Prices. *Quarterly Journal of Economics* 76(1):1–19.

Robinson, J. 1965. *Collected Economic Papers*, vol. 3. Oxford: Basil Blackwell.

Robinson, J. 1971. *Economic Heresies*. London:Macmillan.

Robinson, J. 1973. *Collected Economic Papers*, vol. 4. Oxford: Basil Blackwell.

Robinson, J. 1974. *History Versus Equilibrium*. Thames Papers in Political Economy, Thames Polytechnic, London.

Robinson, J. and J. Eatwell. 1973. *An Introduction to Modern Economics*. London: McGraw-Hill.

Roemer, J. E. 1979. Continuing Controversy on the Falling Rate of Profit: Fixed Capital and Other Issues. *Cambridge Journal of Economics* 3(4):379–399.

Roncaglia, A. 1978. *Sraffa and the Theory of Price*. New York: Wiley.

Samuelson, P. A. 1951. Abstract of a Theorem Concerning Substitutability in Open Leontief Models. In Koopmans, ed., *Activity Analysis* (q.v.), pp. 142–146.

Sass, P. 1975. *Die Untersuchung der Profitraten-Unterschiede zwischen den westdeutschen Industriebranchen nach dem 2. Weltkrieg*. (An analysis of profit rate differentials in West German industry after the Second World War). Tuebingen: Mohr.

Scarf, H. 1960. Some Examples of Global Instability of the Competitive Equilibrium. *International Economic Review* 1:157–172.

Schefold, B. 1976. Relative Prices as a Function of the Rate of Profit: A Mathematical Note. *Zeitschrift fuer National Oekonomie*, 36:21–48.

Schefold, B. 1978. Multiple Product Techniques with Properties of Single Product Systems. *Zeitschrift fuer National Oekonomie*, 38:29–53.

Schefold, B. 1980a. Fixed Capital as a Joint Product and the Analysis of Accumulation with Different Forms of Technical Progress. In Pasinetti, ed., *Essays* (q.v.), pp. 138–208.

Schefold, B. 1980b. Von Neumann and Sraffa: Mathematical Equivalence and Conceptual Difference. *Economic Journal* (March), 90(337):140–156.

Schefold, B. 1981. Nachfrage und Zufuhr in der klassischen Oekonomie (Supply and demand in classical economics). *Schriften des Vereins fuer Socialpolitik*, series 115/I. Studien zur Entwicklung der Oekonomischen Theorie I.

Schumpeter, J. A. 1943. *Capitalism, Socialism and Democracy*. London: George Allen and Unwin.

Schwartzman, D. 1959. Effect of Monopoly on Price. *Journal of Political Economy* (August), 67:352–362.

Scott, J. T. 1981. *Multimarket Contact and Economic Performance*. Bureau of Economics, Federal Trade Commission, Washington, D.C.

Sellekaerts, W. and R. Lesage. 1973. A Reformulation and Empirical Verification of the Administered Price and Inflation Hypothesis: The Canadian Case. *Southern Economic Journal* (January), 39(3):345–360.

Semmler, W. 1977. *Zur Theorie der Reproduktion und Akkumulation* (On the theory of reproduction and accumulation). Berlin: Olle and Wolter.

Semmler, W. 1980. Konzentration und Profitraten Differenzierung? Empirische Ergebnisse zur Industrie der BRD (Concentration and profit rate differentials? Empirical results for West German Industry). WSI-Mitteilungen no. 3, pp. 133–141.

Semmler, W. 1982a. Competition, Monopoly, and Differential Profit Rates: A Reconsideration of the Classical and Marxism Theories. *Revista Internazionale di Scienze Economiche e Commerciali* (August), 29(8):738–762.

Semmler, W. 1982b. Competition, Monopoly and Differentials of Profit Rates: Theoretical Considerations and Empirical Evidence. *Review of Radical Political Economics* (Winter), 13(4):39–53.

Semmler, W. 1984a. On the Classical Theory of Competition, Value and Prices of Production. *Australian Economic Papers*, June (forthcoming).

Semmler, W. 1984b. On Technical Change, Transient Surplus Profit, and Multiple Techniques. *Cahiers d'Economie Politique* (Paris), December (forthcoming).

Shaikh, A. 1976. The Influence of Inter-Industrial Structure of Production on Relative Prices. New School for Social Research, New York. Mimeo.

Shaikh, A. 1978. Political Economy of Capitalism: Notes on Dobb's Theory of Crisis. *Cambridge Journal of Economics* 2(2):233–251.

Shaikh, A. 1979. Notes on the Marxian Notion of Competition. New School for Social Research, New York. Mimeo.

Shaikh, A. 1980. Marxian Competition Versus Perfect Competition: Further Comments on the So-Called Choice of Technique. *Cambridge Journal of Economics* 4(1):75–83.

Shaikh, A. 1983. The Transformation from Marx to Sraffa (Prelude to a Critique of Neo-Ricardians). E. Mandel, *Marx and Sraffa*. London: New Left Books.

Shepherd, W. 1970. *Market Power and Economic Welfare*. New York: Random House.

Shepherd, W. 1972. The Elements of Market Structure. *Review of Economics and Statistics* (February), 54(1):25–37.

Sherman, H. 1968. *Profits in the United States*. Ithaca: Cornell University Press.

Singh, A. and G. Whittington. 1968. *Growth, Profitability and Valuation*. Cambridge: Cambridge University Press.

Smith, A. 1976. *An Inquiry into the Nature and Causes of the Wealth of Nations*. In *The Glasgow Edition of Works and Correspondence of Adam Smith*, R. H. Campbell and A. S. Skinner, eds., vol. 2. Oxford: Clarendon Press.

Sraffa, P. 1960. *Production of Commodities by Means of Commodities: Prelude to a Critique of Economic Theory*. Cambridge: Cambridge University Press.

Stackelberg, H. von. 1948. *Grundlagen der Theoretischen Volkswirtschaftslehre* (Foundations of theoretical economics). Bern: A. Francke.

Steedman, I. 1977. *Marx After Sraffa*. London: New Left Books.

Steedman, I. 1979a. *Trade Amongst Growing Economies*. Cambridge: Cambridge University Press.

Steedman, I. 1979b. *Monopoly, Competition and Relative Prices*. University of Manchester, England. Mimeo.

Steedman, I. 1982. The Empirical Importance of Joint Production. Paper prepared for the conference "Production joint et capital fixe" (Joint production and fixed capital), Economic and Social Research Center, University of Nanterre, Paris.

Steindl, J. 1952. *Maturity and Stagnation of American Capitalism*. New York: Monthly Review Press.

Stekler, H. D. 1963. *Profitability and Size of Firm*. Berkeley: University of California Press.

Stigler, G. J. and J. K. Kindahl. 1973. Industrial Prices as Adminsitered by Dr. *Political Economy* 65(1):1–17.

Stigler, G. J. 1963. *Capital and Rates of Return in Manufacturing Industries*. Princeton: Princeton University Press.

Stigler, G. J. 1975. Buyer Prices, Seller Prices and Price Flexibility: A Reply. *American Economic Review* 63(4):526.

Stigler, G. J. and J. K. Kindahl. 1970. *The Behavior of Industrial Prices*. New York: National Bureau of Economic Research.

Stigler, G. J. and J. K. Kindahl. 1973. Industrial Prices as Administered by Dr. Means. *American Economic Review* (September), 63(3):717–721.

Stone, R., M. Bacharas, and J. Bates. 1963. *Input-Output Relations 1951–1966: A Programme for Growth*, vol. 3. London: Chapman and Hall.

Stonebreaker, R. J. 1976. Corporate Profits and the Risk of Entry. *Review of Economics and Statistics* (February), 58(1):33–39.

Sweezy, P. 1968. *The Theory of Capitalist Development*. New York: Monthly Review Press.

Sylos-Labini, P. 1969. *Oligopoly and Technical Progress*. Cambridge: Harvard University Press.

Teplitz, W. 1977. Werte und Tausch im Kapitalismus (Value and exchange in capitalism). *Mehrwert* (Berlin), no. 13, pp. 165–189.

United Nations Statistical Office. 1968. *A System of National Accounts*. New York: United Nations.

U.S. Bureau of Census. 1975. *1972 Census of Manufactures: Concentration, Ratios of Manufacturing, MC 72 (SR)*, Washington, D.C.: U.S. Government Printing Office.

U.S. Department of Labor. 1979a. *Time Series Data for Input-Output Industries: Output, Price, and Employment*. Washington, D.C.: U.S. Government Printing Office.

U.S. Department of Labor. 1979b. *Capital Stock Estimates for Input-Output Industries: Methods and Data*. Washington, D.C.: U.S. Government Printing Office.

Varga, E. 1969. Probleme der Monopolbildung und Theorie vom Organisierten Kapitalismus (Problems of the formation of monopolies in the theory of organized capitalism). In *Die Krise des Kapitalismus und ihre politischen Folgen* (The crisis of capitalism and its political consequences), E. Altvater, ed., pp. 2531–2536. Frankfurt: Europaeische Verlagsanstalt.

Voievodine, V. 1980. *Algèbre Linéaire* (Linear algebra). Moscow: Editions MIR.

Wachtel, H. M. and P. D. Adelsheim. 1977. How Recession Feeds Inflation: Price Mark-ups in a Concentrated Economy. *Challenge* (September), pp. 6–13.

Walsh, V. and H. Gram. 1980. *Classical and Neoclassical Theories of General Equilibrium: Historical Origins and Mathematical Structure*. Oxford: Oxford University Press.

Weeks, J. 1981. *Capital and Exploitation*. Princeton: Princeton University Press.

Weiss, L. W. 1963. Average Concentration Ratios and Industrial Performance. *Journal of Industrial Economics* (July), 75:237–254.

Weiss, L. W. 1966. Business Pricing Policies and Inflation Reconsidered. *Jounal of Political Economy* (April), 74(2):177–187.

Weiss, L. W. 1971. The Role of Concentration in Recent Inflationary Price Movements: A Statistical Analysis. *Anti-Trust Law and Economics Review*, Spring, pp. 109–121.

Weiss, L. W. 1974. The Concentration-Profits Relationship and Antitrust. In N. J. Goldschmid, M. Mann, and J. F. Weston, eds., *The Industrial Concentration: The New Learning*, pp. 184–233. Boston: Little, Brown.

Wenders, J. T. 1967. Entry and Monopolistic Pricing. *Journal of Political Economy*. 75(5):755–762.

Weston, J. F. 1973. Pricing Behavior of Large Firms. In Weston and Ornstein, eds., *The Impact of Large Firms* (q.v.), pp. 133–166.

Weston, J. F., S. Lustgarden, and N. Grottke. 1974. The Administered Price Thesis Denied. *American Economic Review* 64(1):232–234.

Weston, J. F. and S. J. Ornstein. 1973a. Trends and Causes of Concentration: A

Survey. In Weston and Ornstein, eds., *The Impact of Large Firms* (q.v.), pp. 3–21.

Weston, J. F. and S. J. Ornstein., eds. 1973b. *The Impact of Large Firms on the U.S. Economy.* Lexington, Mass.: Lexington Books.

Wilder, R. P., C. G. Williams, and D. Singh. 1977. The Price Equation: A Cross-Sectional Approach. *American Economic Review* 67(4):732–740.

Winn, D. N. 1977. On the Relations Between Rates of Return, Risk and Market Structure. *Quarterly Journal of Economics* 91(1):157–163.

Winn, D. N. and O. A. Leabo. 1974. Rates of Return, Concentration and Growth—Question of Disequilibrium. *Journal of Law and Economics* 17:97–115.

Wolfstetter, E. 1976. Positive Profit with Negative Surplus Value: A Comment. *Economic Journal* 86(344):864–872.

Wolfstetter, E. 1977. Wert, Profitrate und Beschaeftigung (Value, profit rate, and employment). Frankfurt and New York: Campus.

Wood, A. 1975. *Theory of Profits.* Cambridge: Cambridge University Press.

Yordon, W. J. 1961. Industrial Concentration and Price Flexibility in Inflation: Price Response in Fourteen Industries, 1947–1958. *Review of Economics and Statistics* (August), 43(3):287–294.

Index

Index

Index

6, 18, 33, 63; in Marxian theory, 4, 7–10, 42, 44, 46, 55, 63, 102, 103, 152, 208; and price change, 77–81; relative, 29, 32; in Ricardo, 6, 18, 44; for single production, 151–59; with uniform profit rate, 63–68; and values, 5

Productivity, 68, 77, 86, 87, 110, 117, 123, 125, 131, 186; in cycles, 50, 77

Profit, 4, 5, 6, 15, 17, 18, 24, 29, 38, 41, 42, 46, 48–50, 57, 58, 62, 64, 71, 84, 99, 102, 103, 104, 107, 111, 113–16, 118, 120, 122, 123, 125, 132, 134, 137, 141, 150, 159, 166, 167; average profit, 48, 51; excess profit, 40; integrated profits, 67, 78, 148; monopoly profit, 39, 40, 41, 137; profit differentials, 54, 109, 140, 150; profit margin, 59, 71, 98, 107, 113, 123, 127, 146, 147, 149, 150, 157, 164, 165, 183, 187, 204; share of, 59, 134, 136

Profit margin, 7, 9, 10; and capital/output ratios, 146–47; and differential profit rates, 146–47; measures for, 107; *see also* Mark up

Profit rate, 3, 6, 7, 9, 10, 15, 17, 18, 21, 22, 25, 27, 28, 32–34, 36–38, 41, 45, 47, 49, 55, 60, 64, 65, 68, 70, 79, 81, 87, 106, 107, 109, 110, 115, 118, 119, 120, 122–28, 131, 133, 134, 136, 141, 143, 145, 147, 150, 153, 156, 159, 168, 170, 176, 203, 204, 214; average profit, 35; average rate of, 7, 22, 27, 28, 33, 34, 37, 38, 41, 44, 49, 50, 82, 97, 107, 115, 118, 119, 132, 135, 143, 145, 148, 149, 157, 164, 165, 183; empirical determinants, 111–22; equal profit rate, 27, 37, 45; general profit rate, 33, 34, 38, 51, 152, 183; hierarchy, 41, 131, 133; Marxian/classical theories, 6, 7; measures for, 106–7; normal profit rate, 17, 21, 37, 45; surplus profit, 23, 29, 36, 38; uniform profit rate, 9, 17, 65, 67, 81, 107, 145, 147, 149, 150, 153, 158, 174, 193, 205, 206

Profit rate differential, 2, 3, 7, 10, 12, 36, 44, 45, 110, 111, 127, 128, 134, 136, 142, 143, 145, 192; collusion, 108; and concentration, 109, 110, 111–22; entry

barriers, 109, 110; for joint production, 184–86; and market shares, 126, 127, 145, 146; in Marx, 34–38; and mobility barriers, 133–37; production prices with differential profit rate, 147–51 (*see also* Producton price); in Ricardo, 16, 47; for single production, 147–51; and size classes of firms, 126, 127; in Smith, 16, 47; summary of empirical evidence, 111–22

Rate of return, 63, 64, 65, 66, 67, 75, 80, 81, 103, 119, 127, 152, 154–57, 162, 165, 166, 182, 183, 187, 192; on capital, 63, 75, 103; as financial goal, 61–63; on fixed capital advanced, 65, 80; normal rate of return, 44, 162, 165, 166, 182, 187; pricing, 3, 7, 43 (*see also* Target rate of return); uniform rate of return, 44, 67

Reduction, 180–82, 189; coefficients of heterogenous labor, 180–82, 189

Rent, 14, 16, 34, 35, 40, 44, 48, 50, 159; absolute rent, 35, 50; cartel rent, 40; differential rent, 35, 50; extensive, 50; intensive rent, 50; land rent, 50; marginal rent, 35, 50; and scarcity, 35, 44, 45, 50

Rent theory, 20, 35, 40; Marx, 20, 35, 50; Marxian, 36, 50; neo-Ricardian, 50; Ricardo, 20, 35, 50

Reproduction, 5, 14, 15, 26, 42, 43, 44, 66, 67; cost of, 15, 26, 31, 33, 43, 44, 67, 80; of labor power, 66, 67, 80; price, *see* Production price; and surplus, 14–16

Resources, 11, 12, 44, 45, 51, 144, 191, 207; natural, 37, 50, 159; in neo-classical theory, 50

Returns to scale, 46, 207–9; constant, 207, 209; nonconstant, 46, 207–9

Stability, 12, 33, 40, 49, 126, 145, 212, 213; of centers of gravitation, 27–28, 48; of equilibrium prices, 213, 214; global, 214; local, 12, 214; relative stability, 49; system, 214

Structural change, 28, 29